Negative Liberties

New Americanists

A Series Edited by Donald E. Pease

Negative Liberties

Morrison, Pynchon, and the Problem of Liberal Ideology

Cyrus R. K. Patell

Duke University Press   Durham and London 2001

© 2001 Duke University Press
All rights reserved

Typeset in Quadraat by Keystone Typesetting, Inc.
Library of Congress Cataloging-in-Publication Data appear
on the last printed page of this book.

For Saki

CONTENTS

PREFACE   ix

ONE. Narrating Individualism   1

TWO. Idealizing Individualism   34

THREE. Unenlightened Enlightenment   82

FOUR. Contemplating Community   141

CONCLUSION. Beyond Individualism   186

NOTES   197

WORKS CITED   219

INDEX   231

PREFACE

"These guys sound like Reagan." An undergraduate said this to me during a tutorial sometime in the mid-1980s. He was talking about Emerson and Whitman.

I don't know whether I put this idea into his head or he into mine, but I do know that my interest in the subject of *Negative Liberties* dates from the period now known as *the Reagan era*. Its roots lie in my amazement that so many Americans could find Ronald Reagan's rhetoric to be so persuasive when I found it to be so patently full of rationalizations and deceptions. I had read Christopher Lasch's best-selling study *The Culture of Narcissism* (1979), which claimed that "the culture of competitive individualism" was "a way of life that is dying" (21), destroyed by its own internal contradictions. But, everywhere I looked during the 1980s, I saw American popular culture celebrating individualism, led by Reagan, who described "the dream conceived by our Founding Fathers" as the achievement of "the ultimate in individual freedom consistent with an orderly society" (1989, 212–13). Garry Wills wrote that Reagan "believes the individualist myths that help him to play his communal role," and he described Reagan as "the sincerest claimant to a heritage that never existed, a perfect blend of an authentic America he grew up in and of that America's own fables about its past" (1987, 94). What was it that was so appealing about this rhetoric, that could lead American voters to say, as one retired brewery worker did after the 1984 election, "He really isn't like a Republican. He's more like an American, which is what we really need"?[1]

In speech after speech throughout his political career, Reagan managed to appropriate communal symbols and bend them to serve individualist ends, the most prominent example being his description of the United States as a "shining city upon a hill." He used the phrase in a 1977 speech to the American Conservative Union, declaring "that the preservation and enhancement of the values that strengthen and protect individual freedom, family life, communities, and neighborhoods and the liberty of our beloved nation should be at the heart of any legislative or political program presented to the American people" (1984, 192). Asserting that "liberty can be measured by how much freedom Americans have to make their own decisions—even their mistakes," Reagan reached the conclusion that the Republican party "must be the party of the individual. It must not sell out the individual to cater to the group. No greater challenge faces our society today than insuring that each one of us can maintain his dignity and his identity in an increasingly complex, centralized society. . . . Then with God's help we shall indeed be as a city upon a hill with the eyes of all people upon us" (200–201).

Reagan's appropriation here (and in later speeches) of the symbol of "the shining city upon a hill" inverts the logic of John Winthrop's sermon "A Modell of Christian Charity" (1630), which had stressed the primacy of the community's needs over those of any individual. "Wee must delight in eache other," Winthrop told his fellow colonists on board the *Arbella*, "make others Condicions our owne[,] reioyce together, mourne together, labour, and suffer together, allwayes haueing before our eyes our Commission and Community in the worke, our Community as members of the same body" (294). In Reagan's retelling of Winthrop's message, the individual assumes primacy over the community, and Winthrop himself becomes a rugged individualist: "What he imagined was important because he was an early Pilgrim, an early freedom man. He journeyed here on what today we'd call a little wooden boat; and like the other Pilgrims, he was looking for a home that would be free" (1989, 417).

I began to realize why Ronald Reagan was perceived as "the Great Communicator": not because he rendered the complexities of policy comprehensible to the average citizen (he did not), but because he told stories that average citizens wanted to hear, stories based on a consistently individualist interpretation of what it means to be an American. What Reagan was offering in its most simplified form was a story about the idea of individualism that seemed to have attained a hegemonic force in U.S. culture, that seemed to have become one of those official stories that serve as the foundation for cultural consensus.

Reagan often quoted Winthrop, but to my knowledge he did not quote Emerson until late in his presidency (at the 1987 summit with Gorbachev). Nevertheless, my student and I were not alone in making a connection between Emerson and Reagan.[2] In a controversial address given to the Yale senior class in 1981 (and later published in essay form under the title "Power, Politics, and a Sense of History"), A. Bartlett Giamatti—then president of Yale University—worried about Emerson's valorization of the individual. Tracing the genealogy of Reaganism back to Emersonianism, Giamatti argued that "we are afflicted now, and have been for some time, with solo operators for whom nothing is complex, because nothing is connected to anything else; who believe the function of government is to impose moralistic schemes rather than to forge complex consensuses, and who treat government as an impediment to mandating purity rather than as a means of connecting, and negotiating among, legitimate needs and achieving a practical equitable balance" (99). Giamatti situated the origin of "this worship of power as force, this contempt for restraining or complex connections and the consequent devaluation of political life," in the years after the Civil War, when "prophets of the secular religion that was the new America" were able "to bypass the Founders and to summon up the original strength of Puritan America and to hurl that strength, naked, squalling as if newborn, into the gathering darkness." Singling out Emerson because he "was a potent figure in his time, and his influence is powerful to this day," Giamatti claimed that Emerson has been misunderstood: "You do not have to read the prophet to realize his ideas are all around us. Strangely enough, he lives in the popular imagination as the Lover of Nature, a sweet, sentimental, Yankee Kahlil Gibran. In fact, Emerson is as sweet as barbed wire, and his sentimentality as accommodating as a brick" (102).

I agree with Giamatti that Emerson's influence remains "powerful to this day." He was a major contributor to the national narrative that Reagan presented in simplified form throughout his career. And I agree that we have tended to misunderstand Emerson. I am just not sure, however, that I agree about the precise way in which he has been misunderstood.

Let me give you an example of how the popular imagination tends to conceive of Emerson. In the fall of 1988, the Reebok Corporation ran an advertising campaign for its athletic shoes based on the slogan "Reeboks

Let U. B. U." The television commercials that spearheaded this campaign were shot in bright primary colors and, over a sound track of tango music played on violin and piano, presented the viewer with a montage of brief scenes featuring people dressed in idiosyncratic attire and behaving in idiosyncratic, even eccentric, ways. Each scene was accompanied by a spoken caption drawn from Emerson's famous essay "Self-Reliance"—"Whoso would be a man must be a nonconformist. . . . A foolish consistency is the hobgoblin of little minds. . . . To be great is to be misunderstood . . ."—a total of ten captions in all. The ad campaign raised the hackles of the daily newspaper at Emerson's alma mater: the *Harvard Crimson* ran an opinion piece entitled "Stomping on Individualism" that deplored this appropriation of the work of the man whose name adorns the university's philosophy building. "The postmodern randomness of the ads is meant to stress individuality and uniqueness, as does Emerson's philosophy," writes the author of the piece. But, she complains, "the ads distort that philosophy by implying that Emersonian self-reliance can be found in, of all things, sneakers." Describing Emerson as "the quintessential American philosopher" (a disputed claim in departments of philosophy, including the one housed in Harvard's Emerson Hall), the author argues that the campaign emphasizes "the crucially American dialectic of individual versus community." She claims, however, that the ads are based "on a duplicitous premise" because they "deftly obscure . . . the fact that buying Reeboks is not an act of individualism but an act of conformity" (Brosh, 2).

By extolling the virtues of an authentic "individualism" while sneering at "conformity," the author of the *Crimson* piece places herself squarely within the ideological tradition that has dominated American culture since the early part of the nineteenth century. What she fails to realize, however, is that conformity is crucial to U.S. individualism, which, like all ideologies, serves the function of creating and perpetuating consensus among the members of a particular community or group. The existence of an *ideology of individualism* may at first appear to be a paradox since individualism would seem to be diametrically opposed to any form of social control. But, as we shall see, from the time that the term became a part of the American vocabulary in the early part of the nineteenth century, Americans—including Emerson and his followers—have always conceived of *individualism* as a social formation. Herein lies the genius of the ideology and perhaps the reason for its efficacy: it enforces conformity at the very moment that it extols individuality. The very fact that we conceive of Emerson as a proponent of "solo operators" rather than as a social theorist is a testament to the general acceptance in U.S. culture of the particular social theory that he advocates.

In the pages that follow, I will argue that the problem with U.S. liberal ideology today is its ongoing reliance on Emersonian modes of thinking. I will use the term *Emersonian liberalism* to signify, first, the liberal philosophical tradition that has arisen in the United States around the idea of *self-reliance*, a tradition that represents the crystallization of what might be called the *official narrative* of U.S. individualism. I will also use the term to signify the popular, individualist mythologies that either accompany Emersonianism or are promoted by it. Emersonian liberalism is perhaps the most powerful version of U.S. liberal ideology, and it provides what amounts to a national narrative that teaches us to think in what social scientists call *methodologically individualist* terms. As I will discuss in greater detail in the first chapter, methodological individualism is the idea that all explanations of either individual or social phenomena are valid only insofar as they are grounded in facts about individuals. What I hope to show in the course of *Negative Liberties* is that Americans have become overly reliant on methodological individualism when they think about social problems. Many of the most nettlesome social problems facing Americans today prove resistant to methodologically individualist solutions and therefore seem to us to be insolvable.

Take, for example, the debates over affirmative action. The label *affirmative action* refers to a broad spectrum of programs designed to reverse the effects of systemic discrimination; according to Stephen L. Wasby, "the concept subsumes a set of programs ranging from, at its mildest, wide advertising of positions to prompt more people to apply or extensive recruitment of potential applicants, through the use of ranges and goals in hiring, to, ultimately, at its most severe, the use of fixed hiring and promotion" (ix–x). The most frequent line of attack against affirmative action is what Ronald J. Fiscus describes in *The Constitutional Logic of Affirmative Action* as the "innocent persons" argument: "The charge is that such programs are always unfair to the individuals (white or male) against whom the preferential treatment is directed, unless those individuals themselves participated in the discrimination against the now-preferred minorities. If they have not personally participated in the particular discrimination in question, then they are considered innocent, and the imposition of an affirmative action quota that disadvantages them is considered an unfair act of discrimination against them simply because they are white or male" (4).

During the Reagan administration, this type of argument generally took one of two forms. Frequently, the Justice Department argued that affirmative-action programs violate the Fourteenth Amendment's guarantee of equal protection if they have the effect of taking away a right or a benefit from an individual who was not *personally* guilty of discriminating against the victims of discrimination. At other times, the Justice Department claimed that affirmative-action programs must be restricted to restoring rights or benefits only to "the actual victims of discrimination," to those individuals who can demonstrate that they have been *personally* discriminated against by the entity instituting the program (Fiscus, 46–47). The reaction of the average citizen to affirmative action also typically turns on "actual" individual cases. For example, Vangie Pepper, a Washington State woman interviewed about an anti-affirmative-action ballot initiative, finds it difficult to abandon methodological individualism in the case of her own daughter: "I have always been for affirmative action. If all things are equal you should probably have some kind of affirmative action. But should my daughter not get into school because of it?" (S. A. Holmes, A15). Such arguments are examples of methodologically individualist responses to a problem that demands consideration at the level of the group because it is a matter of group-oriented discrimination. Behind any group-oriented form of discrimination such as racism, sexism, or homophobia lies the unacknowledged abandonment of methodological individualism; predictably, when methodological individualism is invoked in the search for solutions to such problems, it proves to be ineffective.[3]

There is, however, a difference between Emerson's methodological individualism and the reasoning that tends to accompany criticisms of affirmative action. In reframing questions of social choice as questions of individual choice, Emerson tends to describe *the individual* in abstract terms that strip away characteristics, such as gender, race, ethnicity, and class, that we generally consider to be essential parts of our individual identities. In contrast, the methodological individualism that is deployed in today's sociocultural debates often presents particular individual life stories as evidence, relying on a specificity that Emerson avoids in those moments when he might be said to be engaging in political philosophy. The strategy of invoking particular life stories as a form of political discourse draws on what I hope to show is a crucial fact about human culture: its epistemological reliance on storytelling and the creation of narratives.

I will side with those philosophers who argue that philosophy is a form of storytelling, but I will also suggest that philosophy is often insufficiently fictional. In order to attain the goal of internal consistency through the resolution of contradictions and conflicts, philosophy often presents a view of culture that is either simplified or abstracted or both. Such, I will argue, is the case with the abstract conception of the individual presented by Emerson in the nineteenth century and by John Rawls and George Kateb in the twentieth. The invocation of particular life stories remedies some of that abstraction, but it also involves an oversimplification: it generally fails to account for the larger sociocultural contexts within which those life stories must be placed if we are to understand their full significance. Methodological individualism prevents us from doing that contextualizing, in part because it dismisses many sociocultural contexts as irrelevant.

One of the goals of *Negative Liberties* is to revise the traditional view of mainstream liberal political theory by arguing that Rawls must be considered together with Emerson and that the two thinkers share philosophical strategies. *Emersonian liberalism*, in other words, encompasses not only the overt Emersonianism of a thinker like Kateb but also the varieties of individualism espoused by thinkers like Rawls. Acknowledged or not, Emersonianism is the ground upon which contemporary U.S. liberal theory is built.

In addition, I hope to show that some of the most important philosophizing that is going on within late twentieth-century U.S. culture can be found in works of fiction, particularly those works of fiction that we take to be exemplars of literary art. Toni Morrison and Thomas Pynchon are two novelists whose writings have gained them notice as preeminent literary artists. I argue that their literary art arises from an intimate engagement with cultural politics and in particular with the ideology of Emersonian liberalism. Their novels demonstrate why such contemporary philosophers as Ronald Beiner, Stanley Cavell, Alasdair MacIntyre, Martha Nussbaum, Richard Rorty, Michael J. Sandel, Steven Shiffrin, and Judith Shklar have argued that professional philosophy has much to learn from literature's ability to dramatize the complexities and idiosyncrasies of human life. I do not mean to argue that literature enables us to come up with abstract solutions that philosophy cannot supply. Rather, I argue that literature's ability to dramatize philosophical situations enables it to be persuasive about the benefits and costs of particular philosophical arrangements in a way that philosophy cannot be. Literature brings philosophy to life.

Thinking about the costs and benefits of the individualistic tradition represented by Emersonian liberalism, I find myself in agreement with Chantal Mouffe's belief that we must "redress the negative consequences of individualism" (1992, 5) by dissociating "the liberal ideals of individual freedom and personal autonomy" from "the other discourses to which they have been articulated" (1993, 7). Mouffe argues that liberalism's major contribution to modern democratic theory is its emphasis on cultural and political pluralism. The challenge, as I see it, is to theorize forms of individual and communal identity that can draw on pluralism's respect for the dignity of others without slipping into a cultural relativism that prevents us from making philosophical judgments. The triumph of multiculturalism within the U.S. academy in recent years is too often reflected in precisely this sort of cultural relativism, which assumes that an epistemological divide lies between different subject positions, a divide that prevents us from either truly empathizing with or justly criticizing those who occupy subject positions that are significantly different from our own.[4]

Thomas Pynchon and Toni Morrison are typically taken to be authors who occupy radically different subject positions. They are the two most celebrated American novelists of the late twentieth century, canonized postmodernists whose writings have become staples of college English curricula as well as best-sellers, yet critics routinely assign them to separate pigeonholes and thus rarely find cause to consider their novels together.[5] Critics seem to believe that, because Morrison and Pynchon write from what appear to be diametrically opposed authorial subject positions, they must appeal primarily to quite different interpretive communities. Pynchon, after all, is a white male, a descendant of the Puritan Fathers, who guards his privacy jealously, never gives interviews, and publishes rarely. In contrast, Morrison is a woman descended from African American slaves who is not only a prolific novelist and winner of both the Nobel and the Pulitzer Prizes but also a professor at a prominent university; she grants interviews, gives lectures around the country, and has donned the mantle of the public intellectual.

In the current critical climate, the differences in their personal genealogies and their approaches to intellectual life prevent Morrison and Pynchon from being compared to one another, despite the readily apparent formal affinities between their bodies of work. Their novels are experimental and self-consciously difficult pieces of prose that revel in the resources of language and firmly situate themselves within the horizon of postmodernist aesthetics, a stance that becomes immediately apparent as soon as one opens their respective first novels (published seven years apart).[6] Sometimes choppy and harsh, at other times lyrical and mellifluous, their prose styles frequently combine the beautiful and the appalling to create striking images that gnaw at the reader's imagination. In each case, however, this aesthetic prowess is part of an outlook that is deeply political: the novels of Pynchon and Morrison embody a conviction that great art can be simultaneously timeless and time bound, that it can break through to what is transcendent in the human experience by engaging the specific cultural and political issues of its time and place. Their novels and essays bear out Linda Hutcheon's argument about the nature of postmodernism: that it is "engaged in contesting the modernist (humanist) premises of art's apolitical autonomy and of theory and criticism as value-free activities." According to Hutcheon, postmodernist texts teach us "that representation cannot be avoided, but it can be studied to show how it legitimates certain kinds of knowledge and, therefore, certain kinds of power" (230).

By arguing that postmodernism does not depict some generalized condition of subjectivity but rather engages with particular kinds of knowledge and power, Hutcheon here corrects a critical commonplace about postmodernism. Phillip Brian Harper summarizes this view by arguing that "postmodern theory suggests that our sense of the individual human psyche as an integrated whole is a necessary misconception, and that various technological, economic, and philosophical developments of the late twentieth century demonstrate to us the psyche's fundamentally incoherent and fragmentary, or 'decentered,' nature." Harper proposes that, for authors like Morrison, whose work arises out of historical conditions of "social marginality," there is nothing specifically "postmodern" about the experience of fragmented subjectivity; in other words, the "general condition" of fragmentation depicted in postmodern texts "simulates the experience of disenfranchised groups" (29). Although Harper does not treat Morrison's work, his arguments about Maxine Hong Kingston might well be applied to Morrison: "The sociopolitical engagement that Kingston's work . . . manifests effectively sets it apart from the rather more canonized works of postmodern fiction with whom it nonetheless shares key narrative strategies, indicating not that Kingston's work is any the less postmodernist but rather that the criteria according to which certain works are recognized as exemplarily postmodern do not sufficiently engage the sociopolitical issues that are unavoidably implicated in the concept, and thus fall short of constituting its full theorization" (186). Pynchon is among the authors whom Harper includes among the "canonized" postmodernists, and Harper draws a distinction between Pynchon and writers who write from positions of social marginality by suggesting that Pynchon is not interested in "personalizing the crisis of self-cognition" (171). What I will argue below, however, is that Pynchon is, in fact, far more interested in the subjectivities of the disenfranchised than critics have generally been willing to recognize.

To take Pynchon and Morrison seriously as political novelists requires us to understand the ways in which their works engage the official narrative generated by Emersonian liberalism. Their texts pull apart, deconstruct, and reimagine this official narrative, exploring in palpable detail what it means to live in a culture of Emersonian individualism, investigating its benefits and costs, its victories and tragedies, and the kinds of knowledge and power that it promotes. Both novelists portray characters who yearn for what Michael Sandel calls the "powerful liberating vision" of a self that is "free and independent, unencumbered by aims and attachments it does not choose for itself" (1996, 12). Morrison's texts celebrate freedom even when its costs are extraordinarily high, when it is achieved at the expense of community or equal treatment for women. Pynchon's novels view freedom as an endangered value on the verge of extinction in a complex modern world driven by the exigencies of economic gain and technological progress. Both authors depict cultures in which the institutions that are supposed to safeguard freedom have in fact been complicit in its erosion. Their fictions show us that there is nothing inevitable about the happy ending that U.S. culture has grafted onto its official story about self-reliance and the nature of individual freedom. Philosophers like Emerson, Rawls, and Kateb make compelling cases for the potential of individualism as the basis for an ideal democratic society, but as Pynchon and Morrison so dramatically depict, this potential has yet to be realized in American culture, let alone elsewhere in the world.

The story told by Emersonian liberalism is an idealized narrative, an abstraction in which a great many variables are held constant. Morrison and Pynchon force us to think about precisely what has been left out of this narrative. They ask us to recognize that this narrative is a cultural myth; they ask us to measure it against a set of stories that do not end quite so well, stories about those who are disenfranchised, marginalized, and brutalized by the dominant culture even as that dominant culture celebrates its basis in the protection of individual rights.

In chapter 1, I examine the relation between philosophy and official cultural narratives and argue that literary narratives afford us a way of recognizing the limitations of those two forms of discourse. I contend that the tradition of individualism exemplified by Emersonian liberalism renders complementary two conceptions of the nature of freedom that political theorists generally regard as oppositional. The idealizing narrative promoted by Emersonian liberalism promises that self-interest does not conflict with communal interest, that the pursuit of self-interest serves, in fact, as the foundation for the ideals of both community and nationality. And I suggest that critics of this national narrative have tended to fall into two camps: those who believe, on the one hand, that individualism is flawed conceptually and must be eschewed and those who believe, on the other hand, that individualism is a leap forward for human culture and has simply not been sufficiently put into practice.

In chapter 2, I examine the strengths and shortcomings of the particular conception of individualism that lies at the heart of Emerson's philosophy. I then link Emerson's ideas to the theory of justice developed by John Rawls, generally regarded by political theorists as the definitive philosophical statement of individualism in the twentieth century, and I examine George Kateb's attempts to fuse the work of these two thinkers by developing a concept that he calls *democratic individuality*. All these descriptions of individualism suffer, I will suggest, from the abstraction of their philosophical methods, and they fail to provide U.S. culture with adequate conceptual tools for abiding social problems that prove resistant to methodologically individualist description and solutions. Ironically, one solution to this abiding problem within Emersonian liberalism is actually embedded within Emerson's writing. Emerson's rhetorical style, with its eclectic borrowings from a truly global field of reference, offers us a cosmopolitan model of thinking that Emerson himself cannot fully realize. His modes of philosophical abstraction promote in the end not cosmopolitanism but a universalism that has much to tell us about the ways in which we are all the same, but little to tell us about the ways in which we are also all different from one another.

In chapters 3 and 4, I look at the ways in which the novels of Morrison and Pynchon engage the complex cultural dynamics both embodied and effaced by the official narratives generated by Emersonian liberalism. Moreover, I will argue that Morrison and Pynchon are building upon an implicit recognition of the limitations of Emersonian universalism and upon the promise of an Emersonian cosmopolitanism. Chapter 3, "Unenlightened Enlightenment," looks at the ways in which both writers dramatize those flaws that arise from liberalism's Enlightenment inheritance, namely, its overreliance on rationalism and its blindness to its relation with forms of domination such as slavery, racism, and misogyny. At the same time, however, I demonstrate that both Morrison and Pynchon are strongly drawn to the overarching goals of Emersonian liberalism and therefore the power of its ways of thinking about freedom—sometimes despite themselves. In chapter 4, "Contemplating Community," I argue that neither Morrison nor Pynchon finds safe refuge in the idea of community: both writers dramatize situations in which community has been corrupted by its connection to the negative aspects of individualism and in which communities marginalized within the narrative of U.S. individualism create counternarratives that prove to be equally oppressive. My conclusion suggests that, by dramatizing both the power and the limitations of Emersonian liberalism, Morrison's and Pynchon's writings provide us with intellectual resources that might help us break the impasse between those thinkers who believe that there is too much individualism in U.S. culture and those who believe that there is too little. Their writings point to the necessity of conceiving individual, communal, and national components of identity in cosmopolitan terms that respect both the differences between individuals and the links that connect them.

This project has evolved greatly since its genesis as a doctoral dissertation. An earlier version of chapter 2 was published in *Nineteenth-Century Literature* (48 [March 1994]: 440–79) as "Emersonian Strategies: Negative Liberty, Self-Reliance, and Democratic Individuality." I am grateful to the University of California Press for permission to reprint the essay in its expanded and revised form here.

Work on this project has been supported by a President's Postdoctoral Fellowship from the University of California, a Goddard Junior Faculty Fellowship from New York University (NYU), and a publication grant from the Stein Fund of the NYU English Department.

A great many teachers, colleagues, and friends have read and commented on portions of this project over the years. I want in particular to thank Charles Altieri, Paul Aron, Nancy Bauer, Nancy Bentley, Warner Berthoff, Mitchell Breitwieser, Lawrence Buell, Michael Cooper, James Engell, Lianna Farber, Robert Ferguson, Marjorie Garber, Josephine Hendin, George Kateb, John V. Kelleher, Anthony Low, Leo Marx, William Murphy, Barbara Packer, Larry J. Reynolds, Charles Ruberto, Michael Seidel, Eric Sundquist, Werner Sollors, and Albert J. von Frank.

I am grateful to several anonymous readers, whose suggestions and criticisms helped me refine the argument of *Negative Liberties*. I thank Kathleen Fitzpatrick and Priscilla Wald for their readings of a late draft of the manuscript. I am deeply indebted to the series editor, Donald Pease, for his faith in the project and for his critical insights.

I thank Elizabeth Fowler for encouragement and insight during the early stages of this project. Her ability to interrogate my ideas and to ask the right questions helped me refine my vision of what this book should be.

I have been fortunate enough to have had inspirational teachers at every stage of my life. My deepest gratitude is owed to Mary Evelyn Bruce, Thomas Squire, Gregory Lombardo, Gilbert Smith, Donald Hull, John V. Kelleher, Warner Berthoff, and Leo Marx. As the second reader for my dissertation, Philip Fisher had a decisive impact not only on this project but also on the trajectory of my intellectual career. I thank him particularly for prodding me to deepen my engagement with political philosophy.

I have also been fortunate in my friends. I cannot imagine what my life would have been like without the friendship of Cabot and Mollie Brown, Joseph Hershenson and Kent Chang, Jonathan and Irit Kolber, Ingrid and Stefan Pinter, Anne Corbett and Andrew Whitney. I am grateful to them for understanding when work on this project has led me to miss weddings, birthday celebrations, and reunions. It is heartening to know that old friendships can survive the vicissitudes of distance and divergent professional paths.

Of the many new friends that I have made since coming to NYU, I want to single out my colleague Phillip Brian Harper, who has been a steadfast source of encouragement and support.

My family, both here and abroad, has always been a source of strength and inspiration. I cherish the memory of my late aunt Frainy Patell and my late uncle Minocher Patell, fellow scholar and professor. My aunt Banoo Patell, my uncle Noshir Patell, and my grandmother Francisca D. Raña have provided me with models of selflessness and devotion to others. I am deeply grateful to my aunt Diana M. Patell for her continuing support and love. My sister, Shireen, a fellow literary scholar and devotee of Morrison's novels, read drafts of this manuscript with good humor and sharp insight. My parents, Rusi and Estrella Patell, gave me the foundation upon which to build a life in academe; for their love and sacrifices, I will be forever in their debt.

My wife, Deborah Lindsay Williams, is my partner and collaborator in all things. Without her love and encouragement, this book would not have come to fruition. She enabled me to renew my commitment to this project when it was in danger of flagging, and she reminds me every day why it is important to be a teacher as well as a scholar. She has helped me be more like the person I have always wanted to be. Our life together is an object lesson in why unencumbered selves are selves that are woefully incomplete.

My work on individualism had its genesis one afternoon years ago in a seminar taught by Sacvan Bercovitch. Since then he has been a mentor, a friend, and a tireless advocate. In acknowledgement of all that he has meant to my scholarly career, I dedicate this book to him.

New York
February 2000

Negative Liberties

ONE. Narrating Individualism

St. Augustine sets the problem. Mankind has, in its sin, two freedoms, to choose and to choose rightly. It cannot do the second without Divine Grace. Even if we could believe in that, it would not come to us in the ordinary course of history. In the absence of such a god, we are left with what we now call *negative liberty*, but there is no great joy in that for many political theorists, even those who recognize that positive liberty in the hands of human, not divine, hands is an invitation to unrestrained coercion.—Judith N. Shklar (1987)

The problem . . . is that the Constitution is a charter of negative rather than positive liberties. . . . The men who wrote the Bill of Rights were not concerned that government might do too little for the people, but that it might do too much to them.—Richard Posner, *Jackson v. City of Joliet* (1983)

When the communitarians attack liberal society, they are really attacking individualism, because to them it represents the heart of liberalism.—George Kateb (1992)

Two-thirds of the way through Thomas Pynchon's novel *Mason & Dixon* (1997), a Chinese *Feng-Shui* expert named "Capt. Zhang" looks with dismay upon the "Visto"—the line that the novel's protagonists have been hewing through the American wilderness: "Terrible *Feng-Shui* here. Worst I ever saw. You two crazy?" Arguing that "ev'rywhere else on earth, Boundaries follow Nature . . . so honoring the Dragon or Shan within, from which the Landscape ever takes its form," Zhang declares that "to mark a right Line upon the Earth is to inflict upon the Dragon's flesh a sword slash, a long, perfect scar, impossible for any who live out here the year 'round to see as other than hateful Assault" (542; my ellipsis). Later he will tell the surveyors that their Visto may well be "an Agent of Darkness": "To rule forever . . . it is necessary only to create, among the people one would rule, what we call . . . Bad History. Nothing will produce Bad History more directly nor brutally, than drawing a Line, in particular a Right Line, the very Shape of Content, through the midst of a people,—to create thus a Distinction betwixt 'em,— 'tis the first stroke.—All else will follow as if predestin'd, unto War and Devastation" (615; Pynchon's ellipses). Pynchon's earlier novels abound with examples of Bad History at work, from the European incursions into Southwest Africa depicted in *V.* (1963) to Brock Vond's attempts to impose a restrictive communitarian culture on the United States in *Vineland* (1990).

Toni Morrison is another writer who knows all about Bad History and about distinctions between peoples. Her most recent novel, *Paradise* (1998), is set in the all-black town of Ruby, Oklahoma (population 360), whose inhabitants have drawn a line between themselves and the outside world. Morrison describes Ruby as "a sleepy town with three churches within one mile of one another but nothing to serve a traveler: no diner, no police, no gas station, no public phone, no movie house, no hospital" (12). It is a town whose obsession with its own history and traditions is personified in its leading citizens Deacon and Steward Morgan, twin brothers who "have powerful memories," who "between them . . . remember the details of everything that ever happened—things they witnessed and things they have not," who remember above all the "controlling" story "told to them by their grandfather," a story that "explained" why the inhabitants of Ruby could not "tolerate anybody but themselves" (13). It is a story about racism—by whites against blacks, by blacks against blacks—that leads the town to mimic the intolerance once directed against them. In *Paradise*, as in her earlier novels *The Bluest Eye* (1970), *Sula* (1973), and *Beloved* (1987), Morrison shows how black communities subjected to Bad History create bad histories of their own. Morrison's novels indict black communities for the perpetuation of Bad History, but they trace the genealogy of the problem back to the racist narratives generated throughout U.S. history by a dominant culture ruled by whites.

Bad Histories and Official Stories

Morrison confronts the specter of Bad History directly in her introduction to the anthology *Birth of a Nation'hood* (1997). She looks at the events surrounding the first O. J. Simpson trial and sees not just "a hot property of mayhem loaded with the thrill that a mixture of fame, sex, death, money and race produces" but also an example of "the construction of a national narrative, an official story." Such a controlling narrative, she writes, "is born in and from chaos. Its purpose is to restore or imitate order and to minimize confusion about what is at stake and who will pay the price of dissension. Once, long ago, these stories developed slowly. They became over time national epics, written, sung, performed and archived in the culture as memory, ideology and art" (1997, xv–xvi). In democracies like the United States, Morrison contends, "the manufacture of a public truth is harder" than in countries where "the construction of a national narrative is given over to a government agency"; the process occurs more slowly because it is "cautioned and delayed by a free press, an openly dissident citizenry, a reversible electorate" (xvi). What Morrison finds alarming in the case of the first Simpson trial is the rapidity with which the official story was constructed and disseminated, an example of the way in which "democratic discourses" can be "suborned by sudden, accelerated, sustained blasts of media messages—visual and in print—that rapidly enforce the narrative and truncate alternative opinion" (xvi). Nevertheless, Morrison argues, no matter how, or how rapidly, they are produced, official stories have the same "consequence and function": they serve "to impose the will of a dominant culture" (xxviii).

Morrison's description of the relation between storytelling and cultural dominance aligns her with those Americanist historians and literary critics who have found inspiration in the tradition of ideology theory that views ideology as fundamentally "a discursive or semiotic phenomenon" (to use Terry Eagleton's phrase [194]).[1] For example, in *The Problem of Slavery in the Age of Revolution* (1975), David Brion Davis uses the term

> "ideology" to mean an integrated system of beliefs, assumptions, and values, not necessarily true or false, which reflects the needs and interests of a group or class at a particular time in history. By "interest" I mean anything that benefits or is thought to benefit a specific collective identity. Because ideologies are modes of consciousness, containing the criteria for interpreting social reality, they help to define as well as to legitimate collective needs and interests. Hence there is a continuous interaction between ideology and the material forces of history. The salient characteristic of an ideology is that, while it is taken for granted by people who have internalized it, it is never the

> eternal or absolute truth it claims to be. Ideologies focus attention on certain phenomena, but only by arbitrarily screening out other phenomena in patterns that are not without meaning. (14)

This description of ideology as an internalized mode of consciousness that acts as an interpretive lens or filter is indebted, I think, to Louis Althusser's interpretation of the conception of ideology implicit in Karl Marx's *Capital*. Althusser defined ideology as "a system (with its own logic and rigour) of representations (images, myths, ideas or concepts, depending on the case) endowed with a historical existence and role within a given society" (231). In "The Problem of Ideology in American Literary History," Sacvan Bercovitch builds on this representational model by describing ideology as "the system of interlinked ideas, symbols and beliefs by which a culture—any culture—seeks to justify and perpetuate itself; the web of rhetoric, ritual, and assumption through which society coerces, persuades, and coheres." Ideology, for Bercovitch, is "the ground and texture of consensus" (1986, 635).

What Morrison refers to as *official narratives* play a crucial role within an ideology's "system" of representations. Ideology functions first by providing its subjects with a cultural vocabulary, an extended language that includes words, images, symbols, and cultural myths, and then by linking these semantic units together via associative patterns of reasoning that are analogous to such literary devices as metaphor, metonymy, oxymoron, symbolism, and intertextual reference. Elaborating on Althusser's theory, the sociologist Stuart Hall writes that "ideologies do not operate through single ideas"; rather, "they operate, in discursive chains, in clusters, in semantic fields, in discursive formations. As you enter an ideological field and pick out any one nodal representation or idea, you immediately trigger off a whole chain of connotative associations. Ideological representations connote—summon—one another" (104). Each of the representations generated within an ideological field is constructed from one or more associations, but these representations are themselves linked to one another as sequences of thought. Within an ideological field, certain dominant strands, certain characteristic patterns of reasoning, eventually emerge, becoming evident throughout a broad range of different discourses.[2]

Where can we find a counterweight to such official narratives? Pynchon implicitly and Morrison explicitly suggest that we look to the literary imagination. In *Mason & Dixon*, for example, Pynchon uses fiction to create a counternarrative to U.S. frontier mythology. Capt. Zhang is Pynchon's own invention—needless to say, he appears nowhere in *The Journal of Charles Mason and Jeremiah Dixon*—and his presence suggests that Pynchon is telling a story about the eighteenth-century American frontier from the vantage point of twentieth-century border studies. Indeed, it is tempting to read this episode from *Mason & Dixon* as an allegory of late twentieth-century developments within American studies, with Capt. Zhang representing minority discourse theory, Charles Mason representing traditionalists, and Jeremiah Dixon representing the so-called New Americanists. Mason, the older of the two surveyors, refuses to believe in the danger of drawing boundaries; in response to Zhang's diatribe against creating distinctions between peoples, Mason replies, "Poh, Sir, . . . the Provinces are alike as Stacy and Tracy." Dixon, however, is already beginning to learn Zhang's lesson, "point[ing] out" to Mason, "less mildly than he might," that "Negro Slavery" exists "upon one side . . . and not the other" (615). But he does not believe that the line that he and Mason are drawing has anything to do with the problem of slavery. Later, however, he will come to realize the truth of Zhang's belief that "slavery is very old upon these shores,— there is no Innocence upon the Practice anywhere, neither among the Indians nor the Spanish nor in the behavior of the rest of Christendom, if it come to that" (616). By the novel's end, Dixon understands that slavery is "the Element common to all" the adventures on which they have been sent by England's Royal Society and that they are implicated in it: "Didn't we take the King's money . . . whilst Slaves wait upon us[?] Where does it end?" Dixon asks Mason: "No matter where in it we go, shall we find all the World Tyrants and Slaves? America was the one place we should *not* have found them" (692–93). *Mason & Dixon* is thus a revisionist narrative that uses the historical novel to expose the underside of European and American history.

In contrast to Pynchon, Morrison writes openly about literature's ability to engage official narratives. She begins her Nobel Prize acceptance speech by declaring that "narrative has never been merely entertainment for me. It is, I believe, one of the principal ways in which we absorb knowledge" (1994, 77). For Morrison, writing a novel is essentially an act of cultural criticism. "The kind of work I have always wanted to do," she writes in the preface to her critical study *Playing in the Dark* (1992), "requires me to learn how to maneuver ways to free up the language from its sometimes sinister, frequently lazy, almost always predictable employment of racially informed and determined chains" (xi). Speaking of the U.S. literary tradition, Morrison suggests that "living in a nation of people who *decided* that their world view would combine agendas for individual freedom *and* mechanisms for devastating racial oppression presents a singular landscape for a writer" (xiii). The writers whom she prizes most highly are those "who take responsibility for *all* of the values they bring to their art" (xiii), whether those values serve or challenge the dominant culture's official stories. This perspective seems, in retrospect, to have been a part of Morrison's writing all along. "The best art," she writes elsewhere, "is political and you ought to be able to make it unquestionably political and irrevocably beautiful at the same time" (1984, 345).[3]

This conception of the cultural functions of narrative also aligns Morrison with a cadre of late twentieth-century philosophers who have sought to explore the common ground between literature and philosophy. Ronald Beiner, Stanley Cavell, Alasdair MacIntyre, Martha Nussbaum, Richard Rorty, Michael J. Sandel, Steven Shiffrin, and Judith Shklar are among those who have suggested that professional philosophy has much to learn from literature's ability to dramatize the complexities and idiosyncrasies of human life. Describing humans as "storytelling beings," Sandel contends that "political community depends on the narratives by which people make sense of their condition and interpret the common life they share" (1996, 350). Beiner has faulted twentieth-century analytic philosophy for being "self-restricting and self-effacing" in cutting itself off from the kind of imaginative speculation about human life regularly found in literary works (1). These philosophers seek to remind their colleagues that philosophy has always relied on the literary: the precedent for Cavell's use of Shakespeare, for example, is Aristotle's use of Homer and Euripides. Shklar defends the explicit use of stories and storytelling as "something political philosophers used to do quite normally" (1984, 231). Beiner goes further, arguing that all philosophical writing is implicitly a form of storytelling: "In theorizing, . . . we tell a story—preferably a true story" (12).

Philosophy's reliance, however, on abstract theoretical models, which necessarily simplify the complexities of human experience, can lead it to tell stories that fall short of the truth. Commenting on Charles Dickens's *Hard Times*, a novel that satirizes utilitarianism by imagining what it would be like if "the utilitarian norm" were "understood not just as a way of writing up reports, but as a way of dealing with people in daily encounters" (17), Nussbaum claims that philosophical reason would become more powerful if it were supplemented by the literary imagination. She follows Shklar's suggestion that storytelling should be conceived as "an addition" to "more abstract modes of analysis" rather than "a substitute" for them

(1984, 231) by arguing that *Hard Times* does not completely discount the usefulness of political economy. Instead, Nussbaum contends, the novel "indicates that political and economic treatises of an abstract and mathematical sort would be perfectly consistent with its purpose—so long as the view of the human being underlying the treatises was the richer view available in the novel; so long as they do not lose sight of what they are, for efficiency, omitting" (44). For Shklar, this richer view entails the recognition of conflict and irrationality: "The great intellectual advantage of telling stories is that it does not rationalize the irrationality of actual experience and history. Indecision, incoherence and inconsistency are not ironed out or put between brackets. All our conflicts are preserved in all their inconclusiveness. . . . Stories expose rather than create order, and in so doing they can render explicit much that is inarticulate" (1984, 230).

Deprived of the "richer view" that storytelling offers, philosophy becomes more susceptible to appropriation by the forces that create official stories, a process dramatized in *Hard Times*, where utilitarian calculus becomes the basis for both Bad History and bad government. Nussbaum admits that "government cannot investigate the life story of every citizen in the way a novel does with its characters," but it can learn a valuable lesson from the novel: "It can . . . know that each citizen has a complex history of this sort, and it can remain aware that the norm in principle would be to acknowledge the separateness, freedom, and qualitative difference of each in the manner of the novel" (44).[4] What happens when those in power fail to learn this lesson is dramatized in Pynchon's *Gravity's Rainbow* (1973), with its nefarious experiments on human subjects, and in Morrison's *Beloved*, where the cruel slave master known as "Schoolteacher" carefully takes his slaves' measurements, numbers their teeth, and catalogs their attributes—"human characteristics on the left . . . animal ones on the right" (1987a, 193)—in order to evaluate their worth. Both novels can be read as cautionary tales that depict the fundamental inhumanity of abstract scientific rationalism when it is divorced from the "richer view" that Nussbaum finds in novels.

What I want to do in *Negative Liberties* is to take seriously the idea that narrative constitutes "one of the principal ways in which we absorb knowledge." I will focus on the official story that Morrison believes to be at the heart of U.S. national culture, namely, the story that the culture tells itself about its special relation to the idea of *individual freedom*, a story that crystallizes in the Emersonian tradition. This national narrative attempts to persuade us that giving priority to the claims of the individual over the claims of the group does not mean that one set of claims will remain unsatisfied. Indeed, it proposes that satisfying the claims of the individual is the best way of satisfying the claims of any particular group to which the individual belongs. It suggests, for example, that the claims that Morrison makes on behalf of race can—and will—be satisfied by the liberal system of the United States. It asks us to regard the presence of "devastating racial oppression" as immaterial and temporary, a mere side plot soon to be edited away. According to Michael Sandel, one of the most prominent communitarian critics of U.S. liberalism and its basis in individualism, "this vision of freedom" has become "so familiar . . . that it seems a permanent feature of the American political and constitutional tradition" (1996, 5). Describing liberalism as a tradition of thought that emphasizes toleration and respect for individual rights and that runs from John Locke, Immanuel Kant, and John Stuart Mill to John Rawls, Sandel argues that "the public philosophy of contemporary American politics is a version of this liberal tradition of thought, and most of our debates proceed within its terms" (5–6). Sandel's writings describe an official narrative that grows out of "the Enlightenment's quest for the self-defining subject" (1984b, 87) and that has saturated not only U.S. public philosophy but also its popular culture.

The influential study *Habits of the Heart: Individualism and Commitment in American Life* (1985) provides documentary evidence of the extent to which this official narrative continues to influence the ways in which social, political, and moral issues are discussed in the United States. In particular, it demonstrates that this narrative delimits the ways in which Americans think and speak about their communally oriented goals. The book's authors, Robert N. Bellah, Richard Madsen, William M. Sullivan, Ann Swidler, and Steven M. Tipton, state that they seek "to deepen our understanding of the resources our tradition provides—and fails to provide—for enabling us to think about the kinds of moral problems we are currently facing as Americans" (21). *Habits* begins by introducing the reader to four different individuals who are offered as representative character types: a corporate manager, a "concerned citizen," a therapist, and an activist. Claiming that these individuals "each represent American voices familiar to us all," Bellah et al. also suggest that, if the four were to meet, there would be "sharp disagreements" among them and that these disagreements "would be versions of controversies that regularly arise in public and private moral discourse in the United States." Yet, among these four individuals, the authors discern "more than a little consensus about the relationship between the individual and society, between private and public good," a consensus that can be attributed to the fact that "they all to some degree share a common moral vocabulary," which Bellah et al. "propose to call the 'first language' of American individualism in contrast to alternative 'second languages,' which most of us also have" (20). Clarifying this terminology, Bellah et al. state that they use the term *language* "to refer to modes of moral discourse that include distinct vocabularies and characteristic patterns of moral reasoning. We use *first language* to refer to the individualistic mode that is the dominant American form of discourse about moral, social, and political matters. We use the term *second languages* to refer to other forms, primarily biblical and republican, that provide at least part of the moral discourse of most Americans" (334). These second languages are vestigial, fragmentary, and relatively unarticulated.

Bellah et al. claim that, when Americans use "the moral discourse they share, what we call the first language of individualism, they have difficulty articulating the richness of their commitments" (20–21). According to Fredric Jameson, this inability to articulate communal feelings results from the fact that "the first language or discourse of individualism . . . powerfully deflects and deforms everything that passes through it; like a system of cartographic projection, it translates the content offered it into the style and specificity of its own volumes and contours, with the Wittgensteinian consequence that whatever it cannot express falls outside of social reality." Jameson views *Habits of the Heart* as "a kind of 'language experiment' in which, minimally, [the authors] seek to make us aware of the asphyxiating confines and limits of the language into which we are locked; at their most ambitious, they seem themselves to strain to produce a new language capable of bursting the seams of the older one and making new realities and new possibilities appear" (105–6). What *Habits of the Heart* ultimately demonstrates, however, is the strength of those seams. Not only are its authors unwilling to break completely with the ideology of individualism (much to Jameson's chagrin), but they also leave us with profound doubts about the possibility of renovating that ideology. Although Bellah et al. believe that many of those whom they have interviewed are unwittingly engaged in the search for "a moral language that will transcend their radical individualism" (21), they also confess toward the end of the book that, "on the basis of our interviews, and from what we can observe more generally in our society today, it is not clear that many Americans are prepared to consider a significant change in the way we have been living" (294).

Because both Bellah et al. and Jameson do not fully acknowledge the fiction-making capacities of ideology, they have trouble understanding why individualism continues to be so powerfully persuasive for late twentieth-century Americans. What Bellah et al. refer to as *second languages* do not simply coexist, nagging and inarticulate, within the *first language* of individualism; rather, they are actively incorporated into an ideological story that relegates them to a contingent position. The official narrative that has emerged around individualism appropriates the opposition between individual and community that preoccupies both *Habits of the Heart* and Jameson's critique and reconfigures it as a progression. If the subjects interviewed for *Habits of the Heart* find themselves unable to articulate certain types of communal longing, it is not simply because they have lost their ability to use the language of community but also because that language has been appropriated and subordinated by this official narrative. Part of the problem with this narrative is that it has promoted a particularly bloodless and abstract version of community, one that turns out to have little to do with actual communities such as those based on class, race, ethnicity, or sexuality. The vocabulary of community that this narrative employs and makes available is limited: it fails to recognize as legitimate most of the communities that Americans are likely to experience.

Negative Liberties shows how Morrison's and Pynchon's novels engage this national narrative and expose it as a manifestation of Bad History. In so doing, they dramatize both the power and the shortcomings of Emersonian liberalism, a tradition of U.S. liberal philosophy that, I will argue, includes Ralph Waldo Emerson, John Rawls, and George Kateb, a tradition that makes a strong philosophical case for the national narrative of individualism. These three idealist philosophers offer compelling descriptions and defenses of U.S. culture's conception of individual freedom, but (as we shall see in the next chapter) their reliance on both methodological individualism and philosophical abstraction leaves them unable to provide the conceptual resources necessary to counteract such social pathologies as devastating racial oppression. Morrison is surely right to suggest that "living in a nation of people who *decided* that their world view would combine agendas for individual freedom *and* mechanisms for devastating racial oppression presents a singular landscape for a writer." I will argue that both Morrison and Pynchon inhabit this singular landscape and that the formal and thematic differences between their oeuvres are differences of emphasis and degree rather than of kind. In their different ways, Morrison and Pynchon dramatize the fact that the story of individualism that has arisen from Emersonian liberalism in the United States has become a form of Bad History, a coercive narrative that serves to impose the will of a dominant culture.

Varieties of Liberal Individualism

In 1840, Alexis de Tocqueville identified individualism as one of the distinctive characteristics of American democracy. Nearly fifty years later, in the second volume of his study *The American Commonwealth* (1888), the British historian James Bryce argued that "individualism, the love of enterprise, and the pride in personal freedom, have been deemed by Americans not only their choicest, but their peculiar and exclusive possessions" (591). More than a century after Bryce wrote these words, individualism remains at the heart of American ideology. In a grudging tribute to the continuing power of individualism in late twentieth-century U.S. culture, Bellah et al. confess that they "do not argue that Americans should abandon individualism" because "that would mean for us to abandon our deepest identity" (1985, 142).

Habits of the Heart was perhaps the most widely disseminated of the communitarian critiques of U.S. individualism put forward during the 1980s by such thinkers as Benjamin Barber, Amitai Etzioni, Alasdair MacIntyre, Michael Sandel, Charles Taylor, and Michael Walzer. The persistence of individualism in the United States continues to discomfit not only communitarian thinkers but also intellectuals in a variety of fields who are invested in the poststructuralist critique of subjectivity.[5] In the introduction to a collection of essays *Individualism*, originally published in France under the title *Sur l'individualisme: Théories et méthodes* (1986), Pierre Birnbaum and Jean Leca adopt the dire language of an influential nineteenth-century manifesto and proclaim, "A spectre is haunting the West's intellectuals—the spectre of individualism" (1). The editors of the multidisciplinary collection *Reconstructing Individualism* (1986) find themselves compelled to admit that "in America, the post-structuralist critique of individuality has had only a feeble impact on the persistently individualist imagery of our institutions and popular culture. In the political, economic, and artistic spheres of public life, these images have remained unshaken by the theoretical trauma that has led to the subtleties of post-structuralist theory" (Heller and Wellbery, 12–13). Discredited in Europe, individualism continues to provide the ideological field upon which social conflicts and political battles take place in the United States. So ingrained is individualism in late twentieth-century U.S. culture that its propositions often seem to be matters of common sense rather than ideology. In short, U.S. individualism provides an example of ideology at its most persuasive and effective.

U.S. individualism is actually a set of interrelated forms of individualism that include the *methodological*, the *political*, the *economic*, and the *possessive*. Underwriting each of these variants is what social scientists refer to as *ontological individualism*, the belief that the individual has an a priori and primary reality and that society is a derived, second-order construct. Steven Lukes writes that "according to this conception, individuals are pictured abstractly as given, with given interests, wants, purposes, needs, etc.; while society and the state are pictured as sets of actual or possible social arrangements which respond more or less adequately to those individuals' requirements." What is important to notice about this description is the importance of abstraction: ontological individualism presents what Lukes describes as "an *abstract* conception of the individual who is seen as merely the bearer" of "fixed and invariant human psychological features," which "determine his behaviour, and specify his interests, needs and rights" (73).

This conception of the nature of the individual generates a mode of thinking that social scientists call *methodological individualism*. Because it serves to render the workings of ideology invisible, this mode of thinking accounts in large part for the persuasiveness of the official story that has arisen around individualism in the United States. The political theorist Jon Elster describes methodological individualism as "a form of reductionism" according to which "all social phenomena—whether process, structure, institution, or habitus—can be explained by the actions and properties of the participating individuals" (47). Although the term *methodological individualism* was coined by Joseph Schumpeter (889), the concept was first clearly articulated by Thomas Hobbes, whose search for "constitutive causes" consistently led him to ground his analysis in assertions about individual persons and even individual physical bodies: the most notable example is Hobbes's development in *Leviathan* (1651) of the concept of the *artificial person* as a way of describing the commonwealth (Lukes, 110). From Schumpeter on, social scientists have sought to make a distinction between ontological individualism and methodological individualism, viewing the former as a way of characterizing and even legitimizing the institutional structures of a culture, the latter as a mode of social inquiry, a way of thinking about collective phenomena in terms of facts about individuals. The difference between the two, as Birnbaum and Leca have put it, is that methodological individualism is "an attribute of the researcher, not the object of study" (3).

In the patterns of reasoning that characterize U.S. individualism, however, ontological and methodological individualism are fused and mutually reinforcing. American social theorists like Ralph Waldo Emerson who advocate individualism as the most effective mode of social organization for the United States also tend to adopt the theoretical strategy of shifting the ground of social inquiry and debate from society to the individual; they recast situations of social choice into situations of individual choice. For example, in the essay "Circles," Emerson writes that "our culture is the predominance of an idea which draws after it this train of cities and institutions. Let us rise into another idea; they will disappear. . . . The new continents are built out of the ruins of an old planet; the new races fed out of the decomposition of the foregoing. New arts destroy the old." One paragraph later he shifts his attention from culture to the individual, declaring, "The key to every man is his thought. . . . The life of man is a self-evolving circle, which, from a ring imperceptibly small, rushes on all sides outwards to new and larger circles, and that without end" (1841a, 403–4). Emerson's rhetorical shifting here is accompanied by a heightened level of abstraction in which the individual, stripped of social markers, is described as "the soul," the life of the individual is described as "a self-evolving circle," and the concept of power is sanitized, disconnected from its functions in the world of politics, and grounded in the individual. The Emersonian self is an *abstract individual* who exists before and beyond society, a self whose claims are considered to have priority over those of society—a philosophical analogue to the loner so prized by American cultural mythology.

What I am suggesting here is that this pattern of reasoning is not limited to philosophical discourse. Americans characteristically think about the pressing social issues of their day in terms of the rights, needs, and desires of individuals. Both sides of the debate over abortion, for example, define their positions in terms of individual rights: the prolife position defends the fetus's "individual right to life" (to quote, for example, from the 1992 Republican Party platform), while the prochoice position defends the woman's "right to choose." Opponents of affirmative-action policies typically cite the injustice done to particular individuals who were denied jobs or admission to schools; they tend to think about affirmative action only on a case-by-case basis and view its attempt to effect systemic social change as misguided.[6] The campaign rhetoric of American politicians—even of those politicians who preach the value of family and community—invariably cites the experiences of particular individuals as if they were representative and therefore constitute proof of the validity or efficacy of social policy. The pervasiveness of methodological individualism as an interpretive strategy in U.S. culture accounts for the fact that Americans have traditionally been eager to characterize ideology as something that only other societies have, for, as Birnbaum and Leca note, "one of the essential lessons of methodological individualism is that a society is not a system" (11). Part of the reason why individualism is so effective as an ideology is that the official narrative that surrounds it renders it invisible by fostering the belief that group formations like ideology do not really exist.

Ontological individualism is a social theory that regards society as merely a necessary evil, and in the realm of political thought it fosters a "negative" conception of the nature of freedom. According to this conception, the free individual has an innate dignity that is protected through the possession of certain rights that have the effect of creating a sphere of privacy over which the individual is master, free from constraints, protected from the incursions of others. To be deprived of these rights is to be subject to the will of others, in essence, to be a slave. "The only freedom which deserves the name," writes John Stuart Mill in *On Liberty* (1859), "is that of pursuing our own good in our own way, so long as we do not attempt to deprive others of theirs, or impede their efforts to obtain it" (14). The self-fulfillment implied in the idea of "pursuing our own good in our own way" is an important goal of liberal individualism, but it is the conclusion of a process that begins only with self-autonomy. In contrast, the "positive" conception of freedom views self-fulfillment as intimately related to one's communal commitments and attachments.

The distinction between the negative and the positive conceptions of freedom is captured by the difference between the modifying prepositions frequently used to describe them. Negative liberty is "freedom *from*"—freedom from restraint or coercion, from the incursions of authority, from the intrusions of one's neighbors. It denotes the area within which an individual can act without being obstructed by others, and it forms the basis not only for the right to privacy but also for the very idea of rights. Positive liberty, in contrast, is "freedom *to*"—freedom to achieve self-expression, self-realization, and self-mastery as well as freedom to participate in government and political life, activities that prove to be related. Indeed, under a positive conception of freedom, true self-fulfillment depends on active participation in political life.

What I will argue in the course of this book is that a teleological relation between negative liberty and positive liberty is the central feature of the official narrative generated by U.S. culture around the idea of individualism. In other words, the story that U.S. culture tends to tell about the nature of freedom is that negative liberty and positive liberty are not competing but rather complementary and symbiotic conceptions. The appeal of this story should be obvious. Looking after the good of the individual does not thwart but actually produces communal good; individualism leads not to selfishness but rather to self-fulfillment in family life, communal life, or the life of the nation.

An early version of this story can be found in the writings of Benjamin Franklin; indeed, in presenting his life as representative in the *Autobiography*, Franklin offers what amounts to a case study that proves the validity of this cultural narrative. Franklin describes how he "emerg'd from the Poverty & Obscurity in which I was born & bred, to a State of Affluence & some Degree of Reputation in the World" (1307), and in the second part of the *Autobiography*, he relates that his desire for material well-being proves to be inseparable from the cultivation of spiritual well-being, leading him to "conceiv[e] the bold and arduous Project of arriving at moral Perfection" (1383). For Franklin, what is most exceptional and distinctive about America is the fact that it encourages individuals to lead the kind of life that he has led. In his essay "Information to Those Who Would Remove to America" (1784), Franklin describes what he considers to be the typical experience of immigrants arriving in America from Europe: "If they are poor, they begin first as Servants or Journeymen; and if they are sober, industrious, and frugal, they soon become Masters, establish themselves in Business, marry, raise Families, and become respectable Citizens" (979). Here in a nutshell is the official story of U.S. individualism: in the transformation of servant into citizen, we see that U.S. culture first provides the opportunity to attain negative freedom and then transforms negative freedom into the positive form embodied in the ideal of citizenship. Concern for the individual's material well-being transmutes itself into concern for the well-being of the polity.

Both negative liberty and ontological individualism are relatively recent concepts in the history of political thought; indeed, positive liberty has been called "the liberty of the ancients," negative liberty "the liberty of the moderns."[7] In his classic essay "Two Concepts of Liberty" (1958), Isaiah Berlin argues that "there seems to be scarcely any discussion of individual liberty as a conscious political ideal (as opposed to its actual existence) in the ancient world.... The domination of this ideal has been the exception rather than the rule, even in the recent history of the West." He adds that the "sense of privacy itself, of the area of personal relationships as something sacred in its own right, derives from a conception of freedom which for all its religious roots, is scarcely older, in its developed state, than the Renaissance or the Reformation" (129).

One of the earliest and most influential discussions of negative liberty is John Locke's *Two Treatises of Government* (1698). Locke argues that the natural condition of human beings is "a State of perfect Freedom to order their Actions, and dispose of their Possessions, and Persons as they think fit, within the bounds of the Law of Nature, without asking leave, or depending upon the Will of any other Man" (269). Society is conceived as a second-order construct: according to Locke, men remain in that state of perfect freedom until "by their own Consents, they make themselves Members of some Politick Society" (278), and he argues that "government" exists only "for the good of the Governed," to protect "every Mans Right and Property, by preserving him from the Violence or Injury of others" (209–10). Locke's principles of government continue to exert a powerful force in U.S. culture because his *Second Treatise* was a major influence on political thought during the revolutionary era and in particular on Thomas Jefferson. The Declaration of Independence would weave Lockean negative liberty into the very fabric of U.S. cultural life.

Locke and Jefferson are typical of thinkers whose idea of freedom is based on negative liberty: they both emphasize the idea that all individual human beings have certain fundamental rights simply because they *are* human beings. Locke argues that human beings are "born . . . with a Title to perfect Freedom, and an uncontrouled enjoyment of all the Rights and Priviledges of the Law of Nature"; it is only to ensure the effective protection of their property—understood broadly to mean "Life, Liberty, and Estate"—that they allow this freedom and these rights to be circumscribed by civil government (323–24). In the Declaration, Jefferson affirms it to be a "self-evident" truth that all individuals "are endowed by their Creator with certain unalienable Rights" (19).

Both the *Second Treatise* and the Declaration propose a system of *political individualism*, one based on the protection of rights, in which the legitimacy of a government arises from the consent of its citizens—given individually, either directly or through representatives.[8] The role of government is simply to protect the ability of its citizens to choose and pursue their own desires and goals; a legitimate government should have nothing at all to do with influencing or shaping the desires and goals of its citizens. Both Locke and Jefferson seek to preserve as much as possible of what they believe to be the original autonomy of the individual, to protect the identity and agency of the individual from the incursions of society.

In contrast, thinkers whose conception of freedom rests upon the idea of positive liberty tend to emphasize responsibilities and duties instead of rights. One has responsibilities, they argue, to oneself, to the community of which one is a member, and to the polity of which one is a citizen. Like negative liberty, positive liberty originates in the desire to be one's own master, but according to Berlin, in the case of positive liberty, the metaphor of self-mastery acquires an "independent momentum" that enables it to refer not only to literal enslavement but also to metaphysical or spiritual enslavement. Berlin notes, for example, that both Platonists and Hegelians tend to describe human beings as slaves either to nature or to their own "unbridled" passions, resulting in the conviction that there are two selves within each individual, a "higher" self that is identified with reason and a "lower" self that must be "brought to heel" because it is identified with "irrational impulse, uncontrolled desires, [and] the pursuit of immediate pleasures" (132). For the philosopher Charles Taylor, it is the existence of this higher self that makes the negative conception of freedom seem impoverished. In an influential defense of positive liberty, Taylor argues that negative theories rely on an "opportunity-concept" of liberty in which "being free is a matter of what we can do, of what it is open to us to do, whether or not we do anything to exercise these options." The positive conception of liberty, however, turns upon the idea that we must exercise certain options in order to be truly free; according to Taylor, being free means "being able to recognize adequately my more important purposes" and "being able to overcome or at least neutralize my motivational fetters, as well as [having] my way [be] free of external obstacles." This state of being "involves essentially the exercising of control over one's life. On this view, one is free only to the extent that one has effectively determined oneself and the shape of one's life" (1985b, 213).

Because the negative and positive conceptions of liberty both place a high premium on the desire to be one's own master, it is tempting to see them as merely two sides of a coin, negative and positive ways of expressing the same idea. Berlin cautions, however, that "historically [they] developed in divergent directions not always by logically reputable steps, until, in the end, they came into direct conflict with each other." Positive liberty diverges most dramatically from negative liberty when the real or higher self is identified with "a social 'whole' of which the individual is an element or aspect: a tribe, a race, a church, state, the great society of the living and the dead and the yet unborn." This social whole is conceived as "the 'true' self which, by imposing its collective, or 'organic,' single will upon its recalcitrant 'members,' achieves its own, and therefore their, 'higher' freedom" (132).[9] Self-realization, self-expression, and even self-mastery then occur only through the individual's identification with the ideals and goals of this larger social group. In this form, positive liberty is the theoretical underpinning for such social philosophies as communism, socialism, and communitarianism as well as for various religious fundamentalisms.

The classic statement of this form of positive liberty is Jean-Jacques Rousseau's *On the Social Contract* (1762). "Each of us," writes Rousseau, "puts his person and all his power in common under the supreme direction of the general will; and in a body we receive each member as an indivisible part of the whole" (53). In return for giving up "natural freedom" by entering into the social contract, individuals gain "civil freedom," which guarantees them the "proprietorship" (instead of merely the possession) of their goods, and "moral freedom," which "alone makes man truly master of himself" (56). Because he believes that self-realization is intimately connected to fulfilling one's social duties, Rousseau does not shy away from the use of coercion where necessary. "Whoever refuses to obey the general will," he writes, "shall be constrained to do so by the entire body; which means only that he will be forced to be free" (55). For Rousseau, what is important about individuals is not the extent to which they function as autonomous agents but rather the extent to which they function as members of a larger society, for he believes that it is primarily through the assumption of social bonds that the individual's true identity takes shape.[10]

The difference between the champions of negative liberty, like Locke and Jefferson, and the champions of positive liberty, like Rousseau, is ultimately a matter of the way in which each camp assesses the relative claims of the individual, on the one hand, and the community, on the other. The champions of negative liberty attend first and foremost to the claims of the individual; they are interested in the ways in which the individual may be said to *be* individual—to be a single, indivisible, autonomous agent and a possessor of rights. The champions of positive liberty, however, devote their primary attentions to the claims of community, emphasizing the ways in which the individual may be said to be a social being whose identity is realized through communal duties and responsibilities. Typically, such thinkers take the further step of advocating the establishment of particular forms of social organization and the encouragement of particular moral values. As Berlin puts it, those who advocate negative liberty "want to curb authority as such," while those who advocate positive liberty want authority to be "placed in their own hands." What is at issue in the distinction between negative and positive liberty is, he cautions, not "two different interpretations of a single concept, but two profoundly divergent and irreconcilable attitudes to the ends of life. . . . [E]ach of them makes absolute claims [that] cannot both be fully satisfied" (166). Berlin stresses that both negative liberty and positive liberty are "ends in themselves," ends that "may clash irreconcilably" (xlix).

It is my contention, however, that U.S. culture has not generally regarded negative liberty and positive liberty either as contradictory conceptions or as equivalent philosophical ends. Indeed, what I will argue in the pages that follow is that we cannot understand the continuing persuasiveness of individualism as an ideology in the United States without comprehending the way in which its official narrative sets negative liberty and positive liberty into a teleological relation. If negative liberty is the alpha of U.S. culture, its founding premise and point of departure, then positive liberty is its omega, its conclusion and happy ending. The official narrative inherits Locke's negative conception of freedom as freedom from restraint but claims that negative liberty inevitably transforms itself into a form of positive liberty that nurtures communal institutions. This assertion lies at the heart of the official story that tends to accompany the invocation of individualism in the United States: individualism, it is suggested, not only fosters individuality, self-expression, and self-fulfillment but also enables such communal ideals as family, community, and nation to develop and flourish.[11]

In *The Liberal Tradition in America* (1955), a now-classic but much-contested argument about the Lockean basis for U.S. political thought, Louis Hartz described the United States as "a society which begins with Locke, . . . transforms him, stays with Locke, by virtue of an absolute and irrational attachment it develops for him, and becomes as indifferent to the challenge of socialism in the later era as it was unfamiliar with the heritage of feudalism in the earlier one" (6). Indeed, Hartz argues, "here Locke has been so basic that we have not recognized his significance" (26). Hartz's thesis has been prominently contested by Bernard Bailyn (1967), Gordon S. Wood (1969), J. G. A. Pocock (1975, 1980), and Garry Wills (1978), all of whom argue that revolutionary America and Thomas Jefferson in particular were more strongly influenced by republican and communitarian traditions of civic virtue.[12] Although my account of the national narrative of individualism does side with Hartz's assertion of a strong Lockean influence within

U.S. culture, I do believe that Hartz's argument underestimates the power of Jefferson's revision of Locke's doctrine, a revision that was indeed linked to traditions of republican and communitarian thought that coexisted with Lockean liberalism in revolutionary America.

I have referred to both Locke and Jefferson as *champions of negative liberty*, but there is a crucial difference between them. Locke assigns absolute priority to negative liberty; Jefferson assigns it merely lexical priority, setting it into the teleological relation with positive liberty that I have been describing.[13] A crucial chapter in the national narrative of individualism was written when Jefferson chose to substitute the phrase *pursuit of happiness* for Locke's term *property*. Locke's conception of political individualism in the *Second Treatise* is closely linked to *economic individualism*, for Locke defends a form of ontological individualism that conceives of human freedom in terms of possession, proprietorship, and market relations: "Every Man has a *Property* in his own *Person*. This no Body has any Right to but himself. The *Labour* of his Body, and the *Work* of his Hands, we may say, are properly his" (1698, 287–88). The political theorist C. B. Macpherson gave the name *possessive individualism* to this particular fusion of the political and the economic forms of ontological individualism, and he argued that it arose in the seventeenth century because "the relation of ownership, having become for more and more men the critically important relation determining their actual freedom and actual prospect of realizing their full potentialities, was read back into the nature of the individual." In a society based on possessive individualism, being a free individual means being seen as the sole proprietor of one's own person and capacities, and society becomes nothing more than "a human contrivance for the protection of the individual's property in his person and goods, and (therefore) for the maintenance of orderly relations of exchange between individuals regarded as proprietors of themselves" (264). Possessive individualism is thus not only a materialist but also a materialistic philosophy that regards society as nothing but a series of relations between sole proprietors, in other words, as a series of market relations.

Jefferson, however, chose not to enumerate "property" as one of the individual's "inalienable rights," citing instead "the pursuit of happiness," an idealizing rhetorical strategy that was already a staple of writing about the uniqueness of "American" culture.[14] The idealizing rhetoric embodied in the phrase *pursuit of happiness* is a crucial part of the official story of individualism in the United States, linking the transition from negative to positive liberty to a transition from materialistic desires to idealistic pursuits.[15] "Property" and economic individualism are unstated assumptions of Jefferson's new formulation. As Joyce Appleby has argued, "Jefferson rallied his countrymen with a vision of the future that joined their materialism to a new morality. . . . America's economic base and the concept of a benign human potential sustained Jefferson's optimism" (318–19). Appleby also notes the "intellectual appeal that economic liberalism had to men from all walks of life" during the revolutionary and early national eras, and she attributes the "idealistic strain" in revolutionary thought that "[Gordon] Wood has identified with republicanism" instead to a "vision of the democratization of material well-being. . . . Liberalism in America became more than an ideological gloss on market economics; it was a description of a modern utopia which could garner the loyalties of a broad range of Americans" (187).

Appleby identifies the period "between Independence and the election of Thomas Jefferson" as the cultural moment when the "core" values of U.S. liberalism "were expressed explicitly for the first time." She summarizes these core values as follows:

> Human nature manifests itself universally in the quest for freedom. Political self-government emanates from individual self-control. Nature has endowed human beings with the capacity to think for themselves and act in their own behalf. This rational self-interest can be depended upon as a principle of action. Free choice in matters of religion, marriage, intellectual pursuits, and electoral politics is the right of every individual. Free inquiry discloses the nature of reality. True religion teaches the sanctity of each person and the need to glorify God through the cultivation of one's gifts and talents. The rule of law is binding on all citizens as long as its positive statutes conform to the natural law protection of life, liberty, and property. Vicious tyrannies over the body and mind, established in the infancy of human history, have blocked the spread of knowledge and its liberating potential. (1)

Appleby's summary makes it clear that liberalism puts a premium on universalism, individualism, rationalism, and pluralism. It is a utopian vision of progress and enlightenment (in part because it effaces the tensions that exist between universalism and pluralism in the liberal imagination). Appleby is forced, however, to add one final value that seems at odds with the rest: "The human personality presumed in these propositions is male" (1). And, we might add, white.

In other words, the national narrative—idealistic, universalistic, and utopian on its surface—turns out to contain some nasty subtexts that contradict its universalism. The widely used textbook *The Great Republic* offers a typical interpretation of the philosophy behind the Declaration: "The Declaration of Independence set forth a philosophy of human rights that could be applied not only to Americans, but to peoples everywhere. It was essential in giving the American Revolution a universal appeal" (Bailyn et al., 190). This statement, however, represents an idealization of both the theory and the practice of the principles set out by the Declaration. Implicit in the Declaration is the story of negative liberty transcending its origins, but the disjunction that is evident today between the theory and the practice of freedom in the United States demonstrates that the story has not come true because U.S. culture has not yet fully shed the oppressive patterns of reasoning that were dominant in the slaveholding patriarchal mode of culture from which U.S. individualism emerged. The principles stated in the Declaration of Independence *can* apply to all individuals, but at the time in which they were formulated, they did not and were not intended to. Despite the call for political liberty and freedom from oppression that is its central story, the Declaration of Independence fails to extend the benefits of individualism to all individuals; instead, it contains a subtext in which individualism is associated with and even depends on both sexism and racism. These associations may no longer be a part of the legitimate public language of individualism in late twentieth-century U.S. culture, but they have not been purged from its private vocabularies and patterns of reasoning. The ostensibly universal formulation of the principles of U.S. individualism puts women and minorities into a conceptual bind: the ideology of individualism is damaging to them because in practice it continues to countenance sexism and racism, yet it is also powerfully attractive because its central narrative offers such a compelling vision of social progress. As we shall see in examining the conflicting feelings about negative liberty dramatized in the writings of both Pynchon and Morrison, for the victims of sexism, racism, and other forms of group-oriented discrimination, the promises of individualism are simultaneously the source and the frustration of hope.

Encoded into the statement that "all men . . . are endowed . . . with certain unalienable rights" are the sexism and racialism that characterized Enlightenment thought in the American colonies. Even if Jefferson did not expressly seek to deny women those "unalienable rights" when he used the term *men* instead of a gender-neutral term like *individuals*, his choice of words cannot be regarded simply as a matter of convenient diction: only in a culture that was deeply patriarchal could the terms *men* and *individuals* be regarded as synonymous. (Indeed, the Declaration of Sentiments issued by the First Woman's Rights Convention, held in July 1848 in Seneca Falls, New York, took the Declaration of Independence as its model, but its first sentence made the sexism of the earlier document's language apparent: "We hold these truths to be self-evident, that all men and women are created equal.") Emerging from within a patriarchal tradition, individualism in the United States shed certain patriarchal practices, such as primogeniture and entail, but retained its sexist bias, adopting a literal reading of Jefferson's words until 1919, when the Nineteenth Amendment gave the vote to all adults regardless of gender. The extension of suffrage did not, however, break the connection between individualism and sexism, and late twentieth-century U.S. culture still denies women the status that it accords men.

Patriarchy is a communal form, a mode of social organization that directly contradicts the principles of political individualism by distributing rights unequally between men and women. In the late twentieth-century United States, patriarchy no longer has a sanctioned place within the public conception of individualism, as expressed either in laws or in liberal political theory. But it continues to be a part of the private vocabulary of individualism, still at work in versions of the official narrative spun by the popular culture and even, at times, within political theories that profess themselves to be gender blind.

One of the two primary stories told by U.S. individualism is that the individual, the family, the community, and the nation exist in a teleological relation: individualism leads at first to the desire for individuality, self-expression, and self-fulfillment, but the individual soon realizes that true self-fulfillment lies in the family, which represents the extension of the self into posterity.[16] The family is then held up as a model for all communal institutions, and the emphasis on family is conceived as a basic "American" characteristic.[17] In theory, the sexism that is the inevitable by-product of a patriarchal system should threaten to corrode the first term of the teleology by restricting the rights of a whole class of individuals; in practice, however, it serves to enhance the viability of the progression as a whole by creating a powerful (although often submerged) link between the first and the second terms, between the individual and the family.

From Alexis de Tocqueville to John Rawls, many of those who have sought either to describe or to defend U.S. individualism have assumed that the gap between individual and family is far smaller than the gap between individual and community or even between family and community. Rather than regarding the family as a social or communal structure that is fundamentally at odds with the ontological individual, they have seen the family as the extension of the individual, as the mechanism through which some part of the individuality of the individual can be perpetuated through time. Family thus becomes a form of self-expression for the individual—for the individual, that is, who is the head of the family. In late twentieth-century U.S. culture, the dominant model remains the nuclear family, organized around a monogamous, heterosexual relationship and headed by the man of the house: mother and father may both contribute genes to the children, but the children bear the father's surname in the vast majority of households. Single mothers or lesbian mothers serve as heads of households, but their families are often regarded as defective, as examples of the erosion of the family as a cultural institution. The link between individual and family within the logic of U.S. individualism takes for granted the patriarchal structure of the family and implicitly suggests that, to be a real individual, you have to be a man. Patriarchy continues to be powerful in U.S. culture because it operates privately rather than publicly, in the subtexts rather than the sanctioned narratives of U.S. individualism.

The use of the term *men* in the Declaration of Independence also encodes a second exclusion, a further contradiction, for it assumes a restricted definition of the term: the men to whom the Declaration refers are white men. In order to reach a compromise that would enable all members of the Second Continental Congress to sign the Declaration of Independence, Jefferson was forced to omit the condemnation of slavery included in the first draft of the document. Years afterward, Jefferson wrote that the "object of the Declaration of Independence" was "not to find out new principles, or new arguments, never before thought of, . . . but to place before mankind the common sense of the subject, in terms so plain and firm as to command their assent"; it was "intended to be an expression of the American mind, and to give that expression the proper tone and spirit called for by the occasion" (1501). To read *men* as "white men"—to read, in other words, simultaneously literally and metaphorically—is to read under the sway of eighteenth-century American "common sense," under the sway, in other words, of eighteenth-century American ideology.[18] But to deny that the culture still habitually reads in this fashion is to participate in the process of idealization that is a key rhetorical device within the national narrative of U.S. individualism.

At the turn into the twenty-first century, the ostensible universality of the nation's founding principles serves to prolong the nation's inability to recover fully from the evils of slavery. The fact that these principles *could* be universally applied leads many Americans to conclude that they *already are* being universally applied, and this error is magnified by the habit of thinking in methodologically individualist terms, a habit that prevents many Americans from being able to recognize that systemic discrimination does exist in the United States.

Too Much or Not Enough?

Recent critics of U.S. individualism have tended to fall into one of two camps. Members of the first camp, which includes poststructuralist, communitarian, and socialist critiques of the discourse of rights, share an insight that has been powerfully expressed by the sociologist Orlando Patterson. In *Slavery and Social Death* (1982), Patterson argues that the concept of *negative freedom*, "an ideal cherished in the West beyond all others," emerged only as a result of the practice of slavery: "Before slavery people simply could not have conceived of the thing we call freedom. Men and women in premodern, nonslaveholding societies did not, could not, value the removal of restraint as an ideal." According to Patterson, "Slaves were the first persons to find themselves in a situation where it was vital to refer to what they wanted in this way" (340). The idea of negative liberty, in other words, depends conceptually on the existence of the negation of liberty. Isaiah Berlin himself unwittingly corroborates this insight by suggesting that "the fundamental sense of freedom is freedom from enslavement by others. The rest is extension of this sense, or else metaphor" (lvi). For critics of individualism like Patterson, the idea of negative liberty is fatally flawed because it relies conceptually on the domination and oppression of others rather than sympathetic identification with them. As a result, it never rises above either its origins in oppressive ideologies or the tendency to degenerate into selfishness that so worried Tocqueville. A society structured around individualism is therefore unable to produce the kinds of community that it claims to foster, instead setting the individual and the communal into an oppositional relation. Critics who pursue this line of argumentation contend that U.S. culture has overemphasized individuality, and they seek to point out the ways in which individuality is not prior to but dependent on communal bonds. They argue that individualism is pathological at heart and that the United States suffers from an excess of it.

For those who belong to the second camp, such a position appears akin to false consciousness: they contend that the benefits of negative liberty have been denied to a number of groups within the culture—women, people of color, gays and lesbians—and that, far from suffering from an excess of individualism, U.S. culture suffers from a relative lack of it. Deconstructing the culture's conception of freedom is less attractive for those Americans who have not yet been fully granted the tangible benefits of that freedom, and promoting an alternative discourse that does not center on rights runs the risk of leaving certain people ill equipped to escape the effects of discrimination by leaving them content to be group members rather than full-fledged individuals. In contrast to the poststructuralist, communitarian, and socialist critiques, which are all anti-individualist, this second line of argumentation seeks merely to correct individualism's ills.

Late twentieth-century defenders of individualism like John Rawls and George Kateb, both of whom are sympathetic to the complaints offered by disenfranchised groups within U.S. culture, have claimed that individualism is still such a relatively new idea that its potential has yet to be fully realized, even in cultures that cherish it as one of their highest ideals. In contrast to Patterson, these thinkers valorize rights, which provide a protective sphere of immunity around the individual from the unwarranted incursions of others; in their view, negative liberty represents a decisive conceptual break from slavery and the other forms of authoritarian oppression from which it arose. What is wrong with contemporary U.S. individualism is simply that there is not enough of it. The solution is to disseminate negative liberty as widely as possible, ensure that it takes root, prune its excesses, and thereby foster its growth and development.

Both the conceptual and the practical differences between these two positions are adroitly captured in an anecdote told by the African American legal theorist Patricia Williams in *The Alchemy of Race and Rights* (1991). Commenting on the work of her white friend Peter Gabel, a practitioner of the deconstructive approach to jurisprudence known as critical legal studies, Williams writes that, "while the goals of [critical legal studies] and of the direct victims of racism may be much the same, what is too often missing is acknowledgment that our experiences of the same circumstances may be very different; the same symbol may mean different things to each of us" (149). To illustrate her point, Williams tells the story of the way in which Gabel rented an apartment in New York City: he "handed over a $900 deposit in cash, with no lease, no exchange of keys, and no receipt to strangers with whom he had no ties other than a few moments of pleasant conversation" (146). Williams, in contrast, had rented an apartment in New York from friends rather than strangers, but in order "to show good faith and trustworthiness," she had "signed a detailed lengthily negotiated, finely printed lease firmly establishing [her] as the ideal arm's-length transactor" (147).

Gabel's story had a happy ending—his "sublessors showed up at the appointed time, keys in hand to welcome him in"—vindicating his belief that, precisely because of their informality, "the handshake and good vibes were for him indicators of a trust more binding than a form contract" (146). Williams knows, however, that she could not safely participate in such a transaction because she is a black woman: "I am still evolving from being treated as three-fifths of a human, a subpart of the white estate. I grew up in a neighborhood where landlords would not sign leases with their poor black tenants, and demanded that rent be paid in cash; although superficially resembling Peter's transaction, such informality in most white-on-black situations signals distrust, not trust" (147–48). Both Gabel's lifestyle and his legal writing reflect an attempt to move beyond negative liberty, with its language of rights and freedom from restraint, because it is fundamentally based on distrust and a pessimistic view of human nature. For Williams, however, who finds that she must still continue Frederick Douglass's project of establishing herself as a legitimate contracting agent, the language of rights still represents a step forward: "Unlike Peter, I am still engaged in a struggle to set up transactions at arm's length, as legitimately commercial, and to portray myself as a bargainer of separate worth, distinct power, sufficient rights to manipulate commerce" (148).

Is a contract oppressive or empowering? It depends on your subject position. Gabel, according to Williams, applies poststructuralist and communitarian theory to the language of rights and, like most critical legal theorists, finds "that rights may be unstable and indeterminate." In moving away from a negative conception of freedom toward one that is positive, Gabel argues that "the 'needs' of the oppressed should be emphasized rather than their 'rights' " (Williams, 148–49). Williams, however, finds that Gabel's "language of circumstantially defined need, of informality, of solidarity, overcoming distance, sound[s] dangerously like the language of oppression to someone like me who was looking for freedom through the establishment of identity, the formulation of an autonomous social self." Williams speculates that the "distrust" represented by a formal contract might cause Gabel to "suffer alienation, leading to the commodification of his being and the degradation of his person to property" (148). For African Americans still struggling with the legacy of slavery, such metaphoric commodification or degradation is a step forward: no matter how much alienation he may feel, Gabel does not have to contend with a cultural heritage that includes the knowledge that his ancestors were actually treated as property by law. In short, Gabel disputes the premises of individualism; Williams concerns herself less with individualism's premises than with its promises, and she wants them kept.

So the question is, Too much individualism, or not enough? Too much emphasis on the benefits of a negative conception of liberty, or simply not enough negative liberty to go around? Must we deconstruct the discourse of rights, as Gabel contends, or should we be persuaded by Williams's implication that the problem lies in our failure to construct it fully?

Recently, two groups of thinkers have tried to move beyond the impasse suggested by these seemingly opposed positions; both groups occasionally refer to themselves as *radical democrats* seeking to formulate a new, "postliberal" philosophy. The first group is centered around the work of the German philosopher Jürgen Habermas, who has attempted to formulate a Kantian, universalist "discourse ethics" that can nonetheless take the fact of modern pluralism seriously (see Habermas 1990, 45–115). According to Ciaran Cronin, Habermas's "declared goal is to find a middle ground between the abstract universalism with which Kantian ethics is justly reproached and the relativistic implications of communitarian and contextualist positions in the tradition of Aristotle and Hegel" (xi). Like Rawls, Habermas seeks to develop a theory of justice out of a situation of rational deliberation, but without resorting to the kind of stripped-down understanding of what constitutes individuality that Rawls employs.[19] "Habermas's discourse model," writes Thomas McCarthy, "builds the moment of empathy *into* the procedure of coming to a reasoned agreement: each must put him- or herself into the place of everyone else in discussing whether a proposed norm is fair to all" (viii–ix). Extending his own previous work on the idea of *communicative action*, Habermas attempts to accommodate aspects of the communitarian critique of individualism by promoting what Cronin describes as a "moral commitment to *solidarity*. Since personal identity can be achieved only through socialization, the moral concern with autonomy and equal respect is inextricably bound up with an interest in the preservation and promotion of intersubjective relationships of mutual recognition, and hence of forms of communal life in which they can be realized" (xxvii).

What Habermas's perspective ultimately points to is what Chantal Mouffe describes as "a final rational reconciliation of value claims" and "the possibility of a politics from which antagonism and division would have disappeared" (1992, 13). Mouffe, in contrast, aligns herself with a group of thinkers who take the idea of pluralism to mean that conflict and antagonism are unavoidable and indeed fundamental to modern society. The challenge, as Mouffe puts it, is to "defend the gains of the democratic revolution and acknowledge the constitutive role of liberalism in the emergence of a pluralistic democracy, while trying to redress the negative consequences of individualism" (1992, 5). Crucial to Mouffe's conception of pluralism are "the liberal ideals of individual freedom and personal autonomy," and she argues that, "in order to develop fully the potentialities" of these ideals, "we need to dissociate them from the other discourses to which they have been articulated and to rescue political liberalism from its association with economic liberalism" (1993, 7).

These are questions that I believe lie at the heart of both Pynchon's and Morrison's imaginative writings, which dramatize the failings of Emersonian liberalism by dismantling the official story that it promotes. Pynchon and Morrison set their fractured narratives against the grain of this official narrative, vividly portraying the ways in which its continued persuasiveness inflicts damage upon U.S. culture by giving rise to pathological behavior. Both novelists recognize that Emersonian liberalism and U.S. individualism more generally remain marred by an old pathology, namely, the country's historical tolerance for, even its dependence on, slavery and the subjugation of nonwhite peoples. Their novels depict both the phenomenological horror of the slave's experience and the continuing perversion of the practice of individualism by the ideological residue of slavery and subjugation—a residue that includes not only racism but also both the relentless materialism of twentieth-century consumer culture and the continuing power of the myth of rugged individualism.

Thinking of people as things remains a habit of mind that does not go away after slavery is abolished; instead, it takes a different and still corrosive form. What is possessive about possessive individualism in the United States now is less the fact that an individual owns her own body and ability to labor than the fact that an individual is judged according to what possessions (in addition to life and labor) she has. Meanwhile, rugged individualism, the myth of the heroic loner embodied by the frontiersman and the cowboy, is linked historically to an acquisitive hunger for dominion over both lands and peoples, a desire to domesticate the American continent by dividing it into parcels owned by individuals. Paradoxically, it is the relative banality of the popular individualism pursued by twentieth-century consumers that keeps the myth of heroic, rugged individualism alive. Rugged individualism continues to flourish within U.S. popular culture because it provides an experience of wish fulfillment for the middle Americans whose most pressing concerns are pragmatically oriented toward material well-being. But rugged individualism also has material effects, and both Pynchon and Morrison link the oppressive masculinity of its ethos to the continued lack of equality for women in U.S. culture. Too often in their novels male self-esteem proves to be grounded in the ability to dominate and degrade women. Within the imaginative logic of Pynchon's and Morrison's novels, these mutually reinforcing social pathologies are the reasons that the practice of U.S. individualism remains unidealized, relentlessly possessive, and insidiously negative.

Despite the differences in their subject positions, Pynchon and Morrison offer similar diagnoses of the pathologies that arise within U.S. individualism. The difference between their imaginative worlds is far less clear-cut than the difference, for example, between Peter Gabel's and Patricia Williams's approaches to contract. At certain times, each writer seems to adopt Gabel's approach, depicting individualism as inherently pathological and responsible for the ills that beset modern society in the United States. Other moments bring to mind Williams's perspective: individualism seems to be a dream yet to be realized, marred by its historical but not conceptual relation to certain forms of oppression.

One distinction to be made, however, between Pynchon's and Morrison's approaches is that Pynchon tests out different imaginative alternatives to individualism sequentially as his career progresses while Morrison weighs them against one another in each of her novels. Pynchon's first three novels—*V.* (1963), *The Crying of Lot 49* (1966), and *Gravity's Rainbow* (1973)—dramatize a deconstructive and implicitly communitarian response to the narrative of individualism, depicting a version of the alienation that communitarian thinkers like Alasdair MacIntyre and Michael Sandel describe as individualism's inevitable result: individuals are isolated and detached or else entangled in destructive relationships. Indeed, almost all interpersonal relations in these novels seem to be relations of domination, and all social groupings appear to the individual to be conspiracies, part of a "they" that is out to get "you."[20] The imaginative logic of Pynchon's fourth novel, however, is different: Vineland (1990) tries out the typical communitarian prescription for social healing, which begins with an acknowledgment of the communally constituted nature of the self but ultimately presses its communitarian impulses into the service of a revised individualism. Understanding the self as at least in part communally constituted enables the individual to differentiate between the "they" and an "us" that protects and nurtures individuality; such an understanding becomes the opening proposition of an alternative logic in which the concepts that were deconstructed by the earlier novels—self-possession, freedom, individuality, family, community, and nation—are reconstructed and reconnected. Vineland depicts an individualism that manages to sever its connections to repressive social forms and thus make good on its promises.

Morrison, however, explores communitarian alternatives to individualism throughout her novels, and she finds African American communities to be as deformed as those in Pynchon's first three novels. In both cases, the communitarian ideals of family and community offer no panaceas in the worlds of her novels. The difference is that Morrison's communities are not deformed because of some nameless conspiracy or some flaw in the human condition; instead, they are deformed because of particular cultural practices inflicted by white Americans on African Americans. Although, as her analysis in Playing in the Dark (1992c) makes clear, Morrison, like Pynchon, is drawn to critiques that find individualism to be conceptually flawed because of its implicit reliance upon forms of domination, she is less quick to make slavery and racism stand for something else. For the majority of Pynchon's characters, the constraints imposed by modern society seem like a form of bondage; for most of Morrison's characters, however, these abstract constraints seem far less severe than the material constraints and legal bondage imposed until 1865.

Morrison's attention is focused more closely than Pynchon's on the effect of racism and on the particular plight of African Americans: the "they" of her novels is white culture, which seeks, like Pynchon's nefarious Captain Blicero, a.k.a. Weissman ("White Man"), to subjugate black people. While slavery is a topic that appears throughout Pynchon's work, it often seems to assume the status of a trope for more abstract forms of domination. For Morrison, however, slavery and racism are the central pathologies that mar the story about "individual freedom" that U.S. culture wants to tell. Slavery and racism are not particular embodiments of some more general domination that is the problem with individualism; instead, slavery and racism themselves have deformed individualism and made its official story a form of Bad History. Deconstructing the concepts of freedom and individuality often proves to be a luxury that Morrison's novels cannot afford because, despite the fact that those values are continually thwarted by their connection to repressive social forms, they remain the best hope for equality and social progress. Painfully aware that the cultural tools at their disposal are tainted by their history, Morrison's novels depict individualism as both an abettor of oppression and the source of salvation for African Americans. In *The Bluest Eye* and *Jazz*, we even find disturbing moments that celebrate "individual freedom" despite its clear links to violent forms of misogyny.

It is precisely this specific history of oppression that Pynchon sets out to explore in his fifth novel, *Mason & Dixon* (1997); finally, Pynchon finds himself interested in slavery qua slavery. By the novel's end, what the two surveyors come to realize is that slavery has been "the Element common to all" the adventures on which they have been sent by England's Royal Society. "Where does it end?" Dixon asks Mason. "No matter where in it we go, shall we find all the World Tyrants and Slaves? America was the one place we should *not* have found them" (692–93). Both Morrison and Pynchon continually dramatize the appeal of the freedom embodied by the liberal individual, even as they depict the depredations wrought in the name of individualism and portray individuals who long for community with others.

Pynchon's and Morrison's novels suggest that what is wrong with the official narrative of individualism is not that negative liberty and positive liberty are wholly incompatible ideals with fundamentally different goals but rather that it is not that easy to get from the one to the other. Their novels make us realize that the official narrative masks some abiding problems that refuse to go away as well as some difficult choices that can be deferred for only so long.

The official narrative of U.S. individualism thus encompasses a complex structure of contradiction held in abeyance. It tells us that negative liberty and positive liberty are not contradictory but complementary. It tells us that the interests of the individual are not at odds with the interests of family, community, or nation, that to pursue the good of the individual is ultimately to secure the good of the collective. At the same time, it hides the existence of an unholy truce between liberty and various forms of oppression. In short, individualism has come to contain "contradictions and paradoxes," as Bellah et al. (1985) suggest, but it has come to "contain" them in a double sense: the ideology includes contradictions, but it also seeks to rein them in, to prevent them from causing disruptions. As long as contradictions remain controlled, the threats that they pose are lessened; nevertheless, as long as contradictions are allowed to appear, they remain viable threats, sites of potential resistance and change. The official narrative strikes a delicate balance between these two forms of containment, always contingent and always ambiguous.

Official narratives are familiar, persuasive, seemingly beyond question. They have happy endings. And they can deceive us: the fact that the narrative of individualism has a happy ending deflects attention from the fact that this ending has yet to be achieved within U.S. culture. It is the project of *Negative Liberties* to demonstrate how the writings of two of our most celebrated authors—Toni Morrison and Thomas Pynchon—can help us to interrogate this narrative, to uncover its subtexts and subplots, and to tell the stories that it leaves out. Morrison and Pynchon help us to see how U.S. culture's ways of thinking about and representing individualism have thwarted the realization of the very goals that Emersonian liberalism is thought to promote. Fictions like theirs dramatize the appeal and the dangers of the official narrative in a way that philosophy cannot. They suggest that good fiction may well be an indispensable weapon in the struggle against Bad History.

TWO. Idealizing Individualism

In the *divided* or social state, these functions are parcelled out to individuals, each of whom aims to do his stint of the joint work, whilst each other performs his. . . . In this distribution of functions the scholar is the delegated intellect. In the right state he is Man Thinking. In the degenerate state, when the victim of society, he tends to become a mere thinker, or still worse, the parrot of other men's thinking.—Emerson, "The American Scholar" (1837)

Ronald Beiner argues that when philosophers theorize, they inevitably "tell a story—preferably a true story" (12); philosophy, in his account, is inherently fictional. In contrast, when Martha Nussbaum argues that philosophical theorizing often "lose[s] sight" of the "richer view" that is "available in the novel" (44), she is suggesting that philosophy generally is not fictional *enough*. In this chapter, I will argue that both these views are true. Emersonian liberalism draws on the literary imagination in order to articulate an abstract conception of individuality that can serve as the foundation for democratic liberalism. Yet, in relying so heavily on abstraction, philosophers like Emerson, Rawls, and Kateb lose sight of the ways in which the richness of U.S. communal life depends on the particularities and idiosyncrasies of its communal groupings, and they underestimate the extent to which nonindividualist, group-oriented modes of thinking play a constitutive role in the formation of identities in the United States. Communitarian philosophers like Michael Sandel have recognized the thinness of such descriptions of the individual, and indeed Sandel's critique unwittingly fleshes out Rawls's theory by drawing on cultural fictions about rugged individualism.

The Emersonian tradition of idealist philosophy (and I will argue below that Rawls should be included with Kateb in this tradition) has played a major role in the formation, consolidation, and continuing persuasiveness of the national narrative that U.S. culture has constructed around the ideas of negative liberty and individualism. This tradition makes a strong philosophical argument for the defensibility of the national narrative's portrayal of a complementary and sequential relation between the negative and the positive forms of freedom. What I will argue in the chapters that follow this one is that there is a wide gap between philosophical defensibility and practical realization, and that fictions like those produced by Morrison and Pynchon can make us understand the nature of that gap and help us to fill it in. Methodologically individualist in its patterns of reasoning, Emersonian liberalism seeks to find a common denominator that can link all individuals together: it operates by stripping away the richer view that Nussbaum finds in novelistic fiction. Moreover, the stories that it tells—for example, Emerson's "fable" of the "One Man" or the thought experiment that Rawls describes as "original position"—are relentlessly abstract, even when they presume to talk about differences between individuals.

Demonstrating the existence of a common denominator is a way to remove conflict from philosophy and, these philosophers hope, from culture as well. Emersonianism inherits from the Enlightenment a belief in the power of human rationalism: Emerson, Rawls, and Kateb believe that reason can serve as the foundation for a just society in which the promise of individualism can be fulfilled. As the philosopher William Connolly has pointed out, the drawback of this reliance on reason is a normative pressure to be reasonable: "Individualism presupposes a model of the normal or rational individual against which the conduct and interior of each actual self are to be praised. This standard . . . provides the ground for a theory of rights, justice, responsibility, freedom, obligation, and legitimate interests" (1991, 74).[1] What Morrison's and Pynchon's novels vividly dramatize is that the elimination of conflict through this normative mechanism of rationalism is a dangerous fiction that accounts for the appeal of both Emersonian liberalism and the national narrative of individualism to which it contributes. The richer view provided by these novelists shows us that Emersonianism swerves too quickly away from the realities of human irrationality and cultural conflict. It also demonstrates that the idea of democratic sameness, which Emersonianism seeks to establish through its abstraction of individuality, is a methodological strategy that, in the wrong hands, can lead not to freedom but to oppression.

In this chapter, then, I will investigate how the Emersonian tradition has contributed to the U.S. national narrative by telling a story about the potential power of individuality that has proven to be continually compelling, even to writers like Pynchon and Morrison who recognize some of its flaws. Indeed, if we do not get a sense of the power of this Emersonian narrative, we will fail to understand how it unleashes the creative energies of Morrison and Pynchon by simultaneously attracting and repelling them.

From Egoism to Self-Reliance

A crucial moment in the consolidation of the official story that we are considering occurs shortly after the term *individualism* enters common usage in the United States. In 1839, the anonymous author of a piece in the *Democratic Review* entitled "The Course of Civilization" described the "history of humanity" as "the record of a grand march . . . at all times tending to one point—the ultimate perfection of man. The course of civilization is the progress of man from a state of savage individualism to that of an individualism more elevated, moral and refined" (209). This use of the term *individualism*, one of the earliest known in American writing, marks a transitional stage in the evolution of its meaning, away from the negativity of its original coinage toward the positive connotation that it enjoys today within mainstream U.S. culture.

The second volume of Alexis de Tocqueville's *Democracy in America*, published the year after "The Course of Civilization," makes apparent the fact that the word *individualism* was still very much a neologism at this time. "'Individualism,'" wrote Tocqueville, "is a word recently coined to express a new idea. Our fathers only knew about egoism." Henry Reeve, the translator of the American edition, felt obliged to comment on his use of the term: "I adopt the expression of the original," he wrote in a footnote, "however strange it may seem to the English ear, . . . because I know of no English word exactly equivalent to the expression" (1961, 2:1). One measure of the novelty of the word *individualism* is the fact that it does not actually appear in what is now taken to be one of the urtexts of U.S. individualism, Ralph Waldo Emerson's "Self-Reliance," which was published in 1841. In fact, it is not until the following year that Emerson first uses the term in a journal entry, and its initial appearance in his published work is in "New England Reformers" (1844).

The term *individualisme* had been coined in France during the 1820s, and it was deployed by both counterrevolutionary and socialist thinkers as a critique of Enlightenment thought (see Lukes, 16; Arieli, 183–235 passim). The first known use of the word is in the work of the Catholic counter-revolutionary Joseph de Maistre, who believed that the social order had been "shattered to its foundations because there was too much liberty in Europe and not enough Religion." De Maistre viewed government as "a true religion," with "its dogmas, its mysteries, its priests; to submit it to individual discussion," he wrote, "is to destroy it." In 1820 he decried "this deep and frightening division of minds, this infinite fragmentation of all doctrines, political protestantism carried to the most absolute individualism" (quoted in Lukes, 4). At the other end of the political spectrum, *individualisme* was also attacked by the followers of the Comte de Saint-Simon, whose social doctrines advocated a system of government in which all property would be owned by the state, with the worker sharing in it according to the amount and quality of his work. The Saint-Simonians valorized association and believed that the individual had essentially no existence, powers, rights, or capacities independent of society. The Saint-Simonian self is thus a version of what twentieth-century communitarian thinkers call a *radically situated self*, a self whose identity is almost entirely communally constituted. As used by the Saint-Simonians, the term *individualisme* served as a critique of nineteenth-century liberalism, which they believed to be destroying society's common beliefs by emphasizing ruthless competition. The political theorist Steven Lukes notes that, during the 1820s, "Saint-Simonism shared the ideas of the counter-revolutionaries—their critique of the Enlightenment's glorification of the individual, their horror of social atomization and anarchy, as well as their desire for an organic, stable, hierarchically organized, harmonious social order" (6).

It is in this negative sense that Tocqueville uses the term *individualism* in the second volume of *Democracy in America*. Tocqueville defines it as "a calm and considered feeling which disposes each citizen to isolate himself from the mass of his fellows and withdraw into the circle of family and friends; with this little society formed to his taste, he gladly leaves the greater society to look after itself" (1969, 506). According to Tocqueville, egoism "springs from a blind instinct," while "individualism is based on misguided judgment rather than depraved feeling" (506). The distinction, however, ultimately becomes moot: "Egoism sterilizes the seeds of every virtue; individualism at first only dams the spring of public virtues, but in the long run it attacks and destroys all the others too and finally merges in egoism." Unlike egoism, which "is a vice as old as the world," individualism is a new phenomenon "of democratic origin" that "threatens to grow as conditions get more equal" (507). Its existence depends on the fact that democracy dismantles the traditional hierarchical structure that previously linked "everybody, from peasant to king, in one long chain" and thus enabled aristocratic societies to cohere. "Democracy breaks the chain and frees each link," writes Tocqueville, and thus "as social equality spreads there are more and more people who, though neither rich nor powerful enough to have much hold over others, have gained or kept enough wealth and enough understanding to look after their own needs. Such folk owe no man anything and hardly expect anything from anybody. They form the habit of thinking of themselves in isolation and imagine that their whole destiny is in their own hands." As a result, "each man is forever thrown back on himself alone, and there is danger that he may be shut up in the solitude of his own heart" (508).

Tocqueville no doubt would have considered the first paragraph of Emerson's "Self-Reliance" symptomatic of the problem that he was diagnosing. "To believe your own thought," Emerson declares, "to believe that what is true for you in your private heart is true for all men,—that is genius. Speak your latent conviction, and it shall be the universal sense; for the inmost in due time becomes the outmost,—and our first thought is rendered back to us by the trumpets of the Last Judgment" (1841c, 259). Many Americans, however, were more inclined to interpret Emerson's dictum as a sign of health rather than illness, a sign that the United States was finally ready to stand on its own two feet and fulfill the destiny implicit in its genesis. In a journal entry from April 1840, Emerson comments on the way in which his audiences have received his ideas about the individual: "In all my lectures, I have taught one doctrine, namely, the infinitude of the private man. This the people accept readily enough, & even with loud commendation" (1982, 320).[2]

Emerson, however, was not alone in promulgating the idea that individualism is a social good. Barely anointed by Tocqueville's use of it in *Democracy in America*, the term *individualism* was immediately subjected to a process of appropriation and redefinition. The anonymous author of the first American review of *Democracy in America*, which appeared in the *Boston Quarterly Review* in 1841, inverts Tocqueville's argument in order to appropriate the term *individualism* and endow it with a positive connotation ("Catholicism," 326). Regarding individualism as the driving force behind American society, the reviewer describes it as "that strong confidence in self, or reliance upon one's own exertion and resources." The author applauds what Tocqueville laments, arguing that "it is the artificial classification of mankind, into certain unfounded castes of the high and the low, the learned and the ignorant, patricians and plebeians, priests and laymen, princes and subjects . . . rather than the free scope of personal or individual peculiarities, which has enfeebled, and thereby corrupted the race." By destroying the chains forged by aristocratic society and forcing each individual to rely on "the inherent and profound resources of his own mysterious being," individualism has actually created a new "organic unity of the collective race." Individualism is thus perceived, not as a destructive vice that dams the spring of public virtues, but rather as the source of all public virtue and, ultimately, as the mechanism through which America will fulfill its promise: " 'Individualism' has its immutable laws, [which] when allowed to operate without let or hindrance,—however at first . . . their effects may appear destructive and anarchical,—must, in the end, assimilate the species, and evolve all the glorious phenomena of original and eternal ORDER;—that order which exists in man himself, and alone vivifies and sustains him" (333). This new definition idealizes individualism and transforms it into not only a defensible but also a desirable mode of social organization, a solid foundation for U.S. national ideology.

During the 1830s and 1840s, both in Europe and in the United States, the recently coined term *individualism* lay at the heart of a debate, fueled by the rise of Saint-Simonism, about the way in which societies should be organized. Opposed to *individualism* was the newly coined *socialism*, which is thought to have been introduced in 1831 by Alexandre Vinet and which gradually replaced the earlier *associationism* (Arieli, 405 n. 98). After Saint-Simonism was discredited owing to its increasingly authoritarian and quasi-religious tendencies, socialists like Alexandre de Saint-Cheron and Pierre Leroux began to champion the concept *individuality*, which they contrasted emphatically with *individualism*. "Beware of confounding individuality with individualism," wrote Saint-Cheron in *La revue encyclopédique* in 1831. Prefiguring Tocqueville's definition in *Democracy in America* as well as the famous "transparent eyeball" passage in Emerson's *Nature*, Saint-Cheron identifies individualism with "that mean egoism, lonely and disunited, which chokes all dignity, all the elan of the soul, all faith, while the sentiment of individuality is the holy exaltation of man, conscious of the life in him and all others in God and nature" (quoted in Arieli, 232). A year later, in the same journal, Leroux would go so far as to disavow both individualism and socialism in favor of individuality, declaring: "We are neither individualists nor socialists. We believe in individuality, personality, liberty; but we also believe in society" (quoted in Arieli, 233).

A similar concept of individuality can be found in Emerson's thought during this period. In 1833, he writes in his journal, "Democracy/freedom/has its roots in the Sacred truth that every man hath in him the divine Reason or that . . . all men are created capable of so doing. That is the equality & the only equality of all men. To this truth we look when we say, 'Reverence thyself. Be true to thyself' " (1960–82, 4:357). Three years later, Emerson contrasts the individual with society, characterizing the individual as "invulnerable and free" while criticizing society's tendency to fall "under the yoke of the base and selfish." Yet, because he believes that "the private man's heart is the sanctuary and citadel of freedom and goodness," Emerson concludes that "out of the strength and wisdom of the private heart shall go forth at another era the regeneration of society" ("The Individual," 1837b, 186). These ideas crystallize in "Self-Reliance," where Emerson proclaims, "Nothing is at last sacred but the integrity of your own mind. Absolve you to yourself, and you shall have the suffrage of the world" (1841c, 261). To be self-reliant is to trust in your own individuality, in the validity of your own "instincts" and "intuitions." Basing his conception of self-reliance on a highly abstract conception of the self, Emerson, like Saint-Cheron, locates individuality in the human "soul" and links it to the divine: "The sense of being which in calm hours rises, we know not how, in the soul, is not diverse from things, from space, from light, from time, from man, but one with them, and proceeds obviously from the same source whence their life and being also proceed" (1841c, 269).

The individuality extolled in "Self-Reliance" is thus not incompatible with the concepts of individuality found in socialist discourse during the 1830s. What Emerson is beginning to do in "Self-Reliance" and in his other writings during this period is to wrest "individuality" from "socialism" and incorporate it instead into "individualism." And he does it through the use of abstraction.

In one journal entry, he plainly sets individualism against varieties of socialism: "The young people, like Brownson, Channing, Greene, E[lizabeth] P[almer] P[eabody], & possibly Bancroft think that the vice of the age is to exaggerate individualism, & they adopt the word *l'humanité* from

Le Roux, and go for '*the race.*' Hence the Phalanx, owenism [*sic*], Simonism, the Communities" (1960–82, 8:249). Two years later, in the essay "New England Reformers," Emerson lifts almost verbatim a journal entry written a few days after the one cited above, combines it with sentiments that echo passages of "The American Scholar" (1837a) and "Self-Reliance," and describes individualism in highly abstract terms as the foundation of communal values and of the nation:

> The union is only perfect, when all the uniters are isolated. It is the union of friends who live in different streets or towns. Each man, if he attempts to join himself to others, is on all sides cramped and diminished of his proportion; and the stricter the union, the smaller and the more pitiful he is. But leave him alone, to recognize in every hour and place the secret soul, he will go up and down doing the works of a true member, and, to the astonishment of all, the work will be done with concert, though no man spoke. Government will be adamantine without any governor. The union must be ideal in actual individualism. (1844c, 599)

Offered as a critique of the utopian communities such as Brook Farm that were inspired by "the ideas of St. Simon, of Fourier, and of Owen" (597), this definition appropriates the term *individualism* from the Europeans—whether radical like the Saint-Simonians or moderate like Tocqueville—and offers it to America as both a name for its mission and a justification for its existence.[3]

Emerson's depiction of the relation between self and society in these essays is neither truly dialectical nor truly oppositional; it is, rather, complementary and sequential, and it follows the logic of laissez-faire, with one emendation: Emerson's version of Mandeville's fable of the bees is based on the development of individuality rather than on the pursuit of wealth. Individualism becomes the invisible hand that regulates society by enabling individuals to recognize "the secret soul" that each possesses. Like Locke, Emerson believes that the self has an a priori existence independent of society, but thereafter the two philosophers part ways, as Emerson offers what appears to be a parody of the social-contract theory contained in Locke's *Two Treatises of Government*: "Society is a joint-stock company, in which the members agree, for the better securing of his bread to each shareholder, to surrender the liberty and culture of the eater. The virtue in most request is conformity. Self-reliance is its aversion" ("Self-

Reliance"; 1841c, 261). Emerson's definition of individuality represents an abstraction of the possessive individualism found in Locke's *Two Treatises*. Emerson shifts the locus of selfhood from the laboring body to the "secret soul" and thereby leaves philosophical materialism behind in favor of idealism.[4] Property, which forms the foundation for society in Locke's theory, is in Emerson's view a by-product of society that threatens to undermine the development of individuality: "The reliance on Property, including the reliance on governments which protect it, is the want of self-reliance. Men . . . measure their esteem of each other by what each has, and not by what each is" ("Self-Reliance"; 1841c, 281). As currently constituted, society has enveloped its members in something like false consciousness: "Men, such as they are, very naturally seek money or power; and power because it is as good as money,—the 'spoils,' so called, 'of office.' And why not? for they aspire to the highest, and this, in their sleep-walking, they dream is highest. Wake them, and they shall quit the false good, and leap to the true" ("The American Scholar"; 1837a, 66–67). Emerson looks to individualism to provide the wake-up call, to revitalize and perfect democratic society by fostering a self-reliance that can nurture individuality.[5]

One way in which to understand Emerson's use of abstraction is to see it as a strategic response to the increasing commodification of daily life in the Jacksonian era, a necessary corrective to the materialism of the marketplace. Emerson calls for "men and women who shall renovate life and our social state" by being self-reliant: "It is easy to see that a greater self-reliance must work a revolution in all the offices and relations of men; in their religion; in their education; in their pursuits; their modes of living; their association; in their property; in their speculative views" ("Self-Reliance"; 1841c, 274–75). The faith in human perfectibility evident in these lines is typical of Emerson's idealizing rhetorical strategies, which continually attempt to steer his audiences away from materialism, conceived both as a philosophy that bases claims about reality in matter and sensory perception and also as a tendency to valorize possessions and economic success. In "The Transcendentalist" (1842), Emerson argues that human thinkers have traditionally divided themselves into "two sects"—"Materialists and Idealists"—but, as the essay progresses, he suggests that each individual is at once a materialist and an idealist (1842, 193). "The worst feature of this double consciousness," he writes, "is that the two lives, of the understanding and of the soul, which we lead, really show very little relation to each other, never meet and measure each other: one prevails now, all buzz and din; and the other prevails then, all infinitude and paradise; and, with the progress of life, the two discover no greater disposition to reconcile themselves" (205–6). The difference between the materialist and the idealist as Emerson conceives it is roughly the difference between John Locke and Immanuel Kant, between an individualism based on property and grounded in the world of sensory perception and an individualism based on the transcendental subject.[6]

Emerson is clearly drawn to the Kantian position, as he manipulates the tension between materialism and idealism that has animated American aspirations since the time of the Puritan migration. In "The Sin and Dangers of Self-Love" (1621), reputedly the first sermon preached in Puritan America, Robert Cushman, who was both the deacon of the Leyden congregation and the business agent of the colony at Plymouth, depicted individualism as a threat to both the economic well-being of the colony and its Christian spirit. Cushman had an ample interest in the survival of the colony, having just persuaded the colonists to accept a demanding ten-year contract that he had negotiated with merchant-investors in England (see Heimert and Delbanco, 41). The Puritans may have been pilgrims seeking to establish the New Jerusalem, but they were also members of joint-stock companies seeking economic opportunity in the New World who tended to regard a community's material prosperity as a sign of divine approval.[7] John Winthrop's famous lay sermon "A Modell of Christian Charity" (1630) begins with the observation that "God Almightie in his most holy and wise providence hath soe disposed of the Condicion of mankinde, as in all times some must be rich some poore, some highe and eminent in power and dignitie; others meane and in subieccion" (294). Worried that his brethren might devote too much energy to the pursuit of upward mobility on reaching the New World, Winthrop stresses the idealistic underpinnings of their enterprise, laying particular emphasis on the communal values of Christian love and reminding the members of the company that they have entered into a sacred agreement with God:

> Thus stands the cause between God and vs, wee are entered into Covenant with him for this worke, wee haue taken out a Commission, the Lord hath giuen vs leaue to drawe our owne Articles wee haue professed to enterprise these Accions vpon these and these ends, wee haue herevpon besought him of favour and blessing: Now if the Lord shall please to heare vs, and bring vs in peace to the place wee desire, then hath hee ratified this Covenant and sealed our Commission, [and] will expect a strickt performance of the Articles contained in it,

> but if wee shall neglect the observacion of these Articles which are the ends wee haue propounded and dissembling with our God, shall fall to embrace this present world and prosecute our carnall intencions, seekeing greate things for our selues and our posterity, the Lord will sure breake out in wrathe against vs, be revenged of such a periured people, and make vs knowe the price of the breache of such a Covenant. (294)

Here, Winthrop, who had been a lawyer in England, expands the legal connotations of Old Testament "covenant" by bringing it together with an economic vocabulary of contract, debt, and financial instruments, as part of a larger strategy in which the language of materialism is redirected to serve idealistic, spiritual ends. The progression from materialism to idealism is mapped onto the opposition between self and society, with self linked to selfishness and materialism, society linked to Christian love and idealism. Winthrop instructs his brethren to move outward from self to society: "Wee must be knitt together in this worke as one man, . . . wee must delight in eache other, make others Condicions our owne[,] reioyce together, mourne together, labour, and suffer together, allwayes haueing before our eyes our Commission and Community in the worke, our Community as members of the same body" (294). Winthrop's sermon thus turns upon two interlinked progressions: from materialism to idealism and from self to community.

Winthrop and Emerson are both philosophical idealists who believe that truth is to be found, not in the phenomenal world, but in the noumenal realm presided over by God. Moreover, like Winthrop, Emerson deploys the language of materialism in the service of an idealizing rhetoric, using anecdotes and metaphors drawn from the world of commerce, labor, and everyday experience. The difference between Emerson and Winthrop is embodied in Emerson's assertion that society, which he likens to "a joint-stock company," is "in conspiracy against the manhood of every one of its members" ("Self-Reliance"; 1841c, 261). Winthrop's sermon had sought to knit the members of his enterprise into a single social body, but Emerson's essays seek to focus attention on the ways in which society strips idealism away from the individual by encouraging materialistic pursuits. In "The American Scholar," for example, Emerson turns the metaphor of the social body on its head:

> The old fable covers a doctrine ever new and sublime; that there is One Man,—present to all particular men only partially, or through one

faculty; and that you must take the whole society to find the whole man. Man is not a farmer, or a professor, or an engineer, but he is all. Man is priest, and scholar, and statesman, and producer, and soldier. In the *divided* or social state, these functions are parcelled out to individuals, each of whom aims to do his stint of the joint work, whilst each other performs his. The fable implies, that the individual, to possess himself, must sometimes return from his own labor to embrace all the other laborers. But unfortunately, this original unit, this fountain of power, has been so distributed to multitudes, has been so minutely subdivided and peddled out, that it is spilled into drops, and cannot be gathered. The state of society is one in which the members have suffered amputation from the trunk, and strut about so many walking monsters,—a good finger, a neck, a stomach, an elbow, but never a man. (1837a, 53–54)

In Emerson's rewriting of the metaphor, it is society that becomes aligned with the materialistic side of existence and the self with the idealistic; it is society that has "cowed" the individual. "Men are become of no account," Emerson declares in "The American Scholar": "Men in history, men in the world of to-day, are bugs, are spawn, and are called 'the mass' and 'the herd'" (66). Emerson's idealism causes him to spurn the materialism of society and to valorize the individual, but his ultimate goal is a society transfigured by the realization of the potential of individualism.

In "Politics," published in *Essays: Second Series*, Emerson offers a less dire view of society's effects on the individual. Contrasting the "artificial restraints" imposed by his society with "the rewards and penalties" of the individual's "own constitution," he argues that the "tendencies of the times favor the idea of self-government." Emerson's development of this idea exemplifies the idealizing logic that expands the meaning of individualism in U.S. culture:

The movement in this direction has been very marked in modern history. Much has been blind and discreditable, but the nature of the revolution is not affected by the vices of the revolters; for this is a purely moral force. It was never adopted by any party in history, neither can be. It separates the individual from all party, and unites him at the same time to the race. It promises a recognition of higher rights than those of personal freedom, or the security of property. A man has a right to be employed, to be trusted, to be loved, to be revered. (1844d, 569)

The passage simultaneously detaches and links the individual to the rest of the human race, and it expands the idea of rights far beyond the conception handed down by the Declaration of Independence. Once again, however, Emerson's idealization of individualism takes place against a backdrop of socialism, for his references here to "the vices of the revolters" and to the fact that this principle has not been adopted by "any party in history" are veiled attacks on the programs advocated by socialists in both Europe and the United States. In "New England Reformers," the final piece in *Essays: Second Series*, Emerson makes his disdain for "the ideas of St. Simon, of Fourier, and of Owen" explicit and argues that "no society can ever be so large as one man." Emerson concedes that these experiments do indicate that "the world is awaking to the idea of union," but such a union, he contends, "must be inward, and not one of covenants" (597–99). What we see here is a vision of community that is as abstract as Emerson's vision of the individual.

The use of the word *covenants* in this passage is also a veiled attack on Puritan models of social organization, but Emerson does not dispense with all their ideals. For, although he rejects the premises of Winthrop's argument in "A Modell of Christian Charity" by advocating "self-government" and deemphasizing the importance of property, Emerson paradoxically reaches a conclusion similar to Winthrop's: that the ideal society would be bound not by the "artificial restraints" of force but rather by the bonds of love. "The power of love, as the basis of a State, has never been tried," Emerson declares in "Politics," because human beings have grown used to the idea that "a government of force" is necessary for human society to function. "We must not imagine that all things are lapsing into confusion," he argues, "if every tender protestant be not compelled to bear his part in certain social conventions: nor doubt that roads can be built, letters carried, and the fruit of labor secured, when the government of force is at an end." For, when men and women "are pure enough to abjure the code of force, they will be wise enough to see how . . . public ends . . . can be answered" without it (1844d, 569–70). Having eschewed the materialistic foundations that Winthrop accepted as a necessity, Emerson envisions a city on a hill filled with "protestants," a city that is even more idealized than the New Jerusalem imagined by the Puritans.

It is, however, a vision built upon paradox, for Emerson rejects the idea of "covenant" in order to argue that "the union is only perfect, when all the uniters are isolated." The love that exists between them is a love born of reciprocal respect: what will link Emerson's idealistic individuals together is their mutual belief in the value of individuality and the power of individualism. "The union must be ideal," Emerson declares, "in actual individualism" ("New England Reformers"; 1844c, 599). This chiastic formulation of the logic of individualism attempts—both syntactically and thematically—to contain and resolve the contradictions between individual and community, between materialism and idealism.[8]

Emerson's idealism is a form of universalism because it seeks to discover the common forms that underlie all individual manifestations, whether of people or of things. I want to turn now to an aspect of Emerson's thought that seems to offer a counterweight to his universalism: namely, his use of contradictions, multiple perspectives, and an eclectic range of intellectual sources.

Throughout his writings, Emerson displays an openness to contradiction that has troubled many of his commentators.[9] It is, however, precisely Emerson's practice of thinking in contradictions that energizes his defense of ontological individualism. "Cannot I conceive the Universe without a contradiction?" Emerson wrote in his journal on 26 May 1837 (1982, 165). His genius was to answer no and then turn that potential disadvantage into an advantage. Emerson explores the implications of ontological individualism by casting the individual as the arbiter of meaning. "Suppose you should contradict yourself; what then?" he asks in "Self-Reliance," adding, "A foolish consistency is the hobgoblin of little minds, adored by little statesmen and philosophers and divines. With consistency a great soul has simply nothing to do. He may as well concern himself with his shadow on the wall. Speak what you think now in hard words and to-morrow speak what to-morrow thinks in hard words again, though it contradict every thing you said to-day.—'Ah, so you shall be sure to be misunderstood.'—Is it so bad, then, to be misunderstood? . . . To be great is to be misunderstood" (265). George Kateb has described Emerson as "a sustained practitioner of a multiple perspectivism," who "tries to make each element believable, giving it its own essay or passage, or he dwells on its different facets in several essays, while his whole work sets an example of abundant but also sympathetic withholding" (1995, 4). For Emerson, the fact that the individual exists in a contradictory subject position, pulled in different directions by a variety of belief systems, does not vitiate individualism; instead, it attests to the power of the individual, who can transmute contradiction into a unified subjectivity. Emerson suggests that cultural conflicts and contradictions can be subsumed, contained, and resolved by the individual.

As a result, Emerson's awareness of cultural conflict and contradiction does not lead him to a pluralist understanding of human society. In certain respects, Emerson, like Kant, is a cosmopolitan thinker, but, to a far greater extent than Kant, Emerson offers us a version of cosmopolitanism that is universalist rather than pluralist. If, as Bruce Robbins puts it, cosmopolitanism should be "understood as a fundamental devotion to the interests of humanity as a whole" (1), then it is easy to see why it is often described as a form of universalism that is directly opposed to the idea of nationalism. "Cosmopolitanism," writes Robbins, "has often seemed to claim universality by virtue of its independence, its detachment from the bonds, commitments, and affiliations that constrain ordinary nation-bound lives" (1). Kant seems to adopt this sense of the term in his essay "Idea for a Universal History with a Cosmopolitan Purpose" (1784), where he proposes as feasible the philosophical project of attempting "to work out a universal history of the world in accordance with a plan of nature aimed at a perfect civil union of mankind" (51).

Kant, however, begins to alter his assessment of cosmopolitanism in the essay "Theory and Practice" (1793): after briefly setting forth the idea of a world republic bound by a "*cosmopolitan constitution,*" he then suggests as more feasible the idea of "a lawful *federation* under a commonly accepted international *right*" (90). Two years later, in the essay "Perpetual Peace" (1795), Kant theorizes that the only way to achieve permanent world peace is through the formation of a "*pacific federation*" of nations, a "general agreement" to "preserve and secure the *freedom* of each state in itself, along with that of the other confederated states, although this does not mean that they need to submit to public laws and to a coercive power which enforces them, as do men in a state of nature" (104). Because it is organized around the "cosmopolitan right" of "universal hospitality" (105) rather than a uniform set of laws to which all must submit, such a federation is pluralist: Kant grants the legitimacy of the "state," which he describes as "a society of men, which no-one other than itself can command or dispose of. Like a tree, it has its own roots, and to graft it on to another state as if it were a shoot is to terminate its existence as a moral personality and make it into a commodity" (94). (Kant does suggest, however, that a pacific federation will work best when all its members are republics because a republic "by its nature is inclined to seek perpetual peace" [104].) In short, the movement from "Idea for a Universal History" to "Perpetual Peace" represents a shift in Kant's thinking away from a universalist to a more pluralist conception of cosmopolitanism.

This shift indicates a second way in which cosmopolitanism may be conceived: in contradistinction, not to nationalism, but to universalism. The intellectual historian David Hollinger suggests that we should "distinguish between a universalist will to find common ground from a cosmopolitan will to engage human diversity." According to Hollinger, "Cosmopolitanism shares with all varieties of universalism a profound suspicion of enclosures, but cosmopolitanism is defined by an additional element not essential to universalism itself: recognition, acceptance, and eager exploration of diversity. Cosmopolitanism urges each individual and collective unit to absorb as much varied experience as it can, while retaining its capacity to advance its aims effectively. For cosmopolitans, the diversity of humankind is a fact; for universalists, it is a potential problem" (84). As Hollinger points out, however, cosmopolitanism must also be distinguished from the extreme form of pluralism—what Werner Sollors refers to as *pure pluralism* because of its conceptual links to the idea of ethnic purity—that insists on the sanctity of long-standing cultures and therefore on cultural relativism. Pure pluralism is thus oriented around groups, while cosmopolitanism tends to focus on individuals, who have the ability to see themselves as belonging simultaneously to different groups, some overlapping, some distinct, some possibly even conflicting.

Because of this focus on the group, *pure pluralism* is not a concept that would ever have appealed to Emerson, but all his writing is marked by what Hollinger calls "the recognition, acceptance, and eager exploration of diversity" that characterizes cosmopolitanism. Emerson's essays and lectures are deeply allusive and intertextual, drawing from a host of Western and Eastern intellectual sources. Turn to any essay, and you are likely to find ideas from Plato and Plotinus next to quotations from the Bible or from Shakespeare; insights from Kant, Coleridge, or Swedenborg sit cheek by jowl with maxims from the Buddhist, Hindu, and Zoroastrian religious traditions. In one famous paragraph from the "Beauty" chapter of *Nature*, Emerson quotes from Sallust and Gibbon; next cites the examples of the Spartan King Leonidas, the Swiss patriot Arnold Winkelried, Christopher Columbus, Henry Vane (governor of Massachusetts, 1636–37), and the English parliamentarian William Russell (executed by Charles II in 1662); and then concludes the paragraph with references to Homer, Pindar, Socrates, Phocion, and Jesus in quick succession (1836, 16–17).

Emerson, in short, is a rhetorical cosmopolitan, but it is important to see that this diversity of sources results in a uniformity of voice: it all becomes "Emerson." In this sense, Emerson's rhetorical style mimics his conception of the function of "America." In a journal entry from 1845, he writes that "in this continent,—asylum of all nations,—the energy of Irish, Germans, Swedes, Poles, and ⟨the⟩ Cossacks, & all the European tribes,— of the Africans, & of the Polynesians,—will construct a new race, a new religion, a new state, a new literature, which will be as vigorous as the new Europe which came out of the smelting-pot of the Dark Ages, or that which earlier emerged from the Pelasgic & Etruscan barbarism" (1960–82, 9:299–300). Emerson, writes Hollinger, "emphasizes the diversity not of the final product but only of the materials going into it" (87). Despite both this diversity of materials and the openness to contradictions and multiple perspectives that we have already noted, when Emerson theorizes about culture and politics, he does not celebrate the fact of human difference but pulls away from any kind of pluralist vision of the world and grounds his thought instead in universalism. Diverse materials and perspectives are run through a conceptual mill that is powered by methodological individualism and philosophical abstraction.

For example, in the essay "History," Emerson writes that "there is properly no history; only biography" (1841b, 240), but this statement—despite its suggestion of an interest in the particular facts of different lives—turns out to be a vision of sameness rather than difference. History and biography are one discipline for Emerson because he believes, as he tells us in the very first sentences of the essay, that "there is one mind common to all individual men. Every man is an inlet to the same and to all of the same." A few sentences later he adds that "of the universal mind each individual man is one more incarnation" and that "all the facts of history preëxist in the mind as laws." As Kant had in 1784, Emerson describes something that he calls "universal history," according to which "all public facts are to be individualized, all private facts are to be generalized" (246). In "Circles," Emerson writes, "One man's justice is another's injustice; one man's beauty, another's ugliness; one man's wisdom, another's folly" (1841a, 410). As Barbara Packer points out, "These maxims may sound like mere variations on the proverb 'one man's meat is another man's poison,' [but] they are not; since Emerson is careful to add an important qualification— 'as one beholds the same objects from a higher point'" (15). In both essays, the solution to the problem of cultural conflict and contradiction is simply to raise the level of abstraction. Raise it high enough, and individual differences disappear into an abstract vision of the individual that can serve as a common denominator for all human beings, a universal formulation that promotes philosophical idealism.

For Emerson, the ability to think in such abstract terms is closely linked to the ability to think morally. It is, for example, the inability to think abstractly that Emerson believes to be Daniel Webster's greatest defect. In his address "The Fugitive Slave Law," delivered on 7 March 1854, Emerson subtly portrays Webster as a sort of anti-Emerson. Near the beginning of the address, Emerson enumerates Webster's "talents"—his "elocution" and his "rhetoric"—and the descriptions sound very much like the goals that Emerson set for his own writing. Webster, Emerson tells us, was "so thoroughly simple and wise in his rhetoric [that] in his statement, things lay in daylight;—we saw them in order as they were" (1854, 76). Might this remind us of Emerson's stated goal in the introduction to *Nature* of achieving a "true theory" that "will be its own evidence," that will "explain all phenomena" (1836, 7)? Webster's rhetorical power lies in his ability to use rhetoric to make his positions seem self-evident. And, unlike Emerson, often criticized as a brilliant writer of sentences but a poor builder of philosophical arguments, Webster has a rhetorical and philosophical power that is total: "His power, like that of all great masters, was not in excellent parts, but was total. He had a great and everywhere equal propriety" (1854, 76). At his best, Webster was one American who might qualify for Emerson's title *representative man*.

But Webster is not perfect, and Emerson goes on to denounce Webster's support for the Fugitive Slave Bill by asserting that "the history of this country has given a disastrous importance to the defects of this great man's mind" (77). Chief among these defects is the inability to engage in Emersonian abstraction. Arguing that "it is the office of the moral nature to give sanity and right direction to the mind, to give centrality and unity," and that "great thoughts come from the heart," Emerson asserts "that the moral is the occult fountain of genius." He faults Webster for "the sterility of thought, the want of generalization in his speeches, and the curious fact, that with a general ability that impresses all the world, there is not a single general remark, not an observation on life and manners, not a single valuable aphorism that can pass into literature from his writings" (77). This ability to write aphoristically—which Webster lacks—is, of course, a talent for which Emerson is justly famous. And here he suggests that it is also a sign of one's "moral nature." The ability to abstract is the ability to be morally engaged.[10]

The problem is that, while Emerson's strategies of abstraction do enable him to think in more progressive terms than do many of his contemporaries, they ultimately impose a limit on the ways in which he can be morally engaged. Emerson's liberalism depends on stripping away all individual attributes except for "the divine Reason" in order to be able to discuss individuals in universal terms. One result is a relatively enlightened view of the situation of women in his culture. On 15 July 1834, for example, he records a humorous remark in his journal, one that registers an awareness of the privileges conferred on him by his gender: "I wish to be a true & free man, & therefore would not be a woman, or a king, or a clergyman, each of which classes in the present order of things is a slave" (1982, 125–26). Although his essays constantly speak about what "men" can do, at a crucial moment in "Self-Reliance," when he issues a call for a new society, Emerson includes both men and women: "We want men and women who shall renovate life and our social state" (274).

Moreover, "Self-Reliance" provides us with an example of Emerson revising his work in order to soften its sexism. It occurs in the famous quote about "foolish consistency," which I cited above in the version that Emerson revised for the 1847 reprinting of *Essays: First Series*. Here is the original version:

> A foolish consistency is the hobgoblin of little minds, adored by little statesmen and philosophers and divines. With consistency a great soul has simply nothing to do. He may as well concern himself with his shadow on the wall. *Out upon your guarded lips! Sew them up with packthread, do.* Else, *if you would be a man*, speak what you think to-day in words *as hard as cannon balls*, and to-morrow speak what to-morrow thinks in hard words again, though it contradict every thing you said to-day. *Ah, then, exclaim the aged ladies, you should be sure to be misunderstood.* (1841d, 1131; emphasis added)

Emerson removed or significantly revised the phrases in italics for the 1847 edition. Gone is the clause "if you would be a man" and the patronizing phrase "exclaim the aged ladies." The warlike imagery of "words as hard as cannon balls" is replaced simply by the phrase "hard words." The effect of these revisions is to soften the sexist essentialism of the earlier version of this famous—and crucial—passage and thus to heighten the universalism of the essay as a whole. A final example of Emerson's progressive thinking on the subject of gender equality comes from his journal, where he records his support for women's rights on the day of the Worcester Women's Convention in October 1851: "I think that, as long as they have not equal rights of property & right of voting, they are not on a right footing. But this wrong grew out of the savage & military period, when, because a woman could not defend herself, it was necessary that she should be assigned to some man who was paid for guarding her. Now in more tranquil & decorous times it is plain she should have her property, &, when she marries, the parties should as regards property, go into a partnership full or limited, but explicit & recorded" (1982, 431).[11]

Race poses a more difficult problem for Emerson's thinking. Just a few months before writing the journal entry in support of women's rights, Emerson penned a journal entry that made distinctions among whites on the basis of race and ethnicity, describing the Atlantic Ocean as "a sieve through which only or chiefly the liberal, adventurous, sensitive, America-loving part of each city, clan, family are brought. It is the light complexion, the blue eyes of Europe that come: the black eyes, the black drop, the Europe of Europe is left" (June 1851; 1926, 255–56). Logically, Emerson's liberalism demands that he must regard race and ethnicity as attributes that are not essential but rather contingent aspects of individuality. Given the number of U.S. abolitionists who also happened to believe in the inferiority of blacks, this lesson was obviously a difficult one for a mid-nineteenth-century white American to learn, and Emerson was no exception.

Commentators have faulted Emerson for his ostensibly racist beliefs (see, for example, Nicoloff; and West 1939, 35–41), but their most damaging evidence comes from Emerson's journals, private writings that were first edited and published by Emerson's son and grandson between 1909 and 1914. One frequently cited passage comes from late in 1822, when a young Emerson conducts a debate with himself on the issue of African slavery, attempting to marshal arguments on its behalf:

> I believe that nobody now regards the maxim "that all men are born equal," as any thing more than a convenient hypothesis or an extravagant declamation. For the reverse is true—that all men are born unequal in personal powers and in those essential circumstances, of time, parentage, country, fortune. The least knowledge of the natural history of man adds another important particular to these; namely, what class of men he belongs to—European, Moor, Tartar, African? Because Nature has plainly assigned different degrees of intellect to these different races, and the barriers between are insurmountable.

> This inequality is an indication of the design of Providence that some should lead, and some should serve. (8–14 November 1822; 1982, 19)

What begins here as a meditation on the inequities of inheritance quickly becomes a meditation on a human characteristic that Emerson seems to consider essential: race. Emerson is unable to consider race as simply an accident of birth, akin to "parentage," "country," or "fortune"; he finds it difficult to think of other races as capable of the kind of self-reliance for which he calls.

It is significant, however, that these quotations are taken from Emerson's private journals, where he was free to explore the contradictions of his thought as fully as he wished. In the public writings and lectures that he crafts using the journals as raw material, however, Emerson reins himself in. Although his journals are full of passages that register an intellectual engagement with the pressing social and political issues of his day, in public Emerson preferred to speak in universal terms, using specific examples primarily to illustrate general principles. Early in his career, Emerson preferred to abstain from comment on current affairs, in part to give his lectures and essays the authority of the universal and timeless, but also, I think, because he was still struggling to make up his mind about some of the key issues of the day. In particular, what we see in the journals before 1844 is a struggle against the racial and ethnic essentialisms that his culture took for granted. He deemphasizes his doubts about the equality of the sexes and of nonwhite peoples as if he were aware that not all contradictions are created equal; he struggles against the racist essentialisms that he was taught to take for granted, as if he sensed that they would have to be pared away from his doctrine of self-reliance.

Emerson had begun to display a public concern for the rights of nonwhite Americans by 1837, the same year in which he delivered his Phi Beta Kappa address, "The American Scholar." In a now-lost public lecture on the subject of slavery, Emerson argued that "our great duty on this matter is to open our halls to the discussion of this question steadily day after day, year after year until no man dare wag his finger at us" (1960–82, 12:151–54).[12] In the following year, at the urging of friends, Emerson protested the removal of Cherokees from Georgia in a strongly worded letter to President Van Buren that was published in a Washington newspaper (Emerson 1995, 1–6). He dispatched the letter with great reluctance, however, and wrote in his journal the very next day:

> Yesterday went the letter to Van Buren a letter hated of me. A deliverance that does not deliver the soul. . . . I write my journal, I read my lecture with joy—but this stirring in the philanthropic mud, gives me no peace. I will let the republic alone until the republic comes to me.
>
> I fully sympathise, to be sure, with the sentiment I write, but I accept it rather from my friends than dictate it. It is not my impulse to say it & therefore my genius deserts me, no muse befriends, no music of thought or of word accompanies. Bah! (26 April 1838; 1960–82, 5:479)

A breakthrough, however, seems to have come in 1844, the same year in which *Essays: Second Series* was published. Emerson delivered an address in Concord "on . . . the Emancipation of the Negroes in the British West Indies," in which he argued that "the negro race is, more than any other, susceptible of rapid civilization" (1844a, 30). According to Emerson,

> When at last in a race, a new principle appears, an idea;—that conserves it; ideas only save races. If the black man is feeble, and not important to the existing races not on a parity with the best race, the black man must serve, and be exterminated. But if the black man carries in his bosom an indispensable element of a new and coming civilization; for the sake of that element, no wrong nor strength nor circumstance can hurt him: he will survive and play his part. So now, the arrival in the world of such men as Toussaint and the Haytian heroes, or of the leaders of their race in Barbadoes and Jamaica, outweighs in good omen all the English and American humanity. The anti-slavery of the whole world is dust in the balance before this,—is a poor squeamishness and nervousness: the might and the right are here: here is the anti-slave: here is man: and if you have man, black or white is an insignificance. (31)

This lecture presents a far more favorable view of black people than what is to be found earlier in his journal entries, in large part because Emerson is able to reimagine blacks in abstract terms. He transforms race into a category that can accommodate change. Races come and go: as Emerson puts it earlier in the lecture, "Our planet, before the age of written history, had its races of savages. . . . Who cares for these or their wars?" (30). Race is still present as a category here, and Emerson still makes a distinction between blacks and what he calls "English and American humanity," but we see him trying to find a solution to the problem of racism in his thought.[13]

Attempting to fulfill the dictates of methodological individualism and his philosophy of self-reliance, the lecture disengages slavery from race and attempts to abstract race away as a significant category by transforming it from an essential characteristic into something much more mutable.

Emerson's conscious efforts in this regard can be seen by comparing this passage to the journal entry from which it is drawn:

> But if the black man carries in his bosom an indispensable element of a new & coming civilization, for the sake of that element no wrong nor strength nor circumstance can hurt him, he will survive & play his part. So now it seems to me that the arrival in the world of such men as Toussaint *if he is pure blood*, or of Douglas [sic] *if he is pure blood* outweighs all the English & American humanity. The Antislavery of the whole world is but dust in the balance, a poor squeamishness & nervousness[;] the might & the right is here. Here is the Anti-Slave. Here is Man; & if you have man, black or white is an insignificance. (1960–82, 9:125; emphasis added)

Emerson removes the reference to Frederick Douglass when he gives the speech in 1844, substituting instead the "Haytian heroes, or of the leaders of their race in Barbadoes and Jamaica," appropriate enough given that the occasion for the address is the anniversary of West Indian emancipation. More crucially, he omits the phrase "if he is pure blood," a revision that seems at first to signal the desire to dissociate himself from the American obsession with racial purity, a sign perhaps that Emerson is more progressive than many of his contemporaries on the issue of race.

But the revision resists easy interpretation. The original journal entry may be seen as a thought experiment in which Emerson hopes to prove the worth of blackness by stripping it down to its essence and then showing that this essence contains that "indispensable element of a new & coming civilization." Using the examples of men like Toussaint or Douglass to demonstrate the worth of blackness can therefore be effective for Emerson only "if [they are] pure blood" so that the nobility within them cannot be attributed to their possessing white blood (as, for example, in Harriet Beecher Stowe's depiction a few years later of the mulatto George Harris in *Uncle Tom's Cabin*). Barbara Packer has suggested to me that Emerson may have removed the reference to Douglass from the finished speech because he remembered that Douglass's father was thought to be a white man. If this is the case, then, as Packer (personal communication, 6 August 1999) points out, "racial essentialism is essential to a passage that ends by saying that 'black or white is an insignificance.' " Packer's reading gives us a more ambivalent Emerson, one whose movement toward a less essentialist public formulation of the nature of race is the paradoxical result of a private commitment to racial essentialism.[14]

In both versions of the passage, however, we see Emerson's formulations move in the direction of greater abstraction. The passage shifts from the specificity of direct references (Douglass, Toussaint, and the heroes of the West Indian Emancipation) to the abstraction of the declaration that "here is the anti-slave: here is man: and if you have man, black or white is an insignificance" (1844a, 31). As Maurice Gonnaud points out, "Even after the 1844 speech on British West Indian emancipation, Emerson's position on the issue remained loftily abstract; what he valued in abolitionism was the affirmation of a moral principle, and he was little troubled with the situation of the slaves themselves" (394). Emerson's fellow transcendentalist Bronson Alcott complained in his journal that Emerson "does not believe in the actual; his sympathies are all intellectual. He persuades me to leave the actual, devote myself to the speculative, and embody my thought in written works. Emerson idealizes all things. This idealized picture is the true and real one for him—all else is naught" (quoted in Sanborn, 53). In a letter to Carlyle written in December 1844, Emerson professed himself unable to understand why his contemporaries might describe him in this way, but then seemingly answered his own question with a remark about his speeches on public issues that echoes his earlier regrets about the letter to Van Buren:

> But of what you say now & heretofore respecting the remoteness of my writing & thinking from real life, though I hear substantially the same criticism made by my countrymen, I do not know what it means. If I can at any time express the law & the ideal right, that should satisfy me without measuring the divergence from it of the last act of Congress. And though I sometimes accept a popular call, & preach on Temperance or the Abolition of slavery, as lately on the First of August, I am sure to feel before I have done with it, what intrusion it is into another sphere & so much loss of virtue in my own. (31 December 1844; Slater, 373)

Emerson's conception of "real life" is the conception of a philosophical idealist: what is real are things like "the law & the ideal right," not things like an "act of Congress" or public issues like "Temperance or the Abolition of slavery."[15]

This tendency to idealize, to universalize his formulations through the construction of abstractions becomes a driving force in Emerson's thinking about social issues. We might discover an allegory of this philosophical practice in the fate of a passage from the "Lecture on Slavery" that Emerson gave on 25 January 1855: "Secret retributions are always restoring the level, when disturbed, of divine justice. It is impossible to tilt the beam. All the tyrants and proprietors and monopolists of the world in vain set their shoulders to heave the bar. Settles forever more the ponderous equator to its line, and man and mote, and star and sun, must range to it, or be pulverized by the recoil" (1855, 99). The passage reappears verbatim twenty years later in "The Sovereignty of Ethics" (1878, 193), a shift of context foreshadowed years earlier by a journal entry from 1840 on the subject of slavery:

> Strange history this of *abolition*. The negro must be very old & belongs, one would say, to the fossil formations. What right has he to be intruding into the late & civil daylight of this dynasty of the Caucasians & Saxons? It is plain that so inferior a race must perish shortly like the poor Indians. Sarah Clarke said, "the Indians perish because there is no place for them". That is the very fact of their inferiority. There is always place for the superior. Yet pity for these was needed, it seems, for the education of this generation in ethics. Our good world cannot learn the beauty of love in narrow circles & at home in the immense Heart, but it must be stimulated by somewhat foreign & monstrous, by the simular man of Ethiopia. (10 September 1840; 1982, 245)

Here we begin to see the effect of the philosophical strategy of abstraction on Emerson's thinking about slavery and race. At this point in his career, Emerson still takes the inferiority of blacks for granted, but the strategy of abstraction leads him to move away from questions of slavery and race to a more generalized question of ethics. He conceives of the problem of race as if it were simply an abstract test for white culture's ethical development.

This ethical development is the subject of the lecture "The Sovereignty of Ethics," which is animated by an abiding faith in liberal teleology. Emerson tells us that "the civil history of men might be traced by the successive meliorations as marked in higher moral generalizations; . . . bargains of kings with peoples of certain rights to certain classes, then of rights to masses,—then at last came the day when, as the historians rightly tell, the nerves of the world were electrified by the proclamation that all men were born free and equal" (187). Toward the end of the essay, Emerson declares that "man does not live by bread alone, but by faith, by admiration, by sympathy," and he predicts that "America shall introduce a pure religion" (202–3). Emerson, in other words, looks forward to the fruition of the project that he set out years before in *Nature*: the achievement of what he called "our own works and laws and worship" (1836, 7). The transposition of this passage—from the "Lecture on Slavery" to "The Sovereignty of Ethics"—is emblematic of Emerson's strategies of abstraction and universalization.[16] These strategies account for much of Emerson's rhetorical power, but they are also strategies that come with certain built-in limitations.

To speak of "individuals" or "men" in the abstract, idealized terms that Emerson favors is to take seriously the egalitarian potential of U.S. individualism. Abstraction enables Emerson to recognize and to begin to pare away racist elements from his public thought. But this Emersonian abstraction has a cost. Emerson ultimately has little to say about racism per se because it is a group-oriented mode of thinking that violates methodological individualism. He expects racism simply to wither away eventually. So, in the chapter of *English Traits* (1856) entitled "Race," Emerson claims that "race is a controlling influence in the Jew, who, for two millenniums, under every climate, has preserved the same character and employments," adding that "race in the negro is of appalling importance." Yet he softens the essentialism of this assertion by claiming that, "whilst race works immortally to keep its own, it is resisted by other forces. Civilization is a reagent, and eats away the old traits" (1856, 792). In other words, civilization can work like an enzyme to break down the significance of race. Emerson expects the question of race to become moot for his culture, just as it has become moot for his own philosophy of self-reliance.

In "The Sovereignty of Ethics," Emerson looks back to the founding of the United States, to the moment when "the nerves of the world were electrified by the proclamation that all men were born free and equal" (1878, 187). Historians tell us that, because "the Declaration of Independence set forth a philosophy of human rights that could be applied . . . to peoples everywhere," it gave "the American Revolution a universal appeal" (Bailyn et al., 190). Emerson's writings employ a similar strategy of universalism, and thus like the Declaration, they mask the unresolved conflicts over race that exist within the official narrative of U.S. individualism and, as a result, gloss over the difficulties of reconciling the claims of liberty with the claims of equality. Emerson's was the most powerful appropriation of the term *individualism* to emerge in U.S. culture during the first half of the nineteenth century. His writings cement the shift in its meaning from "egoism" to "self-reliance," and his portrayal of a teleological relation between the pursuit of individualism and the achievement of national community underwrites the national narrative that continues to exert a powerful influence on U.S. culture today.

Because, however, they promote strategies of abstraction that efface the relation between individualism and such categories as *gender*, *race*, and *ethnicity*, Emerson's writings do not provide the discursive tools necessary for us to understand how the official narrative of individualism might, in fact, be thwarting the achievement of its cherished ideals. Emerson looms large in the American cultural imagination because his doctrine of self-reliance articulated a compelling vision of the progress of U.S. culture "from a state of savage individualism to that of an individualism more elevated, moral and refined" ("The Course of Civilization," 209). Emerson's comments on the gloomy prospects for the "inferior" races of the world make it clear that he took for granted the idea that the "savage" must ultimately submit to the "civilized." He overlooked—perhaps willfully—the extent to which the civilized is deeply implicated in the savage, a theme that is explored in detail by practitioners of American Gothic like Charles Brockden Brown and Edgar Allan Poe and by ex-slaves like Frederick Douglass and Harriet Jacobs. Emerson's vision is elevated and refined, but it contains moral blind spots that render it inadequate as a conceptual tool.

Emerson's writings present us with an opportunity. His intertextuality and allusiveness, combined with his willingness to pursue multiple perspectives and risk contradicting himself, open the door to a liberal cosmopolitanism that could draw on both individualism and pluralism and negotiate between the often-conflicting claims of liberty and equality. Emerson himself, however, could not walk through that door. In the end, his reliance on abstraction and idealization shuts down the cosmopolitan opportunity and promotes instead a universalism that has much to tell us about the ways in which we are all the same but little to tell us about the ways in which we are also all different from one another.

The Heart of Liberalism

Emerson's oeuvre represents the most powerful philosophical defense of individualism produced by nineteenth-century U.S. culture. In the twentieth century, that mantle is taken up by John Rawls, whose work continues to set the terms of debate for liberals and antiliberals alike. Rawls's treatise

A *Theory of Justice* (1971) marks a crucial moment in the history of U.S. individualism. First presented thirteen years earlier in "Justice as Fairness" (1958), Rawls's influential theory evolved during a period in which the individualistic principles of American liberalism were being strongly challenged, both at the level of theory (by Hegelian and Marxist thinkers within the academy) and at the level of practice (by the civil rights movement and the protests against the Vietnam War).[17] What Rawls set out to do was to demonstrate that liberalism was not morally bankrupt, as many of its critics charged. Upon its publication, A *Theory of Justice* was immediately and widely recognized not only as an ambitious work in the tradition of Anglo-American analytic philosophy but also as a major political statement. In a lead article for the *New York Times Book Review*, Marshall Cohen asserted, "All great political philosophies of the past—Plato's, Hobbes's, Rousseau's—have responded to the realities of contemporary politics, and it is therefore not surprising that Rawls's penetrating account of the principles to which our public life is committed should appear at a time when these principles are persistently being obscured and betrayed" (1). Hugo Adam Bedau, writing in *The Nation*, commented that, "as a work of original scholarship in the services of the dominant moral and political ideology of our civilization, Rawls's treatise is simply without a rival" (180). Rawls would qualify and refine certain aspects of his theory in subsequent articles, eventually producing a restatement entitled *Political Liberalism* (1993), an extension of his contractarian doctrines to the sphere of international law entitled *The Law of Peoples* (1999), and a revised edition of A *Theory of Justice* (1999).

Like Emerson, Rawls seeks to transplant Kantian individualism to American soil: his stated aim in A *Theory of Justice* (and in his later attempts to refine the theory) is "to present a conception of justice which generalizes and carries to a higher level of abstraction the familiar theory of the social contract as found, say in Locke, Rousseau, and Kant" (1971, 11; 1999c, 10). In particular, Rawls writes in a later essay, he hopes "to develop a viable Kantian conception of justice" that is able "to take account of the fully social nature of human relationships" by extricating "the force and content of Kant's doctrine . . . from its background in transcendental idealism" (1977, 165). Rawls grounds his theory in negative liberty and ontological individualism, arguing that the individual self has an a priori existence independent of society. Rawls thus adopts an abstract, Kantian conception of individuals as "free and equal rational beings" (1971, 252; 1999c, 222), taking it as given that "each person possesses an inviolability founded on justice that even the welfare of society as a whole cannot override" (1971, 3; 1999c, 3).[18]

By asserting that individual rights cannot be sacrificed even for the communal good, Rawls sets his theory of justice against utilitarianism, which, like all goal-based theories, relegates the welfare of the individual to the periphery. (In contrast, right-based theories like Rawls's are by definition individualistic because their primary concern is the welfare of the individual [cf. Dworkin, 1959, 40–41].) Rawls's belief in the priority of individual rights leads him to argue that a just society cannot be goal based: it must not specify a particular telos or choose among competing ends, purposes, and definitions of the good; instead, it must respect the right of each citizen to pursue his or her own ends and purposes and to define the good for himself or herself, as long as these pursuits and definitions do not infringe on the ability of others to exercise the same right. Rawls summarizes this view by stating that the "self is prior to the ends affirmed by it" (1971, 560; 1999c, 491). Rawls thus takes for granted the fact of pluralism; he assumes that modern societies are bound to be culturally heterogeneous and therefore forced to contend with alternative and often competing ends and purposes.

In order to derive fair principles of justice that will enable society to adjudicate among competing claims, Rawls invents a hypothetical situation called *the original position of equality*, a thought experiment that occupies the place held by *the state of nature* in earlier contractarian doctrines. Rawls asks us to think of the original social contract, not as an agreement "to enter a particular society or to set up a particular form of government," but rather as an agreement to stipulate "the principles of justice for the basic structure of society," the principles "that free and rational persons concerned to further their own interests would accept in an initial position of equality as defining the fundamental terms of their association" (1971, 11; 1999c, 10). Rawls emphasizes that the original position is not to be "thought of as an actual historical state of affairs, much less as a primitive condition of culture. It is understood as a purely hypothetical situation characterized so as to lead to a certain conception of justice" (1971, 12; 1999c, 11).

To ensure that "the principles of justice are the result of a fair agreement or bargain," Rawls further specifies that persons in this initial position of equality must choose these principles from "behind a veil of ignorance," without knowledge of their social attributes (such as class position or social status), their natural talents (such as intelligence, beauty, or strength), their conceptions of the good, or even "their special psychological propensities"—in short, without knowledge of what kinds of persons they are (1971, 12; 1999c, 11). Rawls's methodology here is to create a set of ground rules that are indisputably fair and thus can ensure a fair outcome; as he puts it in "The Basic Structure as Subject," "the fairness of the circumstances transfers to the fairness of the principles adopted" (1989, 159). For Rawls, this methodological stipulation "explains the propriety of the name" that he gives to his theory—"Justice as Fairness"—because "it conveys the idea that the principles of justice are agreed to in an initial situation that is fair" (1971, 12; 1999c, 11).[19]

The original position is thus a classic instance of methodological individualism in action: like Emerson, Rawls shifts the ground of political inquiry from the social to the individual and presents a highly abstracted version of individuality.[20] Seeking to find the lowest common denominator for all individuals, both thinkers assume that individuality remains even when the self is stripped of social markers. Rawls's "veil of ignorance" produces a version of Emerson's "soul," and both are versions of what political theorists refer to as the abstract individual (see Lukes, 73–78).

Rawls argues that from the vantage point of the original position all individuals would choose two principles of justice. The first principle stipulates that "each person is to have an equal right to the most extensive total system of equal basic liberties compatible with a similar system of liberty for all" (1971, 302; 1999c, 266). It is this principle that assures the individualistic basis of "justice as fairness" and sets the theory apart from utilitarianism. According to Rawls, utilitarianism "balances the individual gains and losses of different persons as if they were one person" (1971, 28; 1999c, 25), treating society as a whole as an individual and thus failing to respect the uniqueness and inviolability of each individual citizen. The second principle of justice—the so-called difference principle—sets the theory apart from the extreme individualism of libertarianism, stipulating that "all social primary goods—liberty and opportunity, income and wealth, and the bases of self-respect—are to be distributed equally unless an unequal distribution of any or all of these goods is to the advantage of the least favored" (1971, 303). In effect, Rawls's two principles follow the model established in the Declaration of Independence: the first principle guarantees liberty, the second strives for equality, and the two are listed in order of lexical priority.[21] In other words, Rawls's theory, like the culture it seeks to justify, identifies liberty as the precondition for equality.

Libertarians like Robert Nozick agree with Rawls about the inviolability of the individual. "There are only individual people, different individual people, with their own individual lives," Nozick writes in *Anarchy, State, and Utopia* (1974). "Using one of these people for the benefit of others, uses him and benefits the others. Nothing more. . . . To use a person in this way does not sufficiently respect and take account of the fact that he is a separate person, that his is the only life he has" (33). Libertarians champion not only individual rights but also laissez-faire, opposing redistribution of wealth on the grounds that the inherent justice of the free market economy underwrites the justice of whatever social distribution of wealth results from its operation. From Rawls's point of view, such an arrangement cannot be called *just* because it fails to compensate for the arbitrariness of fortune. In addition to a "background of equal liberty . . . and a free market economy," a "system of natural liberty," according to Rawls,

> require[s] a formal equality of opportunity in that all have at least the same legal rights of access to all advantaged social positions. But since there is no effort to preserve an equality, or similarity, of social conditions, except insofar as this is necessary to preserve the requisite background institutions, the initial distribution of assets for any period of time is strongly influenced by natural and social contingencies. The existing distribution of income and wealth, say, is the cumulative effect of prior distributions of natural assets—that is, natural talents and abilities—as these have been developed or left unrealized, and their use favored or disfavored over time by social circumstances and such chance contingencies as accident and good fortune. Intuitively, the most obvious injustice of the system of natural liberty is that it permits distributive shares to be improperly influenced by these factors so arbitrary from a moral point of view. (1971, 72; 1991c, 62–63)

Because an individual occupying the original position is unaware of how he or she will fare when natural assets are distributed, he or she applies the principle of *maximum minimorum* ("the most from the least," or "maximin" for short). According to Rawls, "The maximin rule tells us to rank alternatives by their worst possible outcomes: we are to adopt the alternative the worst outcome of which is superior to the worst outcomes of the others" (1971, 152–53; 1991c, 133). A person will choose principles of justice that minimize the effects of the inevitable inequality in the distribution of natural assets, creating an institutional arrangement in which "those who have been favored by nature, whoever they are, may gain from their good fortune only on terms that improve the situation of those who have lost out" (1971, 101; 1991c, 87).

Rawls, however, is not content to maintain that individuals in the original position will choose the difference principle for purely instrumental, self-interested reasons. For him, "The difference principle represents, in effect, an agreement to regard the distribution of natural talents as a common asset and to share in the *greater social and economic benefits made possible by the complementarities* of this distribution whatever it turns out to be" (1971, 101; 1991c, 87; portion in italics added in rev. ed.). Acknowledging that the "theoretical basis" of justice as fairness is "individualistic," Rawls nevertheless argues that "justice as fairness has a central place for the value of community"; indeed, he goes so far as to claim that, without an explanation for the value of community, "the theory of justice cannot succeed" (1971, 264–65; 1991c, 233–34). Rawls contends that "human beings . . . value their common institutions and activities as good in themselves. We need one another as partners in ways of life that are engaged in for their own sake, and the successes and enjoyments of others are necessary for and complementary to our own good" (1971, 522–23; 1991c, 458). An individual's potentialities can never be fully realized; at the same time, those potentialities "fall far short of the powers among men generally." For these two reasons, Rawls argues, it is precisely "through social union founded upon the needs and potentialities of its members that each person can participate in the total sum of the realized natural assets" (1971, 523; 1991c, 459). It is important to recognize, however, what an abstract idea of community this really is; as in Emerson's writing, Rawls's reliance on an abstract conception of the individual can produce only an abstract conception of community. The original position thus proves to be a philosophical fiction that is insufficiently fictional: far from providing the richer view of individuals and communities available in novels, it can produce only an impoverished account of them.

My aim here is not primarily to provide a philosophical critique of Rawls's work but rather to show that his theory is consonant with the teleological conceptions of negative liberty and individualism that characterize Emersonian liberalism. An example of the way in which Rawls's conception of individualism follows this logic can be found toward the end of *A Theory of Justice* when Rawls expands his conception of the individual person as a "free and equal rational being" to include an inherent longing for community. "Human beings," he writes, "have a desire to express their nature as free and equal moral persons, and this they do most adequately by acting from the principles that they would acknowledge in the original position. When all strive to comply with these principles and each succeeds, then individually and collectively their nature as moral persons is most fully realized, and with it their individual and collective good" (1971, 528; 1991c, 462–63). In a passage that might be seen as a rejoinder to Emerson's fable of the "One Man" in "The American Scholar" (1837a, 53–54), Rawls offers a new way of conceptualizing the division of labor in society:

> In a fully just society persons seek their good in ways peculiar to themselves, and they rely upon their associates to do things they could not have done, as well as things they might have done but did not. It is tempting to suppose that everyone might fully realize his powers and that some at least can become complete exemplars of humanity. But this is impossible. It is a feature of human sociability that we are by ourselves but parts of what we might be. We must look to others to attain the excellences that we must leave aside, or lack altogether. The collective activity of society, the many associations and the public life of the largest community that regulates them, sustains our efforts and elicits our contribution. Yet the good attained from the common culture far exceeds our work in the sense that we cease to be mere fragments: that part of ourselves that we directly realize is joined to a wider and just arrangement the aims of which we affirm. The division of labor is overcome not by each becoming complete in himself, but by willing and meaningful work within a just social union of social unions in which all can freely participate as they so incline. (1971, 529; 1999c, 464)

In "The American Scholar," Emerson argues that "the individual, to possess himself, must sometimes return from his own labor to embrace all the other laborers" (54), but Rawls here suggests that this idea is an impossibility. Rawls accepts what Emerson laments, "that we are by ourselves but parts of what we might be" (Rawls 1971, 529; 1991c, 464). For Emerson, such partiality is a sign that most individuals exist in a "degenerate state" that thwarts the realization of any true individualism. Rawls, however, recasts partiality as difference and conceives it not only as a fact of twentieth-century culture but also as a strength. In Rawls's view, the individual's recognition that he or she is partial and incomplete is the first step in understanding that all individuals cannot and should not be alike, that difference is the foundation on which a strong social union is built.

In presenting its argument, Rawls's treatise thus follows the teleological conception of U.S. individualism, although in philosophical terms the doctrine of justice as fairness may well be considered a nonteleological, "deontological" theory (1971, 30). A Theory of Justice moves from an assertion of individualistic principles to an exposition of the ways in which justice as fairness upholds communal values. Grounded in negative liberty, Rawls's theory uses the methodologically individualist device of the original position to produce a social structure that includes both an emphasis on rights and a respect for community. Like that first review of the second volume of *Democracy in America*, and like Emerson's discussions of individualism, Rawls's theory of justice both describes and embodies an expansion of ontological individualism according to a logic that links it to the creation of a national community. It is, however, a bloodless version of community, a community of abstract individuals linked primarily by their belief in the value of individualism. For both radical democrats like Chantal Mouffe and communitarians like Michael Sandel, Rawls's theory promotes only an impoverished conception of community. Mouffe locates the source of this problem in Rawls's reliance on individualism and identifies the emphasis on pluralism and difference as his major contribution to democratic theory. Sandel, however, sees pluralism as part of the problem: what is wrong with Rawls's theory of community is not only its individualistic foundations but also its refusal to recognize that strong communities are held together by far more than a simple belief in the value of individualism.

The Unencumbered Self

Americans, professing themselves to be individualists, nevertheless have habitually thought in racial terms: they have often judged others not on the basis of individual merit but on the basis of race, a group characteristic. The American obsession with race suggests that the abstract individual invoked by both Emerson and Rawls may be an untenable conception of the self because it underemphasizes the importance of communities, institutions, and collectivities in social life.

The most vigorous and influential exposition of the idea that Rawls's theory of justice depends on an untenable conception of the self has been offered by Michael Sandel, who coined the term *unencumbered self* and who regards Rawlsianism as the embodiment of all the assumptions, strengths, and failings of twentieth-century American liberalism. For Sandel, the term *unencumbered self* describes "the way we stand toward the things we have, or want, or seek. It means there is always a distinction between the values I *have* and the person I *am*." Sandel interprets Rawls's claim that "the self is prior to the ends affirmed by it" to mean that, for the unencumbered self, "what matters above all, what is most essential to our personhood, are not the ends we choose but our capacity to choose them" (1984b, 86; 1996, 12). In Sandel's view, "the Rawlsian self is . . . an antecedently individuated subject, standing always at a certain distance from the interests it has," and it therefore excludes any concept of communally constituted identity. Sandel argues that the Rawlsian conception of the self "rules out the possibility of any attachment or obsession able to reach beyond our values and sentiments to engage our identity itself. It rules out the possibility of a public life in which, for good or ill, the identity as well as the interests of the participants could be at stake" (1982, 62; 1998, 62).

The plaintive note sounded by this characterization of the Rawlsian self arises from Sandel's belief that, although the Rawlsian claim for the priority of the right over the good is ultimately a "philosophical failure," it nevertheless represents "the liberal vision . . . by which we live. For us in late twentieth century America, it is our vision, the theory most thoroughly embodied in the practices and institutions most central to our public life" (1984b, 82). The power of this vision, Sandel believes, lies in Rawls's ability to claim that we, as free and equal moral persons, are "self-originating sources of valid claims" (1984b, 86). Sandel is forced to admit the appeal of this idea, acknowledging that "the image of the self as free and independent, unencumbered by aims and attachments it does not choose for itself, offers a powerful liberating vision. Freed from the sanctions of custom and tradition and inherited status, unbound by moral ties antecedent to choice, the liberal self is installed as sovereign, cast as the author of the only obligations that constrain" (1996, 12). It is, writes Sandel, "an exhilarating promise, and the liberalism it animates is perhaps the fullest expression of the Enlightenment's quest for the self-defining subject" (1984b, 87). It is also, Sandel contends, a promise that cannot be kept.

For Sandel and other communitarian thinkers, part of what makes Rawls's theory suspect is the claim that it does not rely on any conception of the good. Thomas Nagel, who is sympathetic to Rawls's emphasis on the priority of right, nevertheless argues that "the original position seems to presuppose not just a neutral theory of the good, but a liberal, individualistic conception according to which the best that can be wished for someone is the unimpeded pursuit of his own path, provided it does not interfere with the rights of others" (1989, 10). Sandel goes further, arguing that Rawlsianism and the liberal vision that it embodies are "not morally self-sufficient but parasitic on a notion of community it officially rejects" (1984b, 91). His central exhibit is the difference principle, which he characterizes as "a principle of sharing" that "must presuppose some prior moral tie among those whose assets it would deploy and whose efforts it would enlist in a common endeavor" (89). Recalling that Rawls claims that "in justice as fairness men agree to share one another's fate" (1971, 102), Sandel suggests that if "those whose fate I am required to share really are, morally speaking, *others*, rather than fellow participants in a way of life with which my identity is bound, the difference principle falls prey to the same objections as utilitarianism," namely, that certain individuals are used as means to achieve the ends of others. What would save the difference principle is some conception of a situated self, in which the individual is seen to be at least partially constituted by his or her bonds to others; instead, both Rawlsianism and American liberalism deny that they rely on attachment to others and, in fact, portray such attachments as "encumbrances." Without "the expansive self-understandings" made possible by admitting that identity is at least partially constituted by communal commitments, the individual is placed in an uncomfortable position, caught between an alienated detachment, on the one hand, and a sense of entanglement, on the other. "Such," writes Sandel, "is the fate of the unencumbered self, and its liberating promise" (1984b, 90–91).[22]

Does Sandel's critique of Rawls present a fair representation of the conception of personhood that underlies justice as fairness? Rawls himself does not think so, despite the fact that Sandel's *Liberalism and the Limits of Justice* (1982, 1998) is frequently cited as an important critique of Rawlsian liberalism. In "Justice as Fairness: Political not Metaphysical" (1985), Rawls clarifies his aims by stating that he seeks to "avoid" certain philosophical claims such as "claims to universal truth, or claims about the essential nature and identity of persons" (388). What he is trying to describe, he contends, is "a political conception of justice for a democratic society," not a prescriptive, universal description of an ideal "basic structure" for all societies (389). "I think Michael Sandel mistaken," he writes in a footnote, "in supposing that the original position involves a conception of the self '... shorn of all its contingently-given attributes,' a self that 'assumes a kind of supra-empirical status, ... and given prior to its end, a pure subject of agency and possession, ultimately thin'" (403n). Rawls suggests that Sandel's interpretation is unwarranted and, essentially, beside the point.[23]

In a more sympathetic commentary on Sandel's work, Charles Taylor avoids the issue of whether Sandel misreads the intent of the original position, arguing instead that Sandel's "important book" represents a "contribution to social ontology" that asks "whether the kind of egalitarian redistribution Rawls recommends can be sustained in a society which is not bound together in solidarity through a strong sense of community; and whether, in turn, a strong community of this kind can be forged around a common understanding which makes justice the principle virtue of social life, or whether some other good does not have to figure as well in the definition of community life" (1989, 162). What Taylor points to here is a disjunction between the kind of "well-ordered society" that Rawls assumes and the kind of society that late twentieth-century America actually is.[24] Taylor's commentary suggests that it is one thing to imagine a hypothetical situation like the original position in which mutually disinterested contracting agents could agree that the distributive justice embodied by the difference principle serves the self-interest of each of them; it is quite another thing, however, to effect distributive justice among self-interested individuals as they actually exist in the world, individuals who already possess certain natural assets and are loathe to give any of them up (cf. Mouffe 1993, 30). Such a situation is imaginable only in a communitarian society that is organized not around the pursuit of individual self-interest but around some conception of collective good—which the United States, a fundamentally pluralist society, is not. Another way to put Taylor's insight is to say that the results that Rawls obtains from his thought experiment might help us if we are planning to found a new liberal society from scratch, but they offer us precious few resources for retrofitting the liberal society with which we are currently stuck.

Taylor thus defends Sandel by arguing that Rawls's well-ordered society is too removed from the reality of American society for his prescriptions to be effective, but it is not an argument that Sandel himself would mobilize in his own defense. For Sandel insists that Rawls's theory is in fact a reflection of American social reality, and he argues that the liberalism embodied by Rawls's theory of justice is "our vision" and that "seeing how it goes wrong as philosophy may help us to diagnose our present political condition" (1984b, 82). Sandel here claims to be moving from political theory to cultural practice, but it seems likely that he has, perhaps unwittingly, done precisely the reverse: refracted Rawls's theory through the lens of American cultural mythology, merging Rawls's methodological individualism with the mythic, rugged individualism that has long been a staple of American popular culture.

Sandel's description of the "unencumbered self" sounds less like a description of the Rawlsian individual than like a description of the frontiersman, or the cowboy, or the hard-boiled detective. What I am suggesting is that the unencumbered self is a particular kind of misreading: it is an exaggeration of the Rawlsian self, in much the same way as the rugged individualist represents an exaggerated embodiment of the desire for self-reliance. The unencumbered self and the rugged individualist are not ontologically identical to the abstract Rawlsian individual; they are, instead, potential avatars, variations that arise when certain aspects of the abstract individual—like self-reliance—are overemphasized.

Rugged individualism is what methodological individualism becomes when it is translated into the mythologized language of popular culture. The idea that "all social phenomena . . . can be explained by the actions and properties of the participating individuals" is simplified, exaggerated, and then personified in characters like Natty Bumppo, Shane, Philip Marlowe, or Indiana Jones, characters whose actions have a decisive and astounding effect on the worlds in which they live. Both the liberalism that Rawls defends and the rugged individualism that these characters embody are central themes within the national narrative of individual freedom—what Sandel calls "the liberal vision . . . by which we live"—but Sandel oversimplifies Rawlsian theory by simply mapping these two components onto one another.

The archetype of the rugged individualist is a subplot within the larger narrative of U.S. individualism that is centered on the transformation of negative liberty into positive liberty. To be effective as a mechanism for the formation of consensus, this narrative must be able to contain and redirect the energies produced by the Thoreauvian impulse to march to the beat of a different drummer. The strategy that it pursues is not to marginalize and deflect attention away from loners but rather to make them central—to emphasize, idealize, and mythologize them—through the archetype of the rugged individualist. The rationale for the myth of the rugged individualist is primarily ontological: it takes as its subject the individualist—self-reliant and unencumbered—and shows us what the world looks like through his or (less often) her eyes. Driven by visions of the individualist as loner and rebel but also agent of justice, this myth has given rise to character types that have attained heroic status in U.S. culture: the frontiersman, the cowboy, the hard-boiled dick. In *Habits of the Heart*, Bellah et al. describe rugged individualism as "a deep and continuing theme in American literature," personified by heroes who "must leave society, alone or with one or a few others, in order to realize the moral good" (144).[25] Thus, while the stories that center on these rugged individualists may appear at first to contradict the teleological conception that is central to the official narrative of individualism, they prove on further scrutiny to bolster its claims instead.

The rugged individualist is a cultural fantasy that compensates for some of the self-imposed limits of the everyday individualism that Herbert Gans has described. Fictions that dramatize rugged individualism give its readers access to the ontology of mastery. The myth of rugged individualism serves as a form of wish fulfillment for a culture that extols varieties of individualism that often lie outside the reach of the average person, who practices a form of individualism that, as Gans puts it, "does not preach the virtues of risk-taking" (3). Although middle Americans tend to live their economic lives according to the dictates of this pragmatic, materialistic form of individualism, they do not eschew mythic, rugged individualism altogether: they merely relegate it to the realm of popular culture, experiencing it vicariously through spectator sports or action films. According to Morris Dickstein, the twentieth century has seen an erosion of "the belief in the power of the individual to solve problems, to correct wrongs, and to control his own destiny," a "kind of mastery [that] survives *only* in popular culture, as a fantasy which compensates for the widespread feeling that larger, more impersonal forces now dominate the destiny of individuals" (56). Many of the most popular films of the late twentieth century depict the efficacy of individual agency through characters like James Bond, Luke Skywalker, Han Solo, and Indiana Jones, to name only a few. The popularity of Ronald Reagan can also be attributed largely to his ability to provide a similar experience of wish fulfillment by presenting a public persona drawn to a great extent from different avatars of rugged individualism: the cowboy, the frontiersman, Rambo, and Dirty Harry.

Narratives that invoke the rugged individualist often allay the fears of potential anarchy that might accompany such a vision of personal autonomy by subtly resituating the self within social bonds or by demonstrating that such bonds have existed all along, thus suggesting that no self can ever be completely asocial but that social bonds do not necessarily destroy personal autonomy or encroach on personal identity. For example, hard-boiled detectives like Raymond Chandler's Philip Marlowe appear at first to be the kind of solo operators that A. Bartlett Giamatti deplored, but, on closer inspection, they prove to be driven by a code of honor that upholds society's ideals. The subplot of rugged individualism thus rationalizes U.S. culture's fascination with loners and resolves the potential contradiction between the valorization of individual agency and the need for communal bonds. The rugged individualist does what he wants, but what he wants is in the best interest of society. In effect, the ontological experience provided by fictions that dramatize rugged individualism often proves to be a version of the teleological story.

Sandel never mentions rugged individualism or the kinds of pop-cultural forms that I have been discussing here, but I believe that they are implicit subjects of his critique. For, ultimately, Sandel's target is not simply the Rawlsian or other philosophical conceptions of liberalism but rather what I have been describing as the official narrative of U.S. individualism. As Samuel H. Beer puts it in a review of Sandel's *Democracy's Discontents* (1996), Sandel is not adopting "the cynical view of man as a self-centered egoist. The individualist Sandel attacks is a worthier and more formidable figure: that often idealized American, the self-made man. Instructed by Benjamin Franklin's *Poor Richard's Almanack* and Ralph Waldo Emerson's 'Self-Reliance,' this individual strives to realize his own freely chosen conception of the good life, constrained only by the right of others to do the same. He is autonomous" (89). Sandel rejects the national narrative in which the negative liberty that protects such an autonomous individual also leads him or her to achieve self-fulfillment by embracing positive liberty. Adopting what Susan Okin has characterized as a "Manichean worldview" (1997, 440), Sandel returns negative and positive liberty to the relation of opposition described by Isaiah Berlin, and, finding them to be mutually exclusive, he chooses positive liberty. Eric Foner has criticized Sandel's "tendency to see republicanism and liberalism as ideologies that flourished sequentially, with one replacing the other, rather than outlooks coexisting throughout our history," suggesting that *Democracy's Discontents* would have been more persuasive had Sandel "portray[ed] Jefferson and other Founders as simultaneously republican and liberal—they exalted both the sense of community and the public good Sandel admires and a devotion to individual rights that cannot be infringed by government" (1996, 35; see also Okin 1997, 440). In rejecting the official narrative of individualism as simplistic and untenable, Sandel offers an alternative that seems equally simplistic and untenable.

Sandel's analysis, like those of his fellow communitarians Alasdair MacIntyre and Christopher Lasch, seems marked by a nostalgia for a good old "republican" past patterned on the Greek idea of the polis or the German ideal of *Gemeinschaft*. But, as Alan Ryan points out, "old-fashioned republicanism lost out to liberalism for very good reasons—it was repressive, anti-individualist, backwardlooking, religiously exclusive, and offered nothing to women. Most forms of communitarianism lost out for similar reasons. People didn't want to stay on the farm once they had seen Paree" (124).[26] Or, as Chantal Mouffe puts it, Sandel's "critique of liberalism ignores the characteristics of modern democracy and leads to a rejection of modernity."[27] Chief among these characteristics are "the separation of public and private and the defence of pluralism" (Mouffe 1993, 36), both of which are deemphasized by Sandel's communitarian vision.

Let me suggest, along with Mouffe, that communitarianism's important contribution to the critique of the national narrative of individualism is its insistence that a social theory that cannot conceive of any collective aspects of social life serving a constitutive role in the formation of identity is a social theory that fails to account for crucial ways in which many of us experience our lives (cf. Mouffe 1993, 33). The idea that both Emersonianism and Rawlsian liberalism can imagine only an abstract and bloodless version of community is an insight suggested by communitarian theory. But, as Mouffe and others have pointed out, this insight does not authorize the leap that Sandel, MacIntyre, Lasch, and others have made in championing the idea that society should be based on "a common moral order," a single idea of what constitutes the good (Mouffe 1993, 31). As we shall see, both Pynchon and Morrison dramatize the alienation that results from the erosion of community within liberal America. They are drawn, in other words, to aspects of the communitarian critique of individualism. But they also realize, along with Isaiah Berlin, how quickly the idea of positive liberty embodied in the idea of *a common moral order* can devolve into oppression and tyranny. Their novels attempt to imagine, along with philosophers like Chantal Mouffe, Charles Taylor, and Michael Walzer, ways in which the defense of individual rights and pluralism can be preserved without losing the idea that individuals are often fundamentally formed by their communal bonds and obligations—and without simply succumbing to the logic of the official story that seeks to whitewash these incompatibilities and contradictions.

Democratic Individuality

In a review of *Liberal Modernism and Democratic Individuality* (1996), a collection of essays devoted to the work of George Kateb, David Weinstein describes "Kateb's Emersonian liberalism" as an "ambitious" attempt to "offer a palpably distinct and heartening alternative to the alleged, suffocating perils of communitarianism, all the while avoiding the equally suffocating conformism of market liberalism."[28] The fusion of the Emersonian and the Rawlsian conceptions of individualism that Kateb calls *democratic individuality* is identified by Weinstein as "a rights-based, negative freedom liberalism peculiar to American civic culture that valorizes self-reliance, authenticity, self-experimentation, and diversity" (953). Kateb agrees with communitarian thinkers that individualism is indeed at the heart of the American political tradition:

> There is common agreement that the individual is the moral center of American life. Tocqueville was one of the first to inject the word "individualism" into discourse about the American character, but the feelings and attitudes that support and grow out of the centrality of the individual had of course to precede his brilliant depiction. Furthermore, American political and judicial institutions were implicated from the start in the enterprise of surrounding individuals with guarantees and protections, just as economic institutions housed individual acquisition. The general sense radiated by the actuality of the American democracy is that the individual is important or prior or precious or sacred. (1992, 77)

Finding individualism embodied in both the theory and the practice of American democracy, Kateb implies that it is the source of what he clearly believes to be American exceptionalism: although he concedes that "the major industrial democracies of the modern world . . . may not truly be the homes of the democratic individual, or may be so in only a significantly mixed or ambiguous manner," Kateb contends that "it is a cardinal fact that the individual is the center in the most modern democracy, the democracy least continuous with nondemocratic systems—in short, in the American democracy" (1992, 78).

What troubles Kateb about late twentieth-century attacks on individualism is the fact "that individualism is not always seen in its fullness and thus is disparaged unfairly or at least prematurely" (1989, 185). He distinguishes between two types of individualism, which he calls "historically related": "The first is the individualism of personal and political rights, profoundly present in Rawls, Dworkin, and Nozick, but, as we know, the creation of the English Protestant seventeenth century: the work of the Levellers, Roger Williams, Milton, Hobbes, and Locke (among others).

This work is carried on, and sometimes improved, by Trenchard and Gordon, Montesquieu, Rousseau, Paine, Kant, Jefferson, Madison, Lincoln, and J. S. Mill (despite his disclaimers about believing in abstract rights" (185). The second type of individualism is Kateb's "democratic individuality," which he describes as "an idealism imagined and theorized initially by Emerson, Thoreau, and Whitman, and with a force that has not been equaled since then, much less surpassed." It is this second form that represents for Kateb both the "fullness" of individualism and the fruition of democracy. According to Kateb, the connection "between the two types of individualism is that democratic individuality is perhaps not the only but probably the best actuality and aspiration that grows or can grow out of a culture in which individual personal and political rights are systematically recognized and appreciated." Just as Kateb sees in the writings of Emerson, Thoreau, and Whitman an idealization of rights-based individualism, so we might see in Kateb's own writing an idealization of Rawls's work, which Kateb calls "the great statement of individualism in this century" (1989, 184).

In contrast to Rawls, whose project is in part an effort to wrest rights-based individualism away from the hold of transcendental idealism, Kateb seeks to reidealize individualism—or, more precisely, to demonstrate that idealism has always been a crucial part of American individualism, implicit in the rights-based tradition, but explicit and paramount in Emersonian liberalism. Kateb detects within rights-based individualism the same weakness identified both by Tocqueville and by twentieth-century communitarian political theorists: Tocqueville calls it the "vice" of "egoism," while the communitarians describe it as an atomism that leads to alienation (see, for example, Taylor 1985a). Kateb, however, depicts the problem in a way that minimizes its severity, calling it simply "the latency in rights-based individualism to make too much of oneself" (1992, 236). What becomes clear as Kateb's argument proceeds is that he is counterpoising this latency against the potentialities of individualism, writing off the costs of the present state of liberal society against the benefits of liberal society in its ideal state.

Among the various criticisms of individualism offered by communitarian thinkers, Kateb is willing to grant the legitimacy of the claim that "people should have greater *mutuality* than they are conditioned to have in liberal society," that they "need greater encouragement to share their lives with others, to care about others for the sake of others, and to cooperate in the attempted solution of common problems" (1992, 224).[29] Kateb recognizes "that espousing mutuality as a constant guide to public policy does not come easily to proponents of individualism," for, "when mutuality passes beyond relief of the needy to a greater effort to persuade or entice people to care actively for each other's well-being, individualists bridle" (225–26). He argues, however, that to "grant the need for greater mutuality" is not "to grant the heart of the communitarian case":

> Communitarianisms are usually reluctant to take in the fact that individualism redefines human bonds; it does not foolishly try to eliminate them. In a liberal society, ideally, the state is changed into government, and ruling into governing; society ceases imagining itself as a natural growth or cyclical process and becomes more consensual and voluntary; and the people become an entity held together by agreement rather than religion, ethnicity, a long and unforgiving memory, or the mimesis of traditional roles and customs. Love and friendship, marriage and the family, are also transformed. A liberal society is explicit, to an unusual degree, in its transactions and therefore in its bonds. (1992, 22)

Communitarians, in other words, present a distorted view of American individualism: their view of rights-based individualism fails to recognize any of its idealistic aspects. Kateb's argument subtly shifts the focus from the present state of affairs (which is most often the focus of communitarian critiques) to an ideal state of affairs in which social bonds are transformed. Like Rawls, Kateb depends on the rationality of individuals, implying that the ideal liberal society is stronger than other forms of society because it is "consensual and voluntary," because its bonds are made "explicit" and are self-consciously enacted. Kateb's first line of defense against communitarian attacks is to put the best possible face onto Rawlsian liberalism and to argue explicitly that such a liberalism will transform not only the individual and the body politic but also all the intermediary bonds and institutions that Rawls tends to take for granted: love, friendship, marriage, and the family. In stipulating that the shift from negative to positive liberty will transform the bonds of love and friendship and the institutions of marriage and the family, this line of reasoning thus recapitulates the teleological conception of individualism that animates Emersonian liberalism and the official narrative that it has generated.

Kateb's second line of defense against the communitarians is to deploy the Emersonian tradition, in which the idealistic side of rights-based individualism is heightened and expressed as democratic individuality. Kateb highlights Emerson's break with Lockean possessive individualism, arguing that, "as Emerson works out his ideas, we are able to see that the defense of self-reliance is an attack on the common tendency to act on the idea that the core of individualism is economic self-centeredness and that the true individual is acquisitive or possessive or consumerist." Kateb's Emerson is an idealist for whom "the exclusively materialistic life is not life, but a misdiagnosed dying" (1995, 18). Indeed, Kateb seems to imply that the selfishness that so worried Tocqueville is a danger of Lockean rights-based individualism that Emerson's thought helps us avoid; Emersonian liberalism, Kateb argues, "corrects the latency in rights-based individualism to make too much of oneself" (1992, 236). For an Emersonian, the development of individuality leads, not to egoism, but to a sense of connectedness: "The nobility of the Emersonian aspiration lies in transcending the ideal of individualism understood as the cultivation and expression of personality, precisely because Emerson, like his great colleagues Thoreau and Whitman, knows how social, and not individualist, such an ideal is. They all go in the direction of self-abandonment, away from egotism, even away from self-expression, and do so as proponents of individualism" (236). Like those who advocated individualism during the early part of the nineteenth century, Kateb deploys the concepts *individuality* and *idealism* as primary weapons in a discursive battle against those who advocate a collectivist form of social organization. "Democracy's most elevated justification," he writes, "lies in its encouragement of individuality." Indeed, Kateb is willing to take the argument one step further, proposing the somewhat mystical "further possibility" that "individuality's meaning is not fully disclosed until it is indissociably connected to democracy" (1992, 78). What Kateb is suggesting here is that the fruition of individuality occurs only when it moves beyond the strictures of negative liberty to encompass the communally oriented goals of positive liberty as well.

To understand the dynamics of democratic individuality as Kateb conceives them, let us turn to his reading of Whitman's "Song of Myself." He prefaces his analysis of the poem by specifying the three components of democratic individuality: self-expression, resistance on behalf of others, and receptivity or responsiveness to others. Kateb argues that this responsiveness was in fact the most important aspect of democratic individuality for the Emersonians. "An individual's insistence on first being oneself expressively is valuable mostly as a preparation for receptivity or responsiveness," writes Kateb, adding that "behavioral nonconformity loosens the hold of narrow or conventional methods of seeing and feeling (as well as preparing a person to take a principled stand in favor of those denied their rights)" (1992, 241).

In Kateb's description of Whitman's word *soul*, we can find the abstract individual who stands in Rawls's original position idealized even further.[30] To create the original position, Rawls transforms social choice into individual choice by stripping individuals down to a common denominator: each person may bring to the initial choice situation only that which all have in common. Kateb finds such a common denominator in Whitman's secular conception of the soul: "In its secular meaning, the soul is what is given in the person, and in all persons the given is the same: the same desires, inclinations, and passions as well as aptitudes and incipient talents. The secular soul is made up of the unwilled, the unbidden, the dreamt, the inchoate and unshaped. It is the reservoir of potentialities. Its roots are wordless. It exists to be observed and worked on, to be realized" (1992, 245). For this reason, Kateb finds himself untroubled by these lines in the first section of "Song of Myself": "What I assume you shall assume, / For every atom belonging to me as good belongs to you" (lines 2–3). Admitting that the first line resembles a demand that Whitman's readers "obey him in their thought," which Kateb calls "a sentiment worse than egotistical," he reads the second line as the premise of the first (and of the poem as a whole), a statement of the essential similarity between poet and reader. Refusing to read this line in a materialist way, for example, as a radical statement about property rights, Kateb argues that it demonstrates Whitman's belief that rights-based individualism "enables and encourages a certain recognition of likeness." Kateb focuses on Whitman's use of the word *atom* to explicate the valences of this "likeness": "An atom is a potentiality, I think. Every individual is composed of potentialities. Therefore, when I perceive or take in other human beings as they lead their lives or play their parts, I am encountering only external actualizations of some of the countless number of potentialities in me, in my soul. These atoms are in everyone; hence 'every atom belonging to me as good belongs to you'" (1992, 244). In this vision of the potentialities that all human beings share in common—before the distribution of natural assets—Kateb creates an idealized version of the logic that underlies Rawls's difference principle. And, in the best Emersonian tradition, Kateb fuses poetics and politics into an idealizing form of political philosophy.

Responding to Kateb's reading of Whitman, Leo Marx writes, "Kateb's argument ... flies directly in the face of so many currently received ideas. At a time when the concept of individualism is widely regarded as an ideological construction designed to justify the power and the privileges of white males affiliated with the dominant, propertied class, Kateb insists on its democratic centrality and integrity" (1990, 596–97). Kateb is not unaware of the possible pitfalls of rights-based individualism (and its materialistic offshoot, economic individualism), which for him include "such things as moronic selfishness; social neglect; varieties of alienation such as disquiet, rage, loneliness, all of which may come from the need or the opportunity to make things up (including an identity) as one goes along in an individualist culture; and anomie (that is, moral confusion amid unprecedented powers that often become new sources of fragility, and unprecedented choices that often become dilemmas or aporias)" (1989, 204). Moreover, he recognizes that Emersonianism itself is not without its problems: "The secret worm that gnaws at the Emersonians," Kateb admits, is "misanthropy. . . . They feel an irritation bred of disappointment that sometimes turns into contempt" when "they see democratic individuals lapsing into economic individuals. The underside of Emersonians' sense of democratic potentiality is a steady censure, a dislike, almost" (191–92). For Kateb, however, such effects are failures of particular individuals rather than faults of Emersonian liberalism. The true vulnerability of Emersonianism arises from the fact that it is ill equipped to contend with certain developments of the modern state: "it fears the entrepreneurial excesses of the market economy" but is unable to foresee "the statist and welfarist responses to those excesses." What Emersonianism needs, according to Kateb, is a more fully developed theory of "individual integrity" to combat the appearance of statism in another guise, a phenomenon that Tocqueville called *democratic despotism* and that Kateb describes as a "painless" form of oppression in which individuals are known "through and through: their behavior is observed and studied, their wants are anticipated, their hurts are assuaged, their lives are mapped out. Everything is permitted but initiative. Paternalism reigns" (1992, 81).

It is finally the defense of individual integrity that emerges as Kateb's primary concern, and his increasingly vehement insistence on the benefits of democratic individuality arises from his sense that anti-individualist ideals participate in "an inadvertent collusion with everything in modern life that leads to the growth of the power of the state. In that growth even anti-individualist ideals would wither or grow cancerous." Statism is what happens when a society seeks positive liberty without first grounding it in the negative liberty that the Emersonian tradition champions: according to Kateb, "Statism must grow with the growth of belief in socialized self-realization because this sort of self-realization is almost indistinguishable from therapeutic and paternalist condescension to ordinary persons who are secretly thought by theorists to be no better than a plebs." Kateb firmly believes that rights-based individualism "provides the best perspective from which to condemn statism, and also to detect in seemingly nonstatist or even overtly antistatist ideals a terrible statist legacy." For him, statism represents the worst possible construction of society: "Not only does statism imperil human dignity as conceived in rights-based individualism, and altogether block the Emersonian conception of democratic individuality, it imperils everything minimally decent or tolerable" (1989, 203).

Even as Kateb attempts to make the best case for the idealized individualism that he calls *democratic individuality*, he cannot share the faith of that anonymous reviewer of Tocqueville who declared that individualism "has its immutable laws, [which] must in the end assimilate the species, and evolve all the glorious phenomena of original and eternal ORDER;—that order which exists in man himself, and alone vivifies and sustains him" ("Catholicism," 326). Confronted with the critiques of individualism embodied in Morrison's and Pynchon's novels, Kateb might reply that individualism must be given time to evolve into democratic individuality: "Time is needed because rights-based individualism is such a strange idea, and so untypical of past human experience, that those who live it and live by it—even though imperfectly, have to keep remembering, or keep learning as if they never knew both the basic meaning and the farther implications of what they profess and enact" (1992, 241). What the writings of Kateb—and of his forebears Emerson and Rawls—seek to demonstrate is that the central idea behind the teleological conception of individualism—that negative liberty can evolve into a form of positive liberty that nurtures social bonds and communal institutions—is not only ideologically persuasive but also philosophically defensible.[31] In their different ways, each of these thinkers affirms what that anonymous review of *Democracy in America* declared in 1841: that individualism can create a new "organic unity of the collective race." They justify and legitimate the ideology of individualism by imagining its ideal manifestation.

THREE. Unenlightened Enlightenment

What is wrong with the narrative that U.S. culture has constructed around the ideas of negative liberty and self-reliance? The writings of Thomas Pynchon and Toni Morrison suggest that the problems begin at the beginning of the story: because negative liberty is a concept born of Enlightenment philosophy, it inherits not only the Enlightenment's humanist ideas of self-possession and self-fulfillment but also its constricted ways of conceiving the individual. Both Morrison and Pynchon recognize that the individual who serves as the subject of the Enlightenment's ostensibly universal formulations is, implicitly, white and male; both writers also suggest that the individual's ability to enjoy and maintain personal autonomy depends on the possession of far more property than just the body with which he or she is born. What Pynchon and Morrison dramatize is the fact that, in too many arenas of modern life, Enlightenment principles have led, not to humanism, but to dehumanization.

Pynchon, perhaps, goes further in his exploration of the inherent flaws within the Enlightenment's conception of the individual, emphasizing more than Morrison the corrosive nature of thinking of individuality in terms of possessions—in terms of things—particularly when this pattern of reasoning is combined with the irrationality that both writers depict as a fundamental part of human nature. In his article "Is It O.K. to Be a Luddite?" (1984), Pynchon describes the rise of the Gothic novel as a response to a certain emptiness within Enlightenment culture:

> The craze for Gothic fiction after "The Castle of Otranto" was grounded, I suspect, in deep and religious yearnings for that earlier mythical time which had come to be known as the Age of Miracles. . . . What had once been true working magic had, by the Age of Reason, degenerated into mere machinery. Blake's dark Satanic mills represented an old magic that, like Satan, had fallen from grace. As religion was being more and more secularized into Deism and nonbelief, the abiding human hunger for evidence of God and afterlife, for salvation—bodily resurrection, if possible—remained. The Methodist movement and the American Great Awakening were only two sectors on a broad front of resistance to the Age of Reason, a front which included Radicalism and Freemasonry as well as Luddites and the Gothic novel. Each in its way expressed the same profound unwillingness to give up elements of faith, however "irrational," to an emerging technopolitical order that might or might not know what it was doing.

The triumph of this technopolitical order has been so absolute, Pynchon suggests, that "20th-century Luddites" now look back "yearningly to . . . the same Age of Reason which had forced the first Luddites into nostalgia for the Age of Miracles." Both Pynchon and Morrison dramatize the ways in which Reason proves inadequate as a way of accounting for the world. To the Enlightenment, they say, like Hamlet to Horatio, "There are more things in heaven and earth than are dreamt of in your philosophy." The moments of magical realism and surrealism that punctuate their novels represent an attempt to reinstate the miraculous into a world that no longer believes in miracles. What I will argue in this chapter, then, is that both Morrison and Pynchon dramatize a particular problem within Emersonian liberalism and the official story of U.S. individualism that arises as part of their Enlightenment inheritance: the unacknowledged reliance on forms of domination such as slavery and racism, combined with an overestimation of the efficacy of rationalist modes of thought.

Slavery and Social Death

Orlando Patterson's contention that the concept of negative freedom emerged only as a result of the practice of slavery is an idea that both Morrison and Pynchon take seriously in their fiction. The ways in which the practice of slavery deformed U.S. culture, and continues to do so even after its abolition, is one of the great topics of Toni Morrison's novels, and it becomes a recurrent motif in Thomas Pynchon's depictions of modernity in *V.* and *Gravity's Rainbow* and of eighteenth-century America in *Mason & Dixon.*

In *Playing in the Dark,* Morrison argues that the presence in U.S. culture of the enslaved African, regarded as the epitome of "rawness and savagery, . . . provided the staging ground and arena for the elaboration of the quintessential American identity," a crucial part of which is "the much championed and revered 'individualism' " (1992c, 44). Commenting on the much-debated conclusion to Mark Twain's *Huckleberry Finn* (in which Tom Sawyer helps Huck free Jim without telling Huck that Jim has already been freed by his owner), Morrison argues that "freedom has no meaning to Huck or to the text without the specter of enslavement, the anodyne to individualism; the yardstick of absolute power over the life of another; the signed, marked, informing, and mutating presence of a black slave" (56).[1] Negative liberty, Morrison suggests, depends conceptually on the existence of the negation of liberty. She is thus drawn here to the kinds of deconstructive critiques of the discourse of rights and of individualism more generally that can be found in the work of critical legal theorists like Peter Gabel.

Slavery in the United States, however, was not simply a matter of being designated free or unfree; it was also a matter of being white or black. Although, historically, racial difference has not been a necessary pretext for the enslavement of particular groups or individuals, in the United States racism played a powerful role in the perpetuation of slavery because it mitigated what would otherwise be a clear contradiction of the idea that "all men are created equal" and "endowed with certain unalienable rights," including "life, liberty, and the pursuit of happiness" (see Patterson, 176–79). If individualism is the product of the Enlightenment, then for Morrison it is also the product of what she calls the Enlightenment's "twin, born at the same time, the Age of Scientific Racism." She notes that "David Hume, Immanuel Kant and Thomas Jefferson, to mention only a few, had documented their conclusions that blacks were incapable of intelligence" (1987b, 108). The master whom the slaves call "Schoolteacher" in *Beloved* is an Enlightenment figure, a scholar and teacher who carefully takes his slaves' measurements, numbers their teeth, and catalogs their attributes in order to evaluate their worth. Locke's *Second Treatise* declares that slaves are "property" and thus akin to the "inferior Creatures" that are "common to all Men." Men like Schoolteacher, however, believe that black people *are* inferior creatures and *therefore* deserve to be nothing but property. One of *Beloved*'s most chilling scenes depicts Schoolteacher inculcating this belief in his students:

> He was talking to his pupils and I heard him say, "Which one are you doing?" And one of the boys said, "Sethe." That's when I stopped because I heard my name, and then I took a few steps to where I could see what they were doing. Schoolteacher was standing over one of them with one hand behind his back. He licked a forefinger a couple of times and turned a few pages. Slow. I was about to turn around and keep on my way to where the muslin was, when I heard him say, "No, no. That's not the way. I told you to put her human characteristics on the left; her animal ones on the right. And don't forget to line them up." (1987a, 193)

Sethe overhears this conversation, and it brings home to her the utter horror and hopelessness of her situation as a slave. So deeply does it affect her that she reveals it to no one, but we learn that this episode underlies her split-second decision, years later in Ohio, to kill her children rather than have them fall back into the hands of Schoolteacher and thus back into slavery. "No one, nobody on this earth," she thinks later, "would list her daughter's characteristics on the animal side of the paper" (251).

Although slavery lies in the background of all Toni Morrison's novels, it is in *Beloved* that she attempts to convey a phenomenological understanding of slavery and to depict the psychological damage that occurs when a human being is treated as property. The process of gaining self-possession that Frederick Douglass describes in his *Narrative* (1845) hinges on entering the individualist order through literacy, work, marriage, and autobiography.[2] But as Morrison points out in her essay "The Site of Memory," Douglass's *Narrative*, like most slave narratives, fails to convey any sense of its protagonist's "interior life" (1987b, 113). It is this task that she sets herself in *Beloved*, which chronicles Sethe's gradual and painful struggle to possess the self she was not allowed to have as a slave, to become human again after being treated as an animal, to experience social rebirth: "Freeing yourself was one thing; claiming ownership of that freed self was another" (1987a, 95).

The guiding trope of the novel is a literary pun: *Beloved* depicts the dispossession of the slave by telling a story about supernatural possession, by overlaying the conventions of the Gothic novel onto the slave narrative. Attempting to kill all her children, Sethe succeeded in killing only her two-year-old daughter, whom she now refers to as "Beloved." "124 was spiteful," the novel begins, describing Sethe's house. "Full of a baby's venom." In 1873, the present time of the novel, Sethe and her surviving daughter, Denver, live there alone. The grandmother, Baby Suggs, has died, and the sons, Howard and Buglar, have run away, unable to stand the haunting—"as soon as merely looking in a mirror shattered it (that was the signal for Buglar); as soon as two tiny hand prints appeared in the cake (that was it for Howard)" (3). If, as Leslie Fiedler's well-known analysis (126–61) suggests, it is the turbulence of revolutionary politics that lies at the heart of the European Gothic novel, then *Beloved* qualifies as a full-blooded descendant. Analyzing her own text after the fact, Morrison claims that "the fully realized presence of the haunting is both a major incumbent of the narrative and sleight of hand. One of its purposes is to keep the reader preoccupied with the nature of the incredible spirit world while being supplied a controlled diet of the incredible political world" (1989, 32).

This technique of narrative distraction enables *Beloved* to take a markedly different approach to the depiction of the memories and life stories of ex-slaves than narratives such as Frederick Douglass's. In "The Site of Memory," Morrison comments that nineteenth-century slave narratives rarely dwelt "too long or too carefully on the most sordid details of their experience," bowing to "popular taste" and "taking refuge in the literary conventions of the day. . . . Over and over, the writers pull the narrative up short with a phrase such as, 'But let us drop a veil over these proceedings too terrible to relate' " (1987b, 109–10). What Morrison makes plain in *Beloved* is that such editing is simultaneously a false and a true representation of the ex-slave's consciousness: false because bad memories—"rememories"—always possess the unconscious mind and frequently take over the conscious as well, unexpectedly and without welcome; true because such memories frequently repress the details and thus the experiential essence of the past. Sethe thinks of the future as "a matter of keeping the past at bay" (43) because she is haunted by memories both of the things that she has done and of the things that were done to her. These "rememories" break into her consciousness without warning and take possession of it:

> Unfortunately, her brain was devious. She might be hurrying across a field, running practically, to get to the pump quickly and rinse the chamomile sap from her legs. Nothing else would be in her mind. . . . Then something. The plash of water, the sight of her shoes and stockings awry on the path where she had flung them; or Here Boy lapping

> in the puddle near her feet, and suddenly there was Sweet Home rolling, rolling, rolling out before her eyes, and although there was not a leaf on that farm that did not make her want to scream, it rolled itself out before her in shameless beauty. It never looked as terrible as it was and it made her wonder if hell was a pretty place too. Fire and brimstone all right, but hidden in lacy groves. Boys hanging from the most beautiful sycamores in the world. It shamed her—remembering the wonderful soughing trees rather than the boys. Try as she might to make it otherwise, the sycamores beat out the children every time and she could not forgive her memory for that. (6)

This passage is typical of Morrison's narrative technique in *Beloved* because its lyrical imagery is transmuted without warning into a description of violence or its aftermath, catching the reader by surprise. The sudden horror of "boys hanging from the most beautiful sycamores in the world" arises, not because it is a graphic description, but because it is a sudden shift in imagery that conveys the banality of violence under slavery. The narrative thus mirrors the stream of Sethe's consciousness, which (like the audience at a horror movie) is lulled into calm so that it can be shocked more effectively later.

What the "rememories" signify is Sethe's inability to possess herself even after the abolition of slavery. When she was a slave, Schoolteacher, the master of Sweet Home, possessed her body and her person, but now that her body and her person are free in post–Civil War Ohio, Sweet Home still possesses her mind. Slaves did not have the right to say what they wanted to say, and sometimes they were restrained from speaking at all by an iron bit. But in *Beloved* the aftermath of slavery is just as brutal, perhaps more so, for Sethe finds now that she cannot think what she wants to think. Sweet Home was the scene of unspeakable horror, yet Sethe can remember only its beauty: she cannot see the boys for the trees. The vaunted faculty of reason thus fails Sethe once again: at Sweet Home, it served as part of the philosophical justification for her enslavement; in Ohio, it proves inadequate to the task of freeing her mind from the tyranny of her imagination.

To end the possession of both her house and her mind, to gain possession of herself once and for all, Sethe must learn to narrate the facts of her life, to control her memories and face up to their horror. The process begins when the ghost becomes silent and a strange young woman appears at 124 calling herself "Beloved." Sethe takes her in and soon finds that Beloved loves to hear stories, particularly stories about Sethe's life. "It amazed Sethe (as much as it pleased Beloved) because every mention of her past life hurt. Everything in it was painful or lost. She and Baby Suggs had agreed without saying that it was unspeakable" (58). But, with Beloved as her audience, Sethe finds herself "wanting to" tell stories about her past, "liking it." The stories start out modestly, with an anecdote about the imitation diamond earrings that Sethe receives from her mistress for her "wedding" (58–60), but they become ever more intimate and painful: Sethe talks about her mother, whom she saw only twice, the second time hung from a tree (60–62); later, she can even imagine telling Beloved the story that she has never revealed to anyone, the story about the listing of her "animal characteristics" (193). Eventually, however, regaining possession of herself will also require Sethe to be rid of Beloved, to exorcise the demon that has been haunting her both metaphorically and literally. Sethe is caught up in a cycle of violence, initiated by white masters who violate the humanity of their slaves by denying them self-possession, by destroying their familial relations, and, when necessary, by mutilating their bodies. This violence breeds more violence: Sethe can think of no way to save her children from the degradation of slavery other than killing them. Beloved represents the incarnation of this vicious circle: she is a vampiric spirit of revenge who sucks life from Sethe in retribution for the loss of her own life and nearly causes a deluded Sethe to keep the cycle of violence alive by murdering a white man who, far from harming Sethe or her family, has been a preserving angel of mercy. It is when this act of violence is thwarted that the ghost of 124 is truly exorcised. *Beloved* dramatizes the idea that human progress can occur only when constricting paradigms can be broken or reimagined.

The link between individualism and slavery is depicted brutally and violently in the ninth chapter of Pynchon's *V.* (1963), which imagines the depredations visited on the natives of Southwest Africa by German colonists in the early part of the twentieth century. The violence of whites against blacks that Pynchon depicts in this chapter is just as graphic as the violence depicted in *Beloved* and possibly even more chilling because it brings the sadomasochism of slavery out into the open. This chapter lies at the very center of the novel, and it takes the form of an inset story, a reminiscence by one Kurt Mondaugen of his days in German Southwest Africa as a young man. What we actually read in the novel is the secondhand version of "Mondaugen's Story": it has been "Stencilized," appropriated and embellished by Herbert Stencil as part of his continuing research into the life history of the mysterious woman to whom he refers only as V. "Mondaugen's Story" recounts events that take place in 1922 during a native uprising against German authority in the protectorate. Forced to flee the remote listening post where he has been monitoring "atmospheric radio disturbances," Mondaugen takes refuge, along with a group of other German colonists, on a large farm owned by one Foppl, who had served as a soldier during "the Great Rebellion of 1904–07." This rather disorganized revolt by "the Hereros and Hottentots, who usually fought one another," had impelled the German administration to send in General Lothar von Trotha, who had "demonstrated to Berlin during his Chinese and East African campaigns a certain expertise at suppressing pigmented populations." Von Trotha ordered his troops "to exterminate systematically every Herero man, woman and child they could find," and Foppl remembers that "it didn't take him long to find out how much he enjoyed it all." Like Morrison in the dedication to *Beloved*, Pynchon uses the Holocaust as a reference point: "Allowing for natural causes during those unnatural years, von Trotha, who stayed only for one of them, is reckoned to have done away with about 60,000 people. This is only 1 per cent of six million, but still pretty good" (245). Gradually, what Mondaugen refers to as "Foppl's Siege Party" becomes a nostalgic attempt to re-create the experience of the Great Rebellion, complete with costumes, makeup, and props, the most notable of which is the "sjambok," a whip used to torture and mutilate native blacks before killing them. In the first days of the siege party, Mondaugen hears a young German girl singing "The sjambok's kiss / Is unending delight" (238), sees Foppl whipping a Bondel servant to death (248), and learns that "another Bondel had been executed, this time by hanging," which was "a popular form of killing during the Great Rebellion" (244). As the siege party progresses, Mondaugen begins to suffer from hallucinations brought on either by scurvy or by some plot against him: he seems to become Foppl and to remember committing acts of unspeakable barbarity.

Pynchon, like Morrison, punctuates his narrative with details designed to shock the reader, as in this example: "Hardening himself the weakling Mondaugen approached the man and stopped to listen for breathing or a heartbeat, trying not to see the white vertebra that winked at him from one long opening" (240). Thematically, however, there is a difference. The violence visited on blacks in *Beloved* is for the most part economically motivated: for Schoolteacher, whipping is a form of discipline designed to render a slave docile and more willing to work, while killing a slave is a regrettable act designed to cut one's losses on a bad investment. Violence for its own sake or for sexual reasons is present in the novel, in Sethe's early speculation that Beloved "had been locked up by some whiteman for his own purposes," something that had actually happened to her neighbor Ella, "except it was two men—father and son" (1987a, 119); but this sort of violence remains at the periphery of the novel. In "Mondaugen's Story," however, the violence almost always involves sadistic sexual practices, as the troops use von Trotha's politically motivated extermination order as a pretext for satisfying their lust. Foppl constructs his manhood and experiences male bonding by torturing the natives: "Before you disemboweled or whatever you did with her to be able to take a Herero girl before the eyes of your superior officer, and stay potent. And talk with them before you killed them without the sheep's eye, the shuffling, the prickly-heat of embarrassment..." (257; ellipsis in original).

Even after the rebellion, the German attitude toward the black natives continues to be more wanton than that of the slaveholders in the American South, for the German regard the natives, not simply as inferior creatures, but as useless creatures, not worth the trouble of enslaving save for the few women who are kept as prostitutes. These women are regarded as property, but property that is communally owned: Foppl's attempt to keep a particular native named Sarah for himself ("manacled to the bed" during the day) is an unacceptable "assertion of the Inanimate" (272). Yet Foppl and his comrades never fully regard their victims as inanimate or nonhuman; to do so would spoil their fun. They derive much of their pleasure from knowing that their victims fully comprehend the horror of their fates: "girls approached with organ at the ready, their eyes filming over in anticipated pleasure or possibly only an anticipated five more minutes of life, only to be shot through the head first and then ravished, after of course being made aware at the last moment that this would happen to them" (264). Ultimately, Mondaugen rejects the siege party's perpetuation of violence, leaving after two and a half months, resigned to taking his chances by crossing hostile territory. He is saved by a mutilated Bondel who has "lost his right arm. . . . He let Mondaugen ride behind him. At that point Mondaugen didn't know where they were going. As the sun climbed he dozed on and off, his cheek against the Bondel's scarred back" (279). Like *Beloved*, "Mondaugen's Story" ends with the cycle of racial violence broken, with an accommodation between whites and blacks.

Throughout the chapter, Pynchon hints that the story of Southwest Africa that we are reading is but a version of the story of the American South: Mondaugen, from Leipzig and thus a Northerner, has "a basic distrust of the South, however relative a region that might be" (230); Foppl's farm is actually a "baroque plantation" (231); and the African natives are occasionally referred to as "niggers." Perhaps these valences are the result of the story's Stencilization: in the next chapter, Stencil watches the reveling being carried on by the friends he calls "the Whole sick Crew" and is reminded of Mondaugen's story (296). But, fixated as he is on the question of V.'s identity, Stencil never seems to be interested in thinking through the ideological implications of Mondaugen's story; Pynchon leaves that task to his reader, providing a final clue in the segue between chapters 9 and 10. The final image of "Mondaugen's Story" shows us the mutilated Bondel singing a song "in Hottentot dialect," which Mondaugen cannot understand; the opening lines of the next chapter focus on the African American jazz musician McClintic Sphere "half listening" to his "horn man . . . soloing" but actually thinking about the racism of the white people in his audience: "Some of them would go through the old liberal routine: look at me, I'll sit with anybody. Either that or they would say: 'Hey fella, how about Night Train?' Yes bwana. Yazzuh boss. Dis darkey, ol' Uncle McClintic, he play you de finest Night Train you evah did hear. An' aftah de set he gwine take dis ol' alto an' shove it up yo' white Ivy League ass" (280–81). Joined by the text across gulfs of time and space, these two moments each picture a black man whose music is an assertion of identity that cannot be understood by the whites who hear it. Paradoxically, the ostensibly bleak image of a mutilated black man and a debilitated white man crossing a devastated landscape conveys a feeling of hopefulness and possible harmony after the racial hatred that has been described to us, but the feeling is short-lived: McClintic Sphere's thoughts indicate that any apparent harmony between the races masks an abiding dissonance.

The marauding German soldiers in "Mondaugen's Story" feel that the "fatherly chastisement" that they administer is "an inalienable right" (267). This paternalistic rhetoric is reminiscent of the language used by the government of the United States to justify its policy of Indian Removal and its doctrine of Manifest Destiny (see Rogin 1975; and Rogin 1987, 134–68), but "inalienable right" takes us further back in American history to the Declaration of Independence itself. Pynchon thus implies that there is a continuity between the individualism on which the United States is founded and the sort of virulent racism depicted in "Mondaugen's Story."

People into Things

Slavery turns people into things. For Pynchon, slavery is but one form of dehumanization among many in Western culture. Unlike Morrison, who (as we shall see) is interested in the particular history of U.S. slavery and its aftermath, Pynchon generalizes his depiction of slavery. This willingness to use slavery as a trope is one of the ways in which the difference between Morrison's and Pynchon's subject positions proves to be significant. Using slavery as a trope is a luxury that Morrison cannot afford. For Pynchon, however, this narrative strategy is an integral part of the critique that he mounts against the Enlightenment origins of both U.S. individualism and Emersonian liberalism.

A seemingly insignificant bit of slapstick in the opening pages of *V.* shows us how this works in Pynchon's fiction. A "gargantuan Negro" sailor "named Dahoud" prevents a little white engineman named Ploy from committing suicide. Ploy, it seems, would rather jump off the side of his ship, the "mine sweeper Impulsive," than wear the full set of dentures that the navy has given him after removing all his teeth:

> "What you want to go and do that for?"
> "Man, I want to die, is all," cried Ploy.
> "Don't you know," said Dahoud, "that life is the most precious possession you have?"
> "Ho, ho," said Ploy through his tears. "Why?"
> "Because without it, you'd be dead."
> "Oh," said Ploy. He thought about this for a week. He calmed down, started to go on liberty again. (1963, 12)

The first thing to notice here is that Dahoud the "Negro" saves Ploy the white man and leads him to freedom: Dahoud's story cures Ploy of his despair, allowing him to "go on liberty" once again. The fact that Ploy's revival requires the aid of a "Negro" seems like a minor detail, until we realize that what is being depicted in shorthand form is the historical link between individualism and slavery in U.S. culture and even in Western culture as a whole, a link that Pynchon dramatizes in "Mondaugen's Story" later in the novel.

There is more, however, to the scene than a critique of the links between negative liberty and the tandem of slavery and racism. For, behind Dahoud's seemingly tautological bromide about life and death lies a profound assumption about the nature of human existence: that life itself is a possession and, therefore, that who you are depends on what you own. Dahoud's words give voice to the possessive individualism that we have seen expressed in Locke's *Second Treatise of Government*: "Every Man has a *Property* in his own *Person*. This no Body has any Right to but himself. The *Labour* of his Body, and the *Work* of his Hands, we may say, are properly his" (287–88). In other words, to be an individual endowed with rights means to be acknowledged as the proprietor of your own person and your capacities: you own yourself and all that you can do. Life itself is classified next to food, clothing, land, and other goods as property, as something to be owned.

Like Emerson, Pynchon worries that this is a dangerous way of thinking about individuality because it leads us to think that what we have determines who we are. Ploy's identity becomes intimately associated with his prosthesis, a possession that functions simultaneously as synecdoche and metonymy: the dentures, to which Ploy is reduced in the minds of those around him, can be seen either as part of a whole or as an object that is substituted for another. He thus becomes one of the "walking monsters" that Emerson describes in "The American Scholar," as he indicts society for bringing about the dehumanization of humankind. The fable of the "One Man" that Emerson recounts in that essay suggests that what he calls "the divided or social state" is a "degenerate state" that has made true self-possession impossible. According to Emerson, "the fable implies that the individual, to possess himself, must sometimes return from his own labor to embrace all the other laborers. But, unfortunately, this original unit, this fountain of power, has been so distributed to multitudes, has been so minutely subdivided and peddled out, that it is spilled into drops, and cannot be gathered." As a result, "man is metamorphosed into a thing" and "the soul is subject to dollars" (1837a, 54).

The transformation of people into things is one of Pynchon's abiding subjects. The characters in his first three novels do indeed exist in a degenerate state in which individuality is under siege. Later in the first chapter of *V.*, Benny Profane, the protagonist of one of the novel's two interwoven narrative strands, thinks about two acquaintances whose relationships to objects dramatize the pathologies of possessive individualism. The first is his old boss at "Scholzhauer's Trocadero," "a mad Brazilian" salad chef named Da Conho "who wanted to go fight Arabs in Israel" (22) and whose prized possession was a .30-caliber machine gun that he got from a customer in exchange for three artichokes and an eggplant. Dreaming of Zionist glory, Da Conho would camouflage the machine gun with salad fixings and pretend to strafe his customers. "Profane had wondered then what it was with Da Conho and that machine gun. Love for an object, this was new to him. When he found out not long after this that the same thing was with Rachel and her MG, he had his first intelligence that something had been going on under the rose, maybe for longer and with more people than he would care to think about" (23). The machine gun, like Ploy's dentures, becomes an intimate part of Da Conho's identity: unable to communicate to others the passion of his vision, Da Conho thinks to himself that the "only voice he had was the machine gun's." Rachel's love for her MG is a similar form of self-expression. "Little, sulky, and voluptuous," Rachel spent the summer during which she met Profane driving the MG "around Route 17's bloodthirsty curves and cutbacks, sashaying its arrogant butt past hay wagons, growling semis, old Ford roadsters filled to capacity, with crewcut, undergraduate gnomes." Profane meets Rachel "through the MG, like everyone else met her. It nearly ran him over." He thinks to himself afterward that he has nearly been killed by an "inanimate object," although he is not sure whether he is using that phrase to refer to Rachel or to the car because in his mind the two are inseparable. Although he does become Rachel's friend, Profane always plays second fiddle to the car; he even catches her one night stroking its stickshift and whispering sweet nothings: "You beautiful stud. I love to touch you. Do you know what I feel when we're out on the road? Alone, just us?" (28). Da Conho and his machine gun, Rachel and her MG—linked chronologically and thematically in Profane's mind, both relationships signify possessive individualism transformed into an unnatural symbiosis with material objects.

The novel as a whole may be said to elaborate on one of the narrator's offhand remarks: that "alignment with the inanimate is the mark of a Bad Guy" (101). Frequently, this alignment is described as "decadence," and it becomes one of the central motifs of the set of stories assembled by Stencil that form the novel's second narrative strand. In "The Confessions of Fausto Maijstral," a manuscript that provides Stencil with crucial information about the mysterious "V.," *decadence* is defined as "a clear movement toward death, or preferably, non-humanity," a process of becoming more and more "inanimate" (321). Later in the novel, in a chapter devoted to the idea of fetishism, a character describes *decadence* as "a falling-away from what is human, and the further we fall the less human we become. Because we are less human, we foist off the humanity we have lost on inanimate objects and abstract theories" (405). Fetishism, too, is conceived as a form of alignment with the inanimate. V. tells the young dancer Mélanie that a "fetish" is "something of a woman which gives pleasure but is not a woman. A shoe, a locket . . . une jarretière. You are the same, not real but an object of pleasure" (404). (Mélanie's stage name is, in fact, "Mlle. Jarretière"—"Miss Garter.") V. herself ends up as a collection of prosthetic body parts and dies on the island of Malta after being pinned by debris during an air raid and then pried apart and dismantled by scavenging children.

This alignment with the inanimate returns as a prominent motif in Pynchon's second novel, The Crying of Lot 49 (1966), where it serves once again as a metaphor for the unnaturalness of modern American life. To Oedipa's husband, used-car salesman Mucho Maas, automobiles offer an unwelcome window into lives of quiet desperation: "seeing people poorer than him come in, Negro, Mexican, cracker, a parade seven days a week, bringing the most godawful of trade-ins: motorized metal extensions of themselves, of their families and what their whole lives must be like, out there so naked for anybody, a stranger like himself, to look at" (13). This passage attempts to take the reader into its confidence, making an appeal to mutual experience in order to establish intimacy:

> frame cockeyed, rusty underneath, fender repainted in a shade just off enough to depress the value, if not Mucho himself, inside smelling hopelessly of children, supermarket booze, two, sometimes three generations of cigarette smokers, or only of dust—and when the actual cars were swept out you had to look at the actual residue of these lives, and there was no way of telling what things had been truly refused (when so little he supposed came by that out of fear most of it had to be taken and kept) and what had simply (perhaps tragically) been lost: clipped coupons promising savings of 5 or 10¢, trading stamps, pink flyers advertising specials at the markets, butts, tooth-shy combs, help-wanted ads, Yellow Pages torn from the phone book, rags of old underwear or dresses that already were period costumes, for wiping your own breath off the inside of a windshield with so you could see whatever it was, a movie, a woman or car you coveted, a cop who might pull you over just for drill, all the bits and pieces coated uniformly, like a salad of despair, in a gray dressing of ash, condensed exhaust, dust body wastes—it made him sick to look, but he had to look. (13–14)

This Nabokovian catalog of cultural detritus draws force from the specificity of its references, from the idiosyncrasy of the details that Pynchon chooses to mention. It testifies to the appalling tendency in a modern culture of possessive individualism to view human lives metonymically, as if they were embodied and encompassed by the things that they possess.

Mucho's customers certainly see their lives metonymically, seeking to express themselves through their possessions, to change their lives by changing their cars. Mucho could "never accept the way each owner, each shadow, filed in only to exchange a dented, malfunctioning version of himself for another, just as futureless, automotive projection of somebody else's life. As if it were the most natural thing" (14). Yet Mucho's firm belief that these cars and their contents *do* sum up the lives of his customers is itself an example of this process of dehumanization through metonymy, which proves to be ubiquitous, enveloping both observer and observed. Even the novel itself is implicated, for it cannot dramatize the horror of this process without relying on its familiarity as a pattern of thought: the success of the descriptive set piece quoted above depends on the reader's ability to envision a whole way of life simply through the evocation of a few cast-off items.

Pynchon brings the motif of dehumanization to a hideous climax in *Gravity's Rainbow* (1973), which depicts the kind of statist nightmare feared by both Isaiah Berlin and George Kateb, in which the growth of state power has effectively replaced democracy with totalitarianism. The story of the way in which the military-industrial complex manipulates the life of Tyrone Slothrop is an extreme example of the devaluation of individual integrity that occurs when a life is completely—in this case, literally—mapped out. Slothrop's humanity has indeed been sacrificed on the altar of abstract theories: "Back around 1920, Dr. Laszlo Jamf opined that if Watson and Rayner could successfully condition their 'Infant Albert' into a reflex horror of everything furry, even of his own Mother in a fur boa, then Jamf could certainly do the same thing for his Infant Tyrone, and the baby's sexual reflex" (84). In exchange for the money to pay for his eventual education at Harvard, Infant Tyrone is subjected to Pavlovian conditioning of his sexual reflexes as part of research for the multinational corporation I. G. Farben. As a young man, he is manipulated by intelligence agencies, who have noticed a surprising correlation between the scenes of Slothrop's sexual conquests and the sites of German rocket landings in London during the Blitz: Slothrop's erections somehow "predict" the falling of rockets, perhaps due to botched deconditioning. He remembers that "once something was done to him, in a room, while he lay helpless," and as he remembers, we are told that "his erection hums from a certain distance, like an instrument installed, wired by Them into his body as a colonial outpost here in our raw and clamorous world, another office representing Their white Metropolis far away" (285). In the course of the novel, Slothrop barely escapes being castrated by scientists eager to understand the physiological basis for his prophetic powers, but he is eventually stripped of his identity, sent by a mysterious organization called "the Counterforce" into the area of occupied lands that Pynchon calls simply "the Zone," and ultimately lost, "broken down," and "scattered." Slothrop simply disappears from the novel, his whereabouts not only unknown but unimportant. "We never cared about Slothrop qua Slothrop" (738), a spokesman for the Counterforce says later. The Counterforce thus ends up merely replicating the military-industrial complex that it was formed to combat: neither group respects the individuality of Slothrop or any other person.

Slothrop is not the only character in *Gravity's Rainbow* whose sexuality is manipulated into an alignment with the inanimate. Captain Blicero has trained and conditioned the young soldier Gottfried—"the word *bitch*, spoken now in a certain tone of voice, will give him an erection he cannot will down" (103)—to prepare him for his final mission aboard the v2 rocket code numbered 00000. Crucial to this mission is a substance known as "Imipolex G . . . a new plastic, an aromatic heterocyclic polymer" developed by Jamf in conjunction with, perhaps even as a result of, his work with Slothrop. The distinguishing property of Imipolex G turns out to be that it "is the first plastic that is actually *erectile*. Under suitable stimuli, the chains grow cross-links, which stiffen the molecule and increase intermolecular attraction" (699). Gottfried does not pilot the rocket 00000; instead, he merges with it: it is "the womb into which Gottfried returns. . . . Not a Procrustean bed, but modified to take him. The two, boy and Rocket, concurrently designed" (750). Gottfried's final alignment with the inanimate brings the novel's sadomasochistic imagery to a climax: "They are mated to each other, Schwarzgerät and next higher assembly. His bare limbs in their metal bondage writhe among the fuel, oxidizer, live-steam lines, thrust frame, compressed air battery, exhaust elbow, decomposer, tanks, vents, valves, right one, the true clitoris, routed directly into the nervous system of the 00000. She should not be a mystery to you, Gottfried. Find the zone of liquid oxygen runs freezing so close to your cheek, bones of frost to burn you past feeling" (751). Thus merged with a machine, Gottfried becomes an instrument of mass destruction, aimed at Los Angeles, California.[3]

Dispossession and the Dispossessed

Near the end of Morrison's novel *Beloved*, Paul D comforts a grieving Sethe by telling her, "me and you, we got more yesterday than anybody. We need some kind of tomorrow." And then he says: "You your best thing, Sethe. You are" (1987a, 273). What Paul D. is telling Sethe is that she now controls her own destiny because she has regained possession of herself. She is no longer the property of the white slaveowner named Schoolteacher, and she is no longer haunted—her mind possessed—by "rememories" of her slave days. She is free: she owns herself.

What happens to African Americans in the aftermath of slavery is, of course, the subject of Morrison's other novels, where we find that the self-possession guaranteed by the Emancipation Proclamation is by no means a right that can be taken for granted, for white culture invents new ways to disenfranchise African Americans and dispossess them of what is legally theirs. Morrison presents a parable of dispossession in the opening chapter of her second novel, *Sula*. The narrator explains that the black community on which the novel focuses is called "the Bottom" because of "a nigger joke" (1973, 6):

> A good white farmer promised freedom and a piece of bottom land to his slave if he would perform some very difficult chores. When the slave completed the work, he asked the farmer to keep his end of the bargain. Freedom was easy—the farmer had no objection to that. But he didn't want to give up any land. So he told the slave that he was very sorry that he had to give him the valley land. He had hoped to give a piece of the Bottom. The slave blinked and said he thought valley land was bottom land. The master said, "Oh, no. See those hills? That's bottom land, rich and fertile."
>
> "But it's high up in the hills," said the slave.
>
> "High up from us," said the master, "but when God looks down, it's the bottom. That's why we call it so. It's the bottom of heaven—best land there is."
>
> So the slave pressed his master to try to get him some. He preferred it to the valley. And it was done. The nigger got the hilly land, where planting was backbreaking, where soil slid down and washed away the seeds, and where the wind lingered all through the winter.
>
> Which accounted for the fact that white people lived on the rich valley floor in that little river town in Ohio, and the blacks populated the hills above it, taking small consolation in the fact that every day they could literally look down on the white folks. (5)

Morrison gives this passage the aura of fable or parable through the use of highly artificial diction in such phrases as *a good white farmer* or *that's why we* call it so as well as through the invocation of God and the anaphoric use of clauses introduced by the word *where* that stress the rawness of the deal that the slave has made. The fable encodes the failure of white culture to honor its promises of freedom and equality for African Americans. "Freedom was easy" for white culture to promise because it was freedom in name only, so long as the conditions of economic and educational inequality remained in force.

The passage pointedly calls the slave a "nigger" only after his ignorance has led him to make the deal that seals his fate and thus the fate of the entire black community. The fable is part of the novel's prologue, which is set in the present and evokes the figure of a "valley man" who "happened to have business in those hills," business that is specified as "collecting rent or insurance payments," occupations that imply the superior economic position of whites. This inequality is evident even in the contrasting ways in which whites and blacks look on this "nigger joke." It is the kind of joke, we are told, that "white folks tell when the mill closes down and they're looking for a little comfort somewhere" (4); it reassures them that up there in the hills there are people who are worse off than they. Poor whites tell the joke during hard economic times, but blacks tell the joke all the time because job discrimination assures that economic hard times are a constant, seemingly natural fact of their lives. We learn that it is the kind of joke that "colored folks tell on themselves when the rain doesn't come, or comes for weeks and they're looking for a little comfort somehow" (4–5). The joke provides comfort for the blacks because it enables them to laugh—albeit at their own expense—rather than cry when they contemplate their situation.

The laughter of the culturally dispossessed is, however, always nervous laughter, for they know how easily economic dispossession can be transformed into physical dispossession: the horror of eviction so vividly dramatized in Ellison's *Invisible Man* (1952) is an abiding horror in the world of Morrison's novels as well.[4] Claudia MacTeer, one of the narrators of *The Bluest Eye* (1970), recalls that even as a child she knew what it meant to live in fear of being put "outdoors": "Outdoors, we knew was the real terror of life. The threat of being outdoors surfaced frequently in those days. Every possibility of excess was curtailed with it. If somebody ate too much, he could end up outdoors. If somebody used too much coal, he could end up outdoors. People could gamble themselves outdoors, drink themselves outdoors" (17). Claudia makes a distinction "between being put *out* and being put *outdoors*. If you are put out," she says, "you go somewhere else; if you are outdoors, there is no place to go. The distinction was subtle but final." Like Ellison's narrator, the now grown-up Claudia recognizes that the dispossession of being put outdoors is nothing but an extreme version of the dispossession that is the mundane reality of life for African Americans in the United States:

> Outdoors was the end of something, an irrevocable, physical fact, defining and complementing our metaphysical condition. Being a minority in both caste and class, we moved about anyway on the hem of life, struggling to consolidate our weaknesses and hang on, or to creep singly up into the major folds of the garment. Our peripheral existence, however, was something we had learned to deal with—probably because it was abstract. But the concreteness of being outdoors was another matter—like the difference between the concept of death and being, in fact, dead. Dead doesn't change, and outdoors is here to stay. (17–18)

The metaphor of the black American as an insect crawling about on the garment of American life captures the sense of insignificance, powerlessness, and precariousness that haunts all Morrison's novels. Living in a state of metaphysical and cultural dispossession that is always in danger of being transformed into physical dispossession, African Americans yearn for the apparent solidity and security of property, not only land but also food and possessions. According to Claudia:

> Knowing that there was such a thing as outdoors bred in us a hunger for property, for ownership. The firm possession of a yard, a porch, a grape arbor. Propertied black people spent all their energies, all their love, on their nests. Like frenzied, desperate birds, they overdecorated everything; fussed and fidgeted over their hard-won homes; canned, jellied, and preserved all summer to fill the cupboards and shelves; they painted, picked, and poked at every corner of their houses. And these houses loomed like hothouse sunflowers among the rows of weeds that were rented houses. Renting blacks cast furtive glances at these owned yards and porches, and made firmer commitments to buy themselves "some nice little old place." In the meantime, they saved, and scratched, and piled away what they could in the rented hovels, looking forward to the day of property. (18)

The accumulation of property can enable an African American to creep up into the folds of white American culture.

Claudia's insight is recapitulated in *Song of Solomon* when a prosperous African American businessman named Macon Dead gives his son, "Milkman," a piece of advice: "Own things. And let the things you own own other things. Then you'll own yourself and other people too" (1987, 55). Property conveys a modicum of respectability and social standing, although, as Macon knows only too well, you have to be careful not to be too much of an annoyance to the owners of the social fabric. Macon's father once owned a farm in Georgia that was an inspiration to all the black folk who knew of it, but he aroused the envy of white folks, who shot "the top of his head off and ate his fine Georgia peaches" (235).

The passage of time makes property owning a less dangerous pursuit for African Americans, and Macon Dead is able to buy land and hang onto it, although he finds himself threatened not only by whites but also occasionally by the poorer blacks who rent from him (and then these are nothing but verbal threats). Macon's father had owned and worked a farm, but Macon owns small houses from which he collects rent. The two generations thus represent different ideas about the nature and meaning of wealth. The Georgia farm is a source of sustenance and communal feeling; prosperity means having enough to nourish yourself, your family, and your friends. The message that the farm conveys to the black folks in Georgia is this: "We got a home in this rock, don't you see! Nobody starving in my home; nobody crying in my home, and if I got a home you got one too! Grab it. Grab this land! Take it, hold it, my brothers, make it, my brothers, shake it, squeeze it, turn it, twist it, beat it, kick it, kiss it, whip it, stomp it, dig it, plow it, seed it, reap it, rent it, buy it, sell it, own it, build it, multiply it, and pass it on—can you hear me? Pass it on!" (235).

This conception of ownership is consonant with Locke's view of the origin of value in human societies. Locke describes labor as the mechanism through which value is created and argues that, in the early stages of society, it was labor that *"gave a Right of Property,* where-ever any one was pleased to imploy it, upon what was common," a view that is reflected in the exhortation to "grab" the land and "make it" (299). In these early stages of society, the right to property was naturally limited by the ability of persons to consume what they produced, there being no incentive to produce an excess of perishable goods. Locke concedes, however, that the introduction into society of money, a "lasting thing that Men might keep without spoiling, and that by mutual consent Men would take in exchange for the truly useful, but perishable Supports of life" (300–301), brought with it the desire and opportunity to enlarge one's possessions. In Locke's view, money seems to represent a deformation of the social contract, in which "Men have agreed to disproportionate and unequal Possession of the Earth" (302), thus stripping from labor its regulating and limiting functions. Labor becomes commodified, conceived primarily as something that can be sold in return for a wage. As a commodity, it is valuable both to the person who sells it and to the person who buys it, but in different ways: it provides sustenance for the laborer, but it creates value for the employer. It thus widens the gap between the laborer and the owner. Moreover, the commodification of labor has dehumanizing tendencies: it encourages those who can afford to buy the labor of others to objectify those who must sell their labor, to regard laborers themselves (and, by extension, all who are poor) as things to be bought and sold. Macon Dead views the world in this way, and, in this respect, he is part of mainstream U.S. culture in the twentieth century.

In such a culture, poor, unpropertied blacks like Cholly Breedlove have no means of gaining social respect, leaving them at a disadvantage in all forms of social transaction. In *The Bluest Eye*, Morrison uses a damaged sofa as an emblem of this kind of cultural dispossession. Racism in this scene is made subtly evident through Morrison's use of dialect in recounting the verbal exchange between salesman and customer:

> "Looka here, buddy. It was O.K. when I put it on the truck. The store can't do anything about it once it's on the truck. . . ." Listerine and Lucky Strike breath.
>
> "But I don't want no tore couch if'n it's bought new." Pleading eyes and tightened testicles.
>
> "Tough shit, buddy. Your tough shit. . . ." (1970, 36; ellipses in original)

Since we know that the customer in this scene is black, the difference in dialect and slang—the difference between "don't want no tore couch if'n" and "Looka here" or "Tough shit, buddy"—stands in for a difference of race. Morrison's words do not necessitate such a reading (the more grammatical slang of the salesman *could*, after all, be spoken by an African American), but they strongly suggest it to anyone familiar with the dynamics of American racism. The detail "pleading eyes and tightened testicles" clearly links the black man's sense of emasculation and impotence to racial, economic, and legal oppression: the black man is in the right, and knows it, but has no practical recourse. U.S. culture now permits African

Americans to own things and thus to attain the status *individual*, but the price is the continual reinscription of racial hatred on them and their possessions. The sofa thus embodies what Morrison calls the "myriad . . . humiliations, defeats, and emasculations" (42) that Cholly has suffered at the hands of white culture.

The story is a small-scale, minor variation on what Morrison presents as one of the defining moments of Cholly's life:

> When he was still very young, Cholly had been surprised in some bushes by two white men while he was newly but earnestly engaged in eliciting sexual pleasure from a little country girl. The men had shone a flashlight right on his behind. He had stopped, terrified. They chuckled. The beam of the flashlight did not move. "Go on," they said. "Go on and finish. And, nigger, make it good." The flashlight did not move. For some reason Cholly had not hated the white men; he hated, despised, the girl. Even a half-remembrance of this episode, along with myriad other humiliations, defeats, and emasculations, could stir him into flights of depravity that surprised himself—but only himself. (42)

The actions of the white men transform what was an act of youthful sexual initiation into an act of rape with two victims: the young girl and Cholly himself. In a longer description of this incident later in the novel, we learn that when Cholly is compelled to continue having sex with the girl (who is named Darlene), he does so with the fury of a rapist: "With a violence born of total helplessness, he pulled her dress up, lowered his trousers and underwear." Rendered impotent and unable to do more than "make-believe," he finds that he "almost wished he could do it—hard, long, and painfully, he hated her so much." Darlene's actions—first "staring out of the lamplight into the surrounding darkness and looking almost unconcerned," then "put[ting] her hands over her face as Cholly began"—suggest the helpless responses of a rape victim. Both passages, however, contain overtones of homosexual rape that serve to emphasize Cholly's own victimization. In the earlier description, Morrison tells us that "the men had shone a flashlight right on his behind," and she confirms the importance of that beam of light to Cholly's consciousness by declaring, not once but twice, that "the flashlight did not move." In the later passage, Morrison's description is more graphic and more suggestive. We learn that one of the men "raced the flashlight all over Cholly and Darlene," before allowing it to settle on Cholly, making "a moon on his behind." Morrison then juxtaposes Cholly's desire to be able to "do it" to Darlene with a graphic description of what Cholly feels is being done to him: "The flashlight wormed its way into his guts and turned the sweet taste of muscadine into rotten fetid bile" (148).

Having led us to believe that Cholly's interrupted backwoods coitus is only the first in a series of deformative incidents, Morrison presents a second: Cholly's attempt to gain acknowledgment from his natural father. Motivated by the "irrational, completely uninformed idea" that he might have gotten Darlene pregnant, he hopes to receive advice from his father, who, it occurs to him, was once in a similar situation. Again, the incident is marked by physical humiliation and loss of control over the self. Rudely dismissed with the words, "Tell that bitch she get her money. Now get the fuck out of my face," Cholly runs to the mouth of the alley where he has found his father playing dice, collapses in tears, and suddenly loses control of his bowels. With the delayed reactions typical of Faulkner's Joe Christmas, Cholly faces his humiliation: "Before he could realize what he knew, liquid stools were running down his legs. At the mouth of the alley where his father was, on an orange crate in the sun, on a street full of grown men and women, he had soiled himself like a baby." All that Cholly can think to do is to flee, and he runs to the river, where he hides under a pier, "knotted . . . in a fetal position, paralyzed, his fists covering his eyes" (156–57). Once again, Cholly's manhood has been stripped away from him, and he can regain it only by treating women as objects.

The humiliation of these moments forever deforms Cholly's attitudes and feelings toward women. Morrison uses the early account of the incident with Darlene to explain why Cholly "poured out on [his wife, Polly,] the sum of all his inarticulate fury and aborted desires" (42). The more detailed description that appears later on is part of a chapter that culminates in Cholly's rape of his daughter, Pecola. Denied his sense of individuality and made to feel impotent by the white men's act of aggression, Cholly becomes locked into a cycle of domination and violence from which he cannot escape. To reconstruct his sense of self, Cholly takes out his rage on his wife and family, doing to others what was done to him. The transformation of his sexual initiation into an act of rape in which he is both aggressor and victim causes a metonymic substitution in his consciousness of violence for affection. When he sees his daughter washing dishes and scratching one leg with the big toe of another, he is reminded of his first glance of his wife and is "filled . . . with a wondering softness. Not the usual lust to part tight legs with his own, but a tenderness, a protectiveness." Morrison captures the paradoxical quality of this moment by writing, "He wanted to fuck her—tenderly" (162–63).

Sula also depicts what might be considered the cultural failure of African American men, whose fruitless attempts to live up to an ideal of economic individualism lead them to vent their frustrations on their mothers, girlfriends, wives, and daughters. The novel explores what it might mean for a woman rather than a man to serve as the embodiment of Emersonian self-reliance. Its opening pages present a strikingly violent image that serves as an emblem for ravaged African American manhood: the body of a soldier whose head has been blown off runs on "with energy and grace, ignoring altogether the drip and slide of brain tissue down its back" (1973, 8). The novel indicts U.S. culture, which is willing to let black men die for its sake in World War I but unwilling to let them share in the benefits of American individualism, for a hypocrisy that is undermining African American communities. An exchange between Sula and her friend Nel's husband, Jude, vividly illustrates the dynamics of this emasculating oppression:

> "Hey, Jude. What you know good?"
> "White man running it—nothing good."
> Sula laughed while Nel, high-tuned to his moods, ignored her husband's smile saying, "Bad day, honey?"
> "Same old stuff," he replied and told them a brief tale of some personal insult done him by a customer and his boss—a whiney tale that peaked somewhere between anger and a lapping desire for comfort. He ended it with the observation that a Negro man had a hard row to hoe in this world. (102–3)

Jude is expecting "milkwarm commiseration" from the women, and Nel is ready and willing to "excrete it." Sula, however, has little sympathy for the lot of men and launches into a diatribe about how good they have it:

> Sula was smiling. "I mean, I don't know what the fuss is about. I mean, everything in the world loves you. White men love you. They spend so much time worrying about your penis they forget their own. The only thing they want to do is cut off a nigger's privates. And if that ain't love and respect, I don't know what is. And white women? They chase you all to every corner of the earth, feel for you under every bed. I knew a white woman wouldn't leave the house after 6 o'clock for fear one of you would snatch her. Now ain't that love? They think rape

soon's they see you, and if they don't get the rape they looking for, they scream it anyway just so the search won't be in vain. Colored women worry themselves into bad health just trying to hang on to your cuffs. Even little children—white and black, boys and girls—spend all their childhood eating their hearts out 'cause they think you don't love them. And if that ain't enough, you love yourselves. Nothing in this world loves a black man more than another black man. You hear of solitary white men, but niggers? Can't stay away from one another a whole day. So. It looks to me like you the envy of the world." (104)

Sula's sardonic reinterpretation of the cultural circumstances of black manhood in America provides a moment of comic relief—even Nel and Jude find themselves laughing—that nevertheless underscores the difficulty of being a black man in a culture ruled by whites.

The story of Jude's life provides a typical tale of thwarted manhood in the Bottom. Stuck working as a hotel waiter, he dreams of doing "real work," of working on the government's road-building project, "not just for the good money, more for the work itself" (81). Continually passed over in favor of "thin-armed white boys from the Virginia hills and bull-necked Greeks and Italians," Jude's energy is transformed into a "rage and a determination to take on a man's role anyhow" that lead him to "press Nel about settling down." For Jude, marriage means having "some of his appetites filled, some posture of adulthood recognized," and, most of all, having "someone to care about his hurt, to care very deeply." Jude realizes that, if he is to be "a man," then "that someone" can "no longer be his mother" (82), although what he wants from Nel is not very different from what a young boy wants from his mother. Marriage to Nel becomes a way for him to complete himself: "The two of them together would make one Jude" (83). Such reasoning proves to be a shaky foundation for a marriage, and he eventually abandons his family.

Morrison uses Jude's story to depict a clear link between economic discrimination and the deformation of African American familial and communal structures, a link that is even more vividly represented in the catastrophic march down the New River Road, the site of the construction project on which Jude dreams of working. Like the dream of entrepreneurial success that motivates so many Americans, the road project represents the possibility of betterment, an incentive to keep believing in the system. When the project is begun in 1927, it soon becomes clear that no

African Americans will be hired, yet it is always rumored that the policy is about to change. Such rumors are enough to keep the Bottom in line, discouraged yet hopeful. In 1941, the narrator tells us, the "rumor that the tunnel spanning the river would use Negro workers became an announcement," and "hope was high in spite of the fact that the River Road leading to the tunnel had encouraged similar hopes in 1927 but had ended up being built entirely by white labor—hillbillies and immigrants taking even the lowest jobs." It is only to those "lowest jobs" that the men of the Bottom aspire, knowing that they would not be given "the craft work," the actual work on the tunnel; but, even still, these jobs would mean that "black men would not have to sweep Medallion to eat, or leave the town altogether for steel mills in Akron and along Lake Erie." No jobs are given, although there is "a definite and witnessed interview of four colored men (and the promise of more in the spring)" (151).

Ordinarily, the faint promise embodied in such an interview would have been taken as a sign of hope, but the hardships brought on by the severe winter of 1941, which arrives early with a freak ice storm at the beginning of November, begin to make the people of the Bottom realize the true desperation of their situation. On the third day of January, when the sun shines again and the temperature shoots up to sixty-one degrees, the Bottom explodes: spontaneously celebrating a mock holiday called National Suicide Day that had previously been celebrated only by the town looney, a shell-shocked veteran named Shadrack, a parade of Bottom dwellers marches down the New Road to the mouth of the tunnel excavation. For the first time, they see the construction site for the shell game that it is: "Their hooded eyes swept over the place where their hope had lain since 1927. There was the promise: leaf-dead. The teeth unrepaired, the coal credit cut off, the chest pains unattended, the school shoes unbought, the rush stuffed mattresses, the broken toilets, the leaning porches, the slurred remarks and the staggering childish malevolence of their employers." Suddenly translated into terms of material deprivation, the tunnel comes to symbolize their dispossession, and they lash out against it, attempting to "kill . . . the tunnel they were forbidden to build." But, instead, the tunnel kills them: "In their need to kill it all, all of it, to wipe from the face of the earth the work of the thin-armed Virginia boys, the bull-necked Greeks and the knife-faced men who waved the leaf-dead promise, they went too deep too far . . ." (161–62; ellipses in original). The unfinished tunnel collapses, dragging the majority of its attackers down with it. The episode serves as yet another parable of what it means to be one of the dispossessed in U.S.

culture: it is to be in a no-win situation, where you lose if you continue to believe in the system and you lose if you try to strike back. Dispossession ultimately leads the dispossessed to destroy themselves.

Of course, the people of the Bottom have not chosen the most effective means of bringing about social change, but their violent, irrational response is the only kind of response that they have been culturally equipped or enabled to have. Dispossession—whether physical or metaphysical—is a violent act that creates a cycle of violence. Spiritually raped by white culture, a black man rapes his own daughter. Denied economic opportunity, a black community vents its rage and self-destructs. The only liberty that it can experience is purely negative, a pathological freedom that is heedless, violent, and destructive.

Similarly, in *The Bluest Eye*, Morrison describes Cholly Breedlove before his marriage as

> dangerously free. Free to feel whatever he felt—fear, guilt, shame, love, grief, pity. Free to be tender or violent, to whistle or weep. Free to sleep in doorways or between the white sheets of a singing woman. Free to take a job, free to leave it. He could go to jail and not feel imprisoned, for he had already seen the furtiveness in the eyes of his jailer, free to say, "No, suh," and smile, for he had already killed three white men.... He was free to live his fantasies and free even to die, the how and the when of which held no interest for him. (1970, 159)

The most shocking part of this description of pathological freedom is its seeming banality. Simply remembering any of the "myriad . . . humiliations, defeats, and emasculations" that have marked his life can "stir" Cholly Breedlove "into flights of depravity that surprised himself—but only himself. Somehow he could not astound. He could only be astounded" (42–43). In other words, no matter how pathologically Cholly behaves, his behavior is in some sense expected: the culture has created a stereotype of black male behavior that is more horrific than anything that a man like Cholly can actually do. The culture expects black men to rape their daughters.

The younger Macon Dead understands the dispossessing power of white American culture. Walking down the street, Macon often thinks about names, particularly his own name, which is identical to his father's, and he reflects bitterly that "his own parents had agreed to abide by a naming done to them by somebody who couldn't have cared less. Agreed to take and pass on to all their issue this heavy name scrawled in perfect thoughtlessness by a drunken Yankee in the Union Army" (18). Ironically, at the moment that he gains his freedom from slavery by gaining possession of his own person, the elder Macon Dead is dispossessed of his only inheritance: his name. Yet he keeps the name that he has been mistakenly given at the Freedman's Bureau in 1869 because his wife argued that "it was new and would wipe out the past" (54). For a time, it does, as the elder Macon Dead becomes the farmer that every black "wanted to be, the clever irrigator, the peachtree grower, the hog slaughterer, the wild-turkey roaster, the man who could plow forty in no time flat and sang like an angel while he did it." To the black men growing up in the vicinity of his farm, he is a legend: later, they remember that "his farm colored their lives like a paintbrush and spoke to them like a sermon." It told them, "Stop sniveling. Stop picking around the edges of the world. Take advantage" (235). Attempting to live the Jeffersonian dream, the elder Macon Dead believed that he could share in the benefits promised by U.S. culture's rhetoric of freedom, a belief that ends when his white neighbors covet his farm and murder him for it.

For the black men who idolized him, the death of the elder Macon Dead signaled the death of their own dreams; when his grandson visits years later, they look to him to "rekindle the dream and stop the death they were dying" (236). When they hear about the property and possessions that the younger Macon Dead has managed to accumulate, their spirits are lifted. For the younger Macon, the death of his father does not invalidate the dream but rather testifies to the power of its central insight: that ownership is everything in a culture of possessive individualism. Locke had said, in effect, "Own yourself, and you can own things," and Macon Dead the elder passes a similar creed on to his son, a creed that Macon Dead the younger will in turn pass on to his son. The irony, of course, is that part of the purchase price is the rejection of one's African American heritage: Macon Dead the elder must give up his original name; Macon Dead the younger must disavow his sister, whose looks are living proof that the Deads hail "from Africa" (54). To gain possession of yourself, in other words, you must suffer cultural dispossession: you must assimilate. And assimilation entails an even more bitter irony: that you must become an avatar of the slaveowner. To truly gain possession of yourself, you must not only dispossess yourself spiritually but also dispossess others literally. "Own things," Dead's motto goes, "then you'll own yourself and other people too" (55): owning yourself is inseparable from, in its fullest expression even depends on, owning others. So Macon Dead must own houses and evict poor black tenants when they can no longer afford the rents. One tenant who is on the verge of being dispossessed tells her grandchildren, "A nigger in business is a terrible thing to see. A terrible, terrible thing to see." These words represent the flip side of Macon Dead's creed, and Morrison tells us, "The boys looked at each other and back at their grandmother. Their lips were parted as though they had heard something important" (22). Like Cholly Breedlove, Macon Dead is caught in a vicious circle in which he can repair the harm done to him only by causing harm to others. Macon's father is dispossessed by whites, so Macon must dispossess blacks. The dilemma that U.S. culture poses to African Americans is this: if you do not wish to be a slave, you must be a slaver. In other words, you can escape enslavement, but you cannot escape from the dynamics of slavery.

Emersonian Nightmares

The name of Ploy's minesweeper—the *Impulsive*—suggests another way in which Pynchon's fictions offer a challenge to the tradition of Emersonian liberalism: they suggest that the concepts of reason and rationality—so fundamental to the philosophy not only of Locke and Kant but also of Emerson and Rawls—are deeply flawed. In *Nature*, Emerson boldly declares that "whatever curiosity the order of things has awakened in our minds, the order of things can satisfy. Every man's condition is a solution in hieroglyphic to those inquiries he would put" (1836, 7). Pynchon's *V.* is a novel that demonstrates how difficult it actually is to read that hieroglyphic and how large a gap exists between "the order of things" and "every man's condition." Herbert Stencil, "the world adventurer," searches for the truth about the "unknown circumstances" of his father's death in 1919 (1963, 52). After discovering a mysterious entry in his father's journal—"There is more behind and inside V. than any of us had suspected. Not who, but what: what is she? God grant that I may never be called upon to write the answer, either here or in any official report" (53)—Stencil embarks on a quest that seems Emersonian in its emphasis on the process rather than the result: "Finding her: what then? Only that what love there was to Stencil had become directed entirely inward, toward this acquired sense of animateness. Having found this he could hardly release it, it was too dear. To sustain it he had to hunt V.; but if he should find her, where else would there be to go but back into half-consciousness? He tried not to think, therefore, about any end to the search. Approach and avoid" (55). Stencil suspects that his father's death is linked to the grandest of all conspiracies, "The Big One, the century's master cabal" (226). At the novel's end, Stencil is off searching for an object—a glass eye—that will tie together the disparate stories that he has heard, having failed to notice another object—an ivory comb worn by his acquaintance Paola—that could have served the same purpose. The question of whether such a master cabal exists is not answered by the novel, but its epilogue—set in 1919—does reveal the circumstances of the elder Stencil's death, and they prove to be trivial: a freakish natural accident that is completely unrelated to any intrigue with which the elder Stencil was involved. The novel's ending is thus a cruel joke: the truth *is* out there, full of sound and fury, but signifying nothing.[5]

V. is thus at least in part a detective story, but it is filtered through the epistemological skepticism of postmodernism. Like other postmodern detective fictions, V. attacks two of the core concepts of the Enlightenment philosophy that underwrites detective fiction: it depicts the futility of any positivist search for the "truth" and deconstructs the very idea of the stable, rational individual.[6] In his second and still most widely read and taught novel, *The Crying of Lot 49*, Pynchon deepens this skepticism. Although the truth behind the death of the elder Stencil remains unknown to the characters in V., it does exist and can be revealed to the reader. In *The Crying of Lot 49*, however, the concept of truth itself is under siege, and the novel can only leave us stranded amid multiple possibilities: as the novel closes, we are left, not on the verge of a revelation, but on the verge of something that may turn out to be a revelation, or may not.

The Crying of Lot 49 sends its protagonist around in circles as it presents a vision of the world in which ambiguity usurps the place of truth and individualism degenerates into narcissism, solipsism, and paranoia. Set in both the San Francisco Bay area and a fictional city in Southern California called San Narciso, *The Crying of Lot 49* pokes fun at the classic California detective novel, replacing the hard-boiled dick with a suburban housewife named Oedipa Maas, who stumbles onto something that might be a nationwide conspiracy but might just as easily be a figment of her imagination. Returning home from a Tupperware party one summer afternoon, Oedipa finds that she "had been named executor, or she supposed executrix, of the estate of [her former lover] Pierce Inverarity, a California real estate mogul who had once lost two million dollars in his spare time but still had assets numerous and tangled enough to make the job of sorting it all out more than honorary" (1966, 9). In the course of attempting to settle Pierce's affairs, Oedipa uncovers what appears to be an underground postal system called "W.A.S.T.E.," which uses cleverly altered waste cans as mailboxes and which may or may not be linked to a vast conspiracy with unclear motives called "the Tristero." In telling the story of Oedipa's obsession with determining whether the Tristero actually exists, Pynchon burlesques not only the genre of the detective story but also the idea of Emersonian self-reliance by dismantling the conceptual framework upon which both rely.

Like the classic hard-boiled detective, Oedipa Maas finds herself living a lonely and isolated existence at the beginning of *The Crying of Lot 49*. Instead of a shabby office, Oedipa spends her time in her suburban home, but she nonetheless feels a "sense of buffering [and] insulation," having "conned herself into the curious, Rapunzel-like role of a pensive girl somehow, magically, prisoner among the pines and salt fogs of Kinneret, looking for somebody to say hey, let down your hair" (20). The affair with Inverarity would, she had hoped, release her from her captivity, but when she visits a museum in Mexico City and sees a painting "by the beautiful Spanish exile Remedios Varo," she realizes that she has not escaped her prison because what is imprisoning her is her own subjectivity: "In the central painting of a triptych, titled 'Bordando el Manto Terrestre,' were a number of frail girls with heart-shaped faces, huge eyes, spun-gold hair, prisoners in the top room of a circular tower, embroidering a kind of tapestry which spilled out the slit windows and into a void, seeking hopelessly to fill the void: for all the other buildings and creatures, all the waves, ships and forests of the earth were contained in this tapestry, and the tapestry was the world" (21). What Oedipa feels is a version of the skepticism that Emerson describes in "Experience": "It is very unhappy, but too late to be helped, the discovery we have made that we exist. That discovery is called the Fall of Man. Ever afterwards we suspect our instruments. We have learned that we do not see directly, but mediately, and that we have no means of correcting those colored and distorting lenses which we are, or of computing the amount of their errors. Perhaps these subject-lenses have a creative power; perhaps there are no objects" (457).

The Varo painting suggests to Oedipa a similar sense of the mediated nature of human vision:

> Oedipa, perverse, had stood in front of the painting and cried. No one had noticed; she wore dark green bubble shades. For a moment she'd wondered if the seal around her sockets were tight enough to allow the tears simply to go on and fill up the entire lens space and never dry.

> She could carry the sadness of the moment with her that way forever, see the world refracted through those tears, those specific tears, as if indices as yet unfound varied in important ways from cry to cry. She had looked down at her feet and known, then, because of a painting, that what she stood on had only been woven together a couple thousand miles away in her own tower, was only by accident known as Mexico, and so Pierce had taken her away from nothing, there'd been no escape. (21)

Emerson's moment of skepticism serves to renew his belief in the need for self-reliance: "I know," he writes toward the end of "Experience," "that the world I converse with in the city and in the farms, is not the world I *think*" (491).[7] Despite his acknowledgment that "manipular attempts to realize the world of thought" have throughout history invariably failed, Emerson persists in asking the question, "Why not realize your world"? for he believes that, with "patience, we shall win at last." Emerson argues that, "in the solitude to which every man is always returning, he has a sanity and revelations, which in his passage into new worlds he will carry with him," and he concludes the essay with this exhortation: "Never mind the ridicule, never mind the defeat: up again, old heart!—it seems to say,—there is victory yet for all justice; and the true romance which the world exists to realize, will be the transformation of genius into practical power" (1844b, 492).

For Oedipa, however, romance can only represent everything from which she is trying to escape. Like the novels of Raymond Chandler, *The Crying of Lot 49* invokes the image of the knight in shining armor, but it transforms the image in the same way that it revises the conventions of hard-boiled detective fiction, sending the maiden out on the quest and making her the individualist:[8]

> Such a captive maiden, having plenty of time to think, soon realizes that her tower, its height and architecture, are like her ego only incidental: that what really keeps her where she is is magic, anonymous and malignant, visited on her from outside and for no reason at all. Having no apparatus except gut fear and female cunning to examine this formless magic, to understand how it works, how to measure its field strength, count its lines of force, she may fall back on superstition, or take up a useful hobby like embroidery, or go mad, or marry a disk jockey. If the tower is everywhere and the knight of deliverance no proof against its magic, what else? (21–22)

In a hostile world not governed by reason, where knights in shining armor lack efficacy, captive maidens must save themselves: self-reliance, debased and suspect, nevertheless provides the only potential avenue for escape. Midway through the novel, when things have begun to look hopelessly confusing, Oedipa will ask herself a version of Emerson's question: "It was part of her duty, wasn't it, to bestow life on what had persisted, to try to be . . . the dark machine in the centre of the planetarium, to bring the estate into pulsing stelliferous Meaning, all in a soaring dome around her? . . . [I]nto her memo book, she wrote *Shall I project a world?*" The question is not transcendent but provisional, and it is immediately qualified and undermined: "If not project then at least flash some arrow on the dome to skitter among constellations and trace out your Dragon, Whale, Southern Cross. Anything might help" (82). Oedipa tries to turn the tables on her epistemological dilemma: instead of fearing that the world she sees is simply the projection of her own mind, as she did when she saw the Varo tapestry, Oedipa realizes that to project a world is to create order out of chaos.

Oedipa's Emersonian optimism proves, however, to be short-lived: finding herself exhausted after a night spent on the streets of San Francisco trying to unravel the mystery behind the seemingly ubiquitous symbol—a muted post horn—that is somehow connected to the Tristero, Oedipa succumbs to a "rare" moment of "fatalism," thinking to herself, "Where was the Oedipa who'd driven so bravely up here from San Narciso? That optimistic baby had come on so like the private eye in any long-ago radio drama, believing all you needed was grit, resourcefulness, exemption from hidebound cops' rules, to solve any great mystery" (124). The very language with which Pynchon invokes the ethos of the hard-boiled detective serves simultaneously to debunk it: the use of the pluperfect tense and the relegation of the private eye to the genre *radio drama* suggest that Philip Marlowe and his ilk are anachronisms in the postmodern world.

If Oedipa associates her quest with radio drama, it is perhaps because Inverarity himself suggested the analogy in what turned out to be their final conversation. Phoning her long-distance in the middle of the night, Pierce performed a series of crazed vocal impersonations, culminating in "his Lamont Cranston voice": " 'But Margo,' earnestly, 'I've just come from Commissioner Weston, and that old man in the fun house was murdered by the same blowgun that killed Professor Quackenbush,' or something" (11). With its outrageous murder weapon and outlandish naming, this parody of the formal detective story recalls Raymond Chandler's disparaging remarks about the genre in "The Simple Art of Murder," but Pynchon soon mocks hard-boiled detective fiction as well, appropriating its traditional topos by setting most of the novel in the fictional city of San Narciso, which like "many named places in California... was less an identifiable city than a grouping of concepts—census tracts, special purpose bond-issue districts, shopping nuclei, all overlaid with access roads to its own freeway" (24). There are other ingredients from hard-boiled detective fiction—gangsters, sleazy bars, suicide, arson—but Pynchon's polymorphous parody spices up this stew with bits of Borgesian scholarly detection, as Oedipa finds herself learning about postage stamp forgery and tracking down the textual variants of a Jacobean revenge play called The Courier's Tragedy by one Richard Wharfinger, itself a nod to the prehistory of detective fiction.[9] Laced with clues and red herrings, The Crying of Lot 49 depicts what is either an ever-widening conspiracy or an ever-deepening paranoia. Oedipa's plight is a parodic version of the story of that original detective, Oedipus, who solves the riddle of the Sphinx but finds himself at the center of a grand conspiracy designed by the Fates to entrap him: like her namesake, Oedipa seeks to answer what turns out to be an ontological riddle and finds herself enmeshed in a series of events and circumstances that may or may not have been designed specifically to entrap her.

Like any good Cartesian individualist, the private eye generally has access to something called truth, but The Crying of Lot 49 makes this concept unavailable to Oedipa. In the world of the novel, truth has been replaced by ambiguity, either because human beings are incapable of discerning truth or because truth itself does not exist, two alternative descriptions of human reality that ultimately become indistinguishable. Beginning with the "quiet ambiguity" of Pierce's untraceable final phone call, conveyed over a phone line that "could have pointed any direction, been any length," every development in Oedipa's investigation is tinged with indeterminacy. The letter informing Oedipa of her appointment as coexecutor of Pierce's estate suggests trivial questions at first: "Had Pierce called last year then to tell her about this codicil? Or had he decided on it later...?" (12). By the end of the novel, however, the questions that haunt Oedipa are similarly unanswerable, but far more significant and disturbing, as she confronts four "symmetrical" and irreducible alternative explanations:

> Either you have stumbled indeed, with the aid of LSD or other indole alkaloids, onto a secret richness and concealed density of dream; on a network by which X number of Americans are truly communicating whilst reserving their lies, recitations of routine, arid betrayals of

spiritual poverty, for the official government delivery system; maybe even onto a real alternative to the exitlessness, to the absence of surprise to life, that harrows the head of everybody American you know, and you too, sweetie. Or you are hallucinating it. Or a plot has been mounted against you.... Or you are fantasying some such plot, in which case you are a nut, Oedipa, out of your skull. (170–71)

The Crying of Lot 49 represents a detective's nightmare, a world into which the substitution of radical ambiguity for truth transmutes individualism and self-reliance into narcissism, solipsism, and paranoia.

If this description also sounds like an Emersonian's nightmare, it is because Pynchon's novel recognizes the fundamental affinity between the hard-boiled detective's quest and the Emersonian's, and it makes fun of them both as part of a larger satire of individualism. Despite his awareness that all human vision is mediated, Emerson believes in the ability of men and women to discern truth and even to experience what might be called *revelation*. In *Nature*, for example, he refuses to acknowledge the existence of any phenomena that might properly be called *inexplicable*. According to Emerson, "We have no questions to ask which are unanswerable." His faith is grounded in the existence of a divine order that is embodied by Nature: "We must trust the perfection of the creation so far, as to believe that whatever curiosity the order of things has awakened in our minds, the order of things can satisfy." Emerson draws an analogy between the rationality of the self and "the order of things," and he implies that the two are mutually reinforcing. "Every man's condition is a solution in hieroglyphic to those inquiries he would put. He acts it in life, before he apprehends it as truth. In like manner, nature is already, in its forms and tendencies, describing its own design" (7). Refusing to believe that an understanding of the order of the universe is beyond human capacity, Emerson asserts that it is simply a matter of correctly interpreting the hieroglyphics that nature places before us.

Attempting to maintain her faith in "the order of things," Oedipa yearns to find evidence of a design behind the various clues and coincidences that confront her, with relatively little success. Throughout the novel, Pynchon tantalizes both his characters and his readers with moments that seem to hold the potential for Emersonian revelation, but in nearly every case the universal current is short-circuited before it reaches its intended outlet. Oedipa is momentarily successful at the outset of her investigation. On the day that she learns about Inverarity's will, Oedipa finds herself thinking about her relationship with him, "shuffling back through a fat deckful of days which seemed (wouldn't she be the first to admit it?) more or less identical, or all pointing the same way subtly like a conjurer's deck, any odd one readily cleared to a trained eye" (11). Promisingly enough, she manages to pinpoint the odd day when Inverarity phoned her and did his Lamont Cranston imitation, which turned out to be the last time that she spoke to him.

She is less successful, however, when she drives down to San Narciso, which "had been Pierce's domicile, and headquarters: the place he'd begun his land speculating in ten years ago." Oedipa expects that fact to "set the spot apart, give it an aura," but she finds that she is mistaken: "If there was any vital difference between it and the rest of Southern California, it was invisible on first glance. She drove into San Narciso on a Sunday, in a rented Impala. Nothing was happening" (24). Things look a little different, however, on second glance. Pynchon's description of Oedipa's second view of San Narciso is riddled with words that suggest the language of Emersonianism, as if Oedipa were somehow standing on the brink of a moment of Emersonian revelation, about to become "a transparent eyeball," able "to see all" and conduct "the currents of the Universal Being" (Emerson 1836, 10):

> She looked down a slope, needing to squint for the sunlight, onto a vast sprawl of houses which had grown up all together, like a well-tended crop, from the dull brown earth; and she thought of the time she'd opened a transistor radio to replace a battery and seen her first printed circuit. The ordered swirl of houses and streets, from this high angle, sprang at her now with the same unexpected astonishing clarity as the circuit card had. Though she knew even less about radios than about Southern Californians, there were to both outward patterns a hieroglyphic sense of concealed meaning, of an intent to communicate. There'd seemed no limit to what the printed circuit could have told her (if she had tried to find out); so in her first minute of San Narciso, a revelation also trembled just past the threshold of her understanding. (24)

In this passage, Pynchon, like Emerson, depicts a moment of potential revelation through the use of a mixed metaphor that conflates vision and electricity. His account of the world is, however, rather less optimistic than Emerson's, for Pynchon can find no solace in the educative and redemptive power of nature. Asserting that "Nature, in the common sense, refers to essences unchanged by man; space, the air, the river, the leaf," Emerson defines "Art" as "the mixture of [man's] will with the same things, as in a house, a canal, a statue, a picture," but he declares that all human "operations taken together are so insignificant . . . that in an impression so grand as that of the world on the human mind, they do not vary the result" (1836, 8).

In Pynchon's world, however, human "operations" on nature are far from "insignificant." The landscape that Oedipa surveys during her "odd, religious instant" is quite different from Emerson's "woods" and even from his "bare common" (1836, 8). Pynchon's California has been domesticated and corrupted in an ironic fulfillment of Emerson's call for "the kingdom of man over nature" (49). In this passage, nature exists only as a simile, something remembered but absent, and even then it is nature cultivated not wild: what Oedipa sees is "a vast sprawl of houses which had grown up all together, like a well-tended crop, from the dull brown earth" (24). Oedipa's mind, however, does not find repose in this image, and her next thought purges nature from the equation altogether as she likens the landscape to a "printed circuit." Nature itself has become alien and unnatural because technology has usurped its place in the human consciousness. When, in one of the novel's slapstick moments, Oedipa finds herself menaced by a ruptured can of hair spray that is whizzing through the air, she thinks to herself that "something fast enough, God or a digital machine, might have computed in advance the complex web of its travel" (37). God, it seems, has competition: the natural order is challenged, perhaps even supplanted, by the technological order. Mike Fallopian, who belongs to an ultraindividualist group called the Peter Pinguid Society, refers to this process as the "creeping horror" of the modern world (54). In these scenes, the novel suggests that the erosion of individuality in modern life is also due to an increasing worship of technology qua technology, which becomes one of the major themes of *Gravity's Rainbow*. In both these novels, Pynchon characterizes modernity as the result of an ontological shift away from the divine toward the technological, a process against which the Luddites were perhaps the first to rebel.

In his article on Luddism, Pynchon argues that "to insist on the miraculous is to deny to the machine at least some of its claims on us, to assert the limited wish that living things, earthly and otherwise, may on occasion become Bad and Big enough to take part in transcendent doings" (1984a, 40). Emerson seems to take part in transcendent doings with some regularity, but, although Oedipa Maas longs for transcendence and revelation, there seems to be little hope of achieving either. Oedipa feels herself to be caught in the pincers of an epistemological double bind that threatens to crush her sense of self. The world around her seems alien, full of meanings that she cannot comprehend, but she cannot be sure that the world she sees is not simply the projection of her own mind. Because the self no longer seems to be the mirror of nature, looking for truth inside the self leads only to solipsism and radical doubt.

Thus, on that slope overlooking San Narciso, the Emersonian moment of transcendental revelation fails to materialize: "the 'religious instant,' whatever it might've been" (24), is broken, its Emersonian potential left unrealized. Oedipa speeds off on her merry way, unenlightened by what she has seen, unsettled by her sense that she has failed to see, nagged by the suspicion that she has missed something. Two pages later, the novel begins to deepen its depiction of the failure of revelation, undermining the very concept of revelation by linking it to delusions, hallucinations, and reliance on drugs. Here, the image of the "printed circuit" is transformed into a far more sinister metaphor. Driving past "the familiar parade of more beige, prefab, cinderblock office machine distributors, sealant makers, bottled gas works, fastener factories, warehouses, and whatever," Oedipa, who has refused to take the pills prescribed for her by her psychiatrist, Dr. Hilarius, because she "didn't want to get hooked in any way," thinks of the road that she is on as "this hypodermic needle, a vein nourishing the mainliner L.A., keeping it happy, coherent, protected from pain, or whatever passes, with a city, for pain." And she thinks of herself as "some single melted crystal of urban horse" (26). Midway through the novel, Oedipa fears that she has had the misfortune of "walk[ing] uncoerced into the presence of madness" when she meets a disgruntled inventor named Stanley Koteks, who tells her about the "Nefastis Machine":

> James Clerk Maxwell, explained Koteks, a famous Scotch scientist who had once postulated a tiny intelligence, known as Maxwell's Demon. The Demon could sit in a box among air molecules that were moving at all different speeds, and sort out the fast molecules from the slow ones. Fast molecules have more energy than slow ones. Concentrate enough of them in one place and you have a region of high temperature. You can then use the difference in temperature between this hot region of the box and any cooler region, to drive a heat engine. . . . [T]he Nefastis Machine contained an honest-to-God Maxwell's Demon. All you had to do was stare at the photo of Clerk Maxwell, and concentrate on which cylinder, right or left, you wanted the Demon to raise the temperature in. The air would expand and push a piston. (86)

Despite her misgivings, Oedipa finds herself intrigued when Koteks tells her that "not everybody can work [the Nefastis Machine] . . . Only people with the gift. 'Sensitives,' John calls them" (87). Oedipa seeks Nefastis out but can find no place for herself in his model of the visionary individual as she proves to be incapable of communicating with Maxwell's Demon. Rationalizing her failure, she concludes that a "sensitive" is merely someone who "can share in the man's hallucinations." In her eyes, Nefastis (whose name is derived from the Latin *nefas*, "that which is contrary to divine law, wickedness") is no visionary, just "a nut, a sincere nut" (107). She reaches a similar conclusion about her husband, Mucho, when she learns that he has turned to drug-induced hallucinations in order to make his life bearable. LSD gives him the feeling of connectedness that he has yearned for: "It's not like you're some hophead," he tells Oedipa. "You take it because it's good. Because you hear and see things, even smell them, taste like you never could" (143–44).

It is easy at first for Oedipa to dismiss Nefastis as "a nut" and her husband for being "too sensitive," too "thin-skinned," but, in the course of the novel, Oedipa finds herself become increasingly "sensitized" to potential clues, until her search for the Tristero begins to become an obsession. Oedipa begins to think that she is constantly having revelations and that everything she sees is somehow connected to the Tristero: "Though she saw Mike Fallopian again, and did trace the text of *The Courier's Tragedy* a certain distance, these follow-ups were no more disquieting than the other revelations which now seemed to come crowding in exponentially, as if the more she collected the more would come to her, until everything she saw, smelled, dreamed, remembered, would somehow come to be woven into The Tristero" (81). The word *revelation* has ceased to have the portentous significance with which it was invested during Oedipa's first look at San Narciso: Oedipa has many "revelations," but she comes no closer to understanding the "concealed meaning" of what she has discovered. In the next chapter, the word *revelation* comes to signify the entire web of ambiguous facts and circumstances that have enveloped Oedipa: what it now signifies is something akin to "delusion." Oedipa decides not to pursue certain clues, "anxious that her revelation not expand beyond a certain point. Lest, possibly, it grow larger than she and assume her to itself" (166). Revelation has become a virus or cancer that threatens to take over Oedipa's entire being.

What is at work here is, however, a peculiar conception of revelation, all form and no content. Oedipa senses that revelation is going on all around her, but she never quite understands what it is that is being revealed.[10] Indeed, the novel suggests that true revelation may simply lie outside human capacity. When Genghis Cohen, "the most eminent philatelist in the L.A. area," offers Oedipa some wine made from dandelions picked in a cemetery that was demolished to make room for the East San Narciso Freeway—the second time she has encountered the fact of this demolition in the course of her investigation—she begins to feel as if she is on the verge of making an important connection:

> She could, at this stage of things, recognize signals like that, as the epileptic is said to—an odor, color, pure piercing grace note announcing his seizure. Afterward it is only this signal, really dross, this secular announcement, and never what is revealed during the attack, that he remembers. Oedipa wondered whether, at the end of this (if it were supposed to end), she too might not be left with only compiled memories of clues, announcements, intimations, but never the central truth itself, which must somehow each time be too bright for her memory to hold; which must always blaze out, destroying its own message irreversibly, leaving an overexposed blank when the ordinary world came back. In the space of a sip of dandelion wine it came to her that she would never know how many times such a seizure may already have visited, or how to grasp it should it visit again. Perhaps even in this last second—but there was no way to tell.

Once again, revelation and truth are short-circuited, but the process, as Pynchon describes it here, is far more disturbing than the simple inability to discern truth that Oedipa experiences when looking at San Narciso for the first time. Something is "revealed" during an epileptic's attack, but inevitably forgotten. If truth is merely hidden, then there is always the possibility—no matter how remote—of uncovering it. But what to do if human beings are flawed, if the "central truth itself" is always "too bright for . . . memory to hold"? Pynchon writes that Oedipa "glanced down the corridor of Cohen's rooms in the rain and saw, for the very first time, how far it might be possible to get lost in this" (95).

Once the private eye has discovered the identity of the criminal, he or she can set clues and events into a narrative order and thus describe the way in which the crime was committed. Once the oracles have revealed his true identity to him, Oedipus can rewrite the narrative of his experience in a way that solves its mysteries. Oedipa, however, never manages to sort out the clues from the red herrings, to separate meaningful patterns from misleading coincidences. During the night in which she encounters post horn after post horn in the streets of San Francisco, she realizes that what she shares with the private eye is something other than the ability to solve mysteries; it is instead the fact that "the private eye sooner or later has to get beat up on." Marlowe is slugged, drugged, and pistol-whipped with regularity, but it never discourages him enough to make him give up a case. Oedipa, however, finds that she is less resilient: "This night's profusion of post horns, this malignant, deliberate replication, was their way of beating up. They knew her pressure points, and the ganglia of her optimism, and one by one, pinch by precision pinch, they were immobilizing her" (124).

To understand what Oedipa is up against, we might consider what the name *Narcissus* and the concept *narcissism* signify in *The Crying of Lot 49*. Pynchon overloads the name *Narcissus* with symbolic meaning, using it to refer both to Ovid's self-infatuated youth and to the legendary Saint Narcissus, bishop of Jerusalem, who used water to light his Easter lamp in the absence of oil. As Wendy Steiner points out, "The mythic Narcissus is a symbol of modernist solipsism and isolation; the Narcissus of sacred legend introduces the possibility of revelation, miracle, and rebirth" (1986, 325). These two figures stand in figurative opposition to one another in the novel, but Pynchon complicates things further by invoking each of them in contradictory ways. He likens Oedipa to Ovid's Narcissus by constantly associating her with mirrors, but he also links her to Narcissus's unrequited lover, Echo. When Oedipa drives up to the Echo Courts Motel in San Narciso, she is surprised to find a large sign depicting a nymph: "The face of the nymph was much like Oedipa's, which didn't startle her so much as a concealed blower system that kept the nymph's gauze chiton in constant agitation, revealing enormous vermilion-tipped breasts and long pink thighs at each flap. She was smiling a lipsticked and public smile, not quite a hooker's but nowhere near that of any nymph pining away with love either" (26). Pynchon's polymorphous parody thus casts doubt on the identification of Oedipa as a Narcissus figure (and also on her self-reliance and independence from males, a doubt that is magnified when Oedipa proceeds to succumb to the amorous wiles of coexecutor Metzger in her motel room). Pynchon invokes Saint Narcissus in similarly ambiguous fashion: in the course of the novel, he represents short-circuited revelation (in his guise as "San Narciso"), becomes an instrument of death (appearing in *The Courier's Tragedy* as a statue with poisoned feet), and finally (in the form of a picture on a wall) presides over the novel's one genuine scene of tenderness, Oedipa's encounter with the old sailor suffering from delirium tremens. The nexus of meanings surrounding the name *Narcissus* and the concept of *narcissism* resists being subsumed into any system of determinate meaning, posing an interpretive problem for the reader of the novel that is similar to the problems faced constantly by Oedipa.

Throughout the novel, Oedipa attempts to create meaning out of indeterminacy, to restore order to the process of signification, which has gone mad, producing a proliferation of equally plausible signifieds for each signifier. But despite the best efforts of both Oedipa and the reader, narrative becomes hopelessly fractured in *The Crying of Lot 49*. When Oedipa and Metzger turn on a television and stumble across a film called *Cashiered* in which Metzger starred as a child, the experience provides a microcosm of the novel as a whole. The film is punctuated by commercials that all seem to be related to interests owned by Pierce Inverarity; its apparent order is really disorder (the reels are shown out of sequence); and, as he watches, Metzger functions in a manner analogous to that of the novel's narrator: he knows the ending (although he is not telling), and yet even he becomes confused by the scrambling of the plot.

The novel thus dismantles the sense of teleology on which classic detective fiction and Emersonian liberalism both depend. The only mystery that will be solved as the novel draws to its close is the meaning of its title (and, even then, we will still not learn the meaning of the utterance that the title turns out to describe). Of course, the title itself encodes this fact through its relation to the Pentecostal imagery that the novel both deploys and burlesques.[11] *Pentecost*, derived etymologically from the Greek word *pentokostos*, meaning "fiftieth," is the name given to the Jewish festival celebrated fifty days after Passover in commemoration of Moses' receipt of the law, but it is also a Christian holiday (known alternatively as Whitsunday) that marks the descent of the Holy Ghost from heaven to confer on the Apostles the gift of tongues—the ability to speak in foreign languages—so that they could spread the teachings of Christ around the world. Pentecost and the number 50 are thus linked to both revelation and the ability to communicate, but Pynchon's single use of the word *Pentecost* occurs in *The Courier's Tragedy*, in the form of a sadistic joke about the inability to communicate. The first act of the play ends with one of its characters using a pair of pincers to tear out an enemy's tongue: "With the tongue impaled on his rapier Ercole runs to a burning torch set in the wall, sets the tongue aflame and waving it around like a madman concludes the act by screaming,

> The pitiless unmanning is most meet,
> Thinks Ercole the zany Paraclete.
> Descended this malign, Unholy Ghost,
> Let us begin thy frightful Pentecost. (68–69)

The satiric effect of this passage depends on a literalization of the biblical image of the Apostles crowned by tongues of flame. The novel as a whole is more decorous but equally subversive in its invocation of Pentecost. If the number associated with the Pentecost is 50, then Lot 49 symbolically represents the moment before revelation, the threshold that must be crossed to move from babble to communication.

The Crying of Lot 49 transforms this liminal moment into a continuing ontological state: its characters and its readers never cross over into revelation. "Power," Emerson claimed, "ceases in the instant of repose; it resides in the moment of transition from a past to a new state, in the shooting of the gulf, in the darting to an aim" ("Self-Reliance"; 1836, 271). Oedipa is in a state of constant transition, but it is never empowering: in The Crying of Lot 49, Emersonian process appears in the debased form of Pierce Inverarity's dictum, "Keep it bouncing" (178). At the end of the novel, Oedipa seems poised for a revelation: she is attending an auction where she expects agents of the Tristero to bid for a lot containing Pierce's stamp collection—Lot 49. The concluding image of the novel invokes Pentecostal symbolism, as if Oedipa were truly poised on the brink of a revelation: "An assistant closed the heavy door on the lobby windows and the sun. She heard a lock snap shut; the second echoed a moment. [The auctioneer] spread his arms in a gesture that seemed to belong to the priesthood of some remote culture; perhaps to a descending angel. . . . Oedipa settled back, to await the crying of lot 49" (183). The novel thus proves to be a circular text, and its final words—"Oedipa settled back, to await the crying of lot 49"—return us to its title page still searching for that concealed meaning.

The novel's final words thus embody one of its recurrent motifs. When Oedipa looks down on San Narciso for the first time, she sees in its "outward patterns a hieroglyphic sense of concealed meaning" but fails to unravel that meaning. Instead of feeling what Emerson calls "the currents of the Universal Being" circulating through her, instead of becoming "part or particle of God," Oedipa drives down the hill and becomes a particle on the circuit that is San Narciso. And, like an electron stuck in a circuit, she will spend the novel seeming to make progress but actually going around in circles. Metzger's film *Cashiered* provides another emblem for the circularity depicted by the novel. Metzger tells Oedipa, "The film is in an air-conditioned vault at one of the Hollywood studios, light can't fatigue it, it can be repeated endlessly" (33). The printed circuit, the hermetically sealed but endlessly repeatable film, and, finally, the circular structure of the novel itself embody what Oedipa calls "the exitlessness . . . that harrows the head of everybody American" that she knows (170).

What is harrowing about the exitlessness of American culture is its corrosive effect on individuality. The metaphor of the printed circuit encodes an atomistic view of American life—literally, even exaggeratedly, so—since an electron is a far smaller particle than an atom. On the one hand, the characters in Pynchon's novel yearn to break out of the narcissism and solipsism that envelops them, seeking to understand their world as a network of connections rather than a set of entropic particles. Yet the quest for connection merely reconstitutes narcissism and solipsism in an even more unbearable form. In the final pages of the novel, Oedipa is brought back full circle to experience another form of the solipsism from which she began, finding herself alone, "her isolation complete" (177). Emerson had begun his interrogation of nature by asserting the priority of the self, which serves as the principle against which he defines nature: "Philosophically considered, the universe is composed of Nature and the Soul. Strictly speaking, therefore, all that is separate from us, all which Philosophy distinguishes as the NOT ME, that is, both nature and art, all other men and my own body, must be ranked under this name NATURE" (*Nature*; 1836, 8). Oedipa Maas, however, discovers to her chagrin that this seemingly trivial distinction between self and other, between the me and the not me, cannot be taken for granted. Unable to orient herself, Oedipa finds her sense of individuality slipping away, "as if there could be no barriers between herself and the rest of the land," and she makes a startling discovery: "San Narciso at that moment lost (the loss pure, instant, spherical, the sound of a stainless orchestral chime held among the stars and struck lightly), gave up its residue of uniqueness for her; became a name again, was assumed back into the American continuity of crust and mantle" (177). San Narciso becomes an emblem for America and its culture of narcissism: "There was the true continuity, San Narciso had no boundaries. No one knew yet how to draw them. She had dedicated herself, weeks ago, to making sense of what Inverarity had left behind, never suspecting that the legacy was America" (178). The alternative to the isolated self proves to be self-loss. Oedipa's vision of San Narciso stretching without boundaries across America is merely another version of the Varo tapestry, both "seeking hopelessly to fill the void" (21).

The novel thus suggests that paranoid narcissism may be the only form in which individuality survives in modern U.S. culture. Dr. Hilarius's advice, which Oedipa initially rejects as delusional, comes to seem like the only answer: refusing to accede to Oedipa's request to "talk [her] out of a fantasy," Hilarius had urged her to "Cherish it! . . . What else do any of you have? Hold it tightly by its little tentacle, don't let the Freudians coax it away or the pharmacists poison it out of you. Whatever it is, hold it dear, for when you lose it you go over by that much to the others. You begin to cease to be" (138). At the end of the novel, Oedipa's paranoid narcissism, driven by a vision of the self under siege and surrounded by conspirators, becomes a form of self-preservation. Knowing that "behind the hieroglyphic streets there would either be a transcendent meaning, or only the earth" (181). Oedipa realizes that, if there is no transcendent meaning, she must invent one, even if it means sinking into paranoia: "For there either was some Tristero beyond the appearance of the legacy America, or there was just America and if there was just America then it seemed the only way she could continue, and manage to be at all relevant to it, was as an alien, unfurrowed, assumed full circle into some paranoia" (182). The alternative for Oedipa is to slip into what Pynchon calls in *Gravity's Rainbow* "anti-paranoia, where nothing is connected to anything, a condition not many of us can bear for long" (1973, 434). To preserve her individuality and fend off nihilism, Oedipa must embrace paranoia as if it were truth. A losing battle against impossible odds is better than no battle at all. When paranoid delusion is indistinguishable from truth and serves as a necessary antidote to nihilism, then a rational self is an impossibility. Oedipa Maas has come a long, long way from the Cartesian individualism that undergirds even the most nasty and brutish of hard-boiled detectives. Pynchon's revision of the detective genre thus offers a pointed critique of the rationalism on which Emersonian liberalism's and U.S. culture's official narratives both depend.

From Reason to Miracle

Pynchon's first three novels are marked by moments of the fantastic: we might remember the "dismantling" of the Bad Priest in *V.*, the story of the Tristero in *The Crying of Lot 49*, Tyrone Slothrop's journey down into a toilet in search of his beloved harmonica in *Gravity's Rainbow*. Pynchon, writes Douglas Fowler, "does not enter into any covenant with the reader as to what is 'real' and what is 'fantastic.' His fiction is fantastic in its essence, not incidentally or symbolically. He does not hold up a mirror to nature, but steps through the looking glass into a realm governed by magical forces rather than logical ones, and we will misread his fiction if we expect it to be confined to the empirical world" (1980, 55). What I will show here, however, is that, with *Vineland*, a shift occurs in Pynchon's use of the fantastic: it becomes, to use Pynchon's own term, the manifestation of the *miraculous*.

Like *The Crying of Lot 49*, *Vineland* (1990) is set in California. Pynchon links it to the earlier book by allowing Wendell "Mucho" Maas to make a cameo appearance in a chapter devoted to filling in the story of how one of the novel's protagonists, a musician named Zoyd Wheeler, originally "disappeared" with his infant daughter Prairie into Vineland County in order to escape the wrath of Brock Vond, a rather tenacious and vindictive federal prosecutor. Zoyd and Prairie spend a few nights at Mucho's "posh Telegraph Hill town house" in San Francisco. A few years have passed since the events of *The Crying of Lot 49*: Richard Nixon is now president, the Paranoids (just a garage band in *The Crying of Lot 49*) are playing at places like the Fillmore, and Mucho has become "a music-business biggie." We learn a little bit about Mucho's post-Oedipal phase:

> Psychedelicized far ahead of his time, Mucho Maas, originally a disk jockey, had decided around 1967, after a divorce remarkable even in that more innocent time for its geniality, to go into record producing. The business was growing unpredictable, and his take-off was abrupt—soon, styling himself Count Drugula, Mucho was showing up at Indolent [Records], down in the back-street Hollywood flats south of Sunset and east of Vine, in a chauffeured Bentley, wearing joke-store fangs, and a black velvet cape from Z & Z, scattering hits of high-quality acid among the fans young and old who gathered daily for his arrival. "Count, Count! Lay some dope on us!" they'd cry. Indolent Records had rapidly become known for its unusual choices of artists and repertoires. Mucho was one of the very first to audition, but not, he was later to add hastily, to call back, fledgling musician Charles Manson. He almost signed Wild Man Fischer, and Tiny Tim, too, but others got to them first. (309)

Always ahead of his time, Mucho subsequently became addicted to cocaine and then underwent a conversion experience (with a little help from "a dedicated and moralistic rhinologist" named Dr. Hugo Splanchnick [310] as well as a VW busload of "long-haired desperadoes . . . clamoring for acid" [311]): shedding his image as Count Drugula (a.k.a. Mucho the Munificent), he has lately devoted himself to a drug-free lifestyle that he refers to as "The Natch," which seems to include a propensity for proselytizing about "the evils of drug abuse" to all his friends and acquaintances.

Zoyd cannot believe his eyes or his ears: "Mucho, what happened, you were the Head of Heads, and not that long ago. This can't be you talking, it must be the fuckin' government, which this is all their trip anyway, cause they need to put people in the joint, if they can't do that, what are they? ain't shit, might as well be another show on the Tube" (311). But Mucho knows what it will take Zoyd many more years to realize—that the 1960s are over:

> "We're on into a new world now, it's the Nixon Years, then it'll be the Reagan years—"
>
> "Ol' Raygun? No way he'll ever make president."
>
> "Just please go careful, Zoyd. 'Cause soon they're gonna be coming after everything, not just drugs, but beer, cigarettes, sugar, salt, fat, you name it, anything that could remotely please any of your senses, because they need to control all that. And they will."
>
> "Fat Police?"
>
> "Perfume Police. Tube Police. Music Police. Good Healthy Shit Police. Best to renounce everything now, get a head start." (313)

This episode, which is revealed late in the novel (although it occurred fourteen years before the events that form the novel's present time), reminds us just how different *Vineland* is from *The Crying of Lot 49*. Unlike the earlier book, its first sentence sets us squarely in the summer of 1984, and the novel constructs its vision of this historical moment using not only the sort of pop-cultural references that dot *The Crying of Lot 49*—the first pages of *Vineland* give us Count Chocula, Nestle's Quik, "So Lonesome I Could Cry," and *Return of the Jedi*—but also direct references to politicians, primarily Nixon and Reagan. At the dark center of the novel is an episode that recalls the violence at Kent State University in 1968, when four students were killed by national guardsmen. Mucho's "prediction" about Reagan's accession to the presidency does, of course, come true, and his prescience is both a joke (since Pynchon writes with twenty/twenty hindsight) and an announcement that the world of *Vineland* is one in which communication, prophecy, and revelation are all possible. *Vineland* begins with a dream about failed communication, but it proves merely to be a tease: in place of the ambiguity and entropic arbitrariness that haunt *The Crying of Lot 49*, this novel substitutes truth and justice. The narrative structure of *Lot 49* is circular, modeled on a printed circuit, but the structure of *Vineland* is convergent, its various narrative strands all coming together in a scene of reunion and reconciliation. What makes this conclusion is the possible intervention of the miraculous into a world of authoritarian politics.

Vineland takes up where *The Crying of Lot 49* leaves off, providing an account of the transformation of American culture that occurred between the 1960s and the 1980s. *Vineland* tells the story of the strikingly beautiful Frenesi Gates, a former radical activist whose sexual obsession with Brock Vond leads her to betray 24fps, the radical collective of filmmakers to which she belongs, thereby causing the death of her lover, Weed Atman, a mathematics professor turned guru. She later marries Zoyd Wheeler but abandons both him and her infant daughter, Prairie. Eventually, she escapes from Vond by becoming an FBI sting specialist shielded by the Federal Witness Protection Program, and she marries a fellow operative named Flash. *Vineland* is full of characters trying to find Frenesi (some more obsessively than others): not only Vond and Zoyd and Prairie, but also her old comrade DL Chastain (now a ninja warrior specializing in karmic adjustment) and former DEA agent Hector Zuñiga, who calls Frenesi "a legendary observer-participant" from the 1960s and wants to "bring her up out of her mysterious years of underground existence" in order "to make a film about all those long-ago political wars, the drugs, the sex, the rock an' roll" (53). When *Vineland* begins, Ronald Reagan's budget cutting has caused Frenesi and Flash to be deleted from the rolls of the protected, making her fair game for Brock Vond, who has descended on Zoyd's house in Vineland County with an army of Justice Department types attempting to snatch Prairie and use her as bait.

Pynchon uses the mutual sexual obsession between Brock Vond and Frenesi Gates as an emblem for a startling suggestion: that the struggles of the 1960s were really a form of foreplay between the political Left and the political Right and that the conservative repressiveness of the Nixon and Reagan years was, in fact, the natural—even the desired—result of the radical expressiveness of the 1960s. "Brock Vond's genius," Pynchon tells us, "was to have seen in the activities of the sixties left not threats to order but unacknowledged desires for it" (269). Pynchon proceeds to formulate Brock's insight as a metaphor but cunningly includes a phrase that recalls Oedipa Maas's description of metaphor as "a thrust at truth and a lie, depending where you were: inside, safe, or outside, lost." Here, Pynchon writes: "While the Tube was proclaiming youth revolution against parents of all kinds and most viewers were accepting this story, Brock saw the deep—if he'd allowed himself to feel it, the sometimes touching—need to stay children forever, *safe inside* some national extended Family" (269; emphasis mine). Pynchon's phrasing suggests that Brock's insight is simply one way of viewing the 1960s, a fiction constructed to legitimate his authority and to appropriate the vision to which Zoyd still clings.

In retrospect, the seeds of Brock's ostensibly preposterous idea may well have been planted in *The Crying of Lot 49*, where Pynchon depicts Oedipa's obsessive search for the Tristero finally as a desire for order and significance at all costs, a desire above all to be "inside, safe" instead of "outside, lost." To be sure, Oedipa Maas is a self-professed Young Republican, although Metzger does mistake her for one of "these lib, overeducated broads with the soft heads and bleeding hearts" and then, once he has learned the truth about her political outlook, implies that it is nothing but a variation on the same crusading theme: " 'Hap Harrigan comics,' Metzger now [speaking] even louder, 'which she is hardly old enough to read, John Wayne on Saturday afternoon slaughtering ten thousand Japs with his teeth, this is Oedipa Maas's World War II, man. Some people today can drive VW's, carry a Sony radio in their shirt pocket. Not this one folks, she wants to right wrongs, 20 years after it's all over. Raise ghosts" (76). Oedipa Maas is a Republican who looks like a liberal; *Vineland*'s Frenesi Gates, however, is a radical who acts in cahoots with the Right in order to cuckold and otherwise betray the Left.

When Reaganomics brings an end to her days in the snitch community, Frenesi thinks to herself that it was "as if they'd been kept safe in some time-free zone all these years but now, at the unreadable whim of something in power, must reenter the clockwork of cause and effect" (90). Frenesi's "time-free" zone is like a parody of the sense of timelessness that seems to have characterized the radical Left during the 1960s. Zoyd and Mucho manage to recapture the feeling for just a moment:

> "Well I wish it was back then, when you were the Count. Remember how the acid was? Remember that windowpane, down in Laguna that time? God, I knew then, I knew...."
>
> They had a look. "Uh-huh, me too. That you were never going to die. Ha! No wonder the State panicked. How are they supposed to control a population that knows it'll never die? When that was always their last big chip, when they thought they had the power of life and death. But acid gave us the X-ray vision to see through that one, so of course they had to take it away from us." (313–14)

Once betrayed, this dream of eternal youth degenerates into parody, in the form of the "time-free zone" of the snitch underground or in the form of Thanatoia, a state between life and death that becomes the fate of Frenesi's betrayed and murdered lover, Weed Atman.

The Thanatoids serve as the agents of magical realism in the novel. One Thanatoid tells DL and her partner in the karmic adjustment business, Takeshi Fumimoto, that " 'Thanatoid' means 'like death, only different' " (170). Thanatoids are victims of "karmic imbalances—unanswered blows, unredeemed suffering, escapes by the guilty—anything that frustrated their daily expeditions on into the interior of Death." As a result, they have learned "to limit themselves . . . to emotions helpful in setting right whatever was keeping them from advancing further into the condition of death. Among these, the most common by far was resentment, constrained as Thanatoids were by history and by rules of imbalance and restoration to feel little else beyond their needs for revenge" (171). The Thanatoid village in Vineland County represents "a psychic jumping-off town—behind it, unrolling, regions unmapped, dwelt in by these transient souls in constant turnover, not living but persisting, on the skimpiest of hopes" (173). Neither ghosts nor the ghouls conjured up by George Romero's *Night of the Living Dead*, Thanatoids are instead a comic bunch, who eat junk food, watch television constantly, and find themselves plagued by credit problems (since all their property now belongs to their heirs).

With their addictions to junk food and television and their feelings of resentment, the Thanatoids are simply an extreme version of the ordinary person in the era of "Nixonian repression." According to Mucho, the state has found insidious ways to take away the empowering feeling of deathlessness: "They just let us forget. Give us too much to process, fill up every minute, keep us distracted, it's what the Tube is for, and though it kills me to say it, it's what rock and roll is becoming—just another way to claim our attention, so that beautiful certainty we had starts to fade, and after a while they have us convinced all over again that we really are going to die. And they've got us again" (314). Takeshi Fumimoto has a similar theory about television, "which with its history of picking away at the topic with doctor shows, war shows, cop shows, murder shows, had trivialized the Big D itself. If mediated lives, he figured, why not mediated deaths?" (218). The "deadish green eye of the TV tube" that appears on the first page of *The Crying of Lot 49* becomes omnipresent in the world of *Vineland*: not just the Thanatoids but everyone watches "the Tube," and some, like Hector Zuñiga, Zoyd's nemesis from the DEA, become so addicted that they end up in Tubal Detoxification programs run by the National Endowment for Video Education and Rehabilitation (NEVER).

In short, the world of *Vineland* seems to be yet another Pynchonian statist nightmare, continuous with the world of *Gravity's Rainbow*, but the presence of the Thanatoids signals the possibility of the restoration of karmic balance through retributive justice. During the large reunion of Frenesi's family that serves as the finale of the novel, the clan listens to the patriarch Jess Traverse give his

> annual reading of a passage from Emerson he'd found and memorized years ago, quoted in a jailhouse copy of *The Varieties of Religious Experience*, by William James. Frail as the fog of Vineland, in his carrying, pure voice, Jess reminded them, " 'Secret retributions are always restoring the level, when disturbed, of divine justice. It is impossible to tilt the beam. All the tyrants and proprietors and monopolists of the world in vain set their shoulders to heave the bar. Settles forever more the ponderous equator to its line, and man and mote, and star and sun, must range to it, or be pulverized by the recoil.' "

Jess supplements his reading from Emerson with a concrete, personal example of the existence of justice in the universe: " 'And if you don't believe Ralph Waldo Emerson,' added Jess, 'ask Crocker "Bud" Scantling,' the head of the Lumber Association whose life of impunity for arranging to drop the tree on Jess had ended abruptly down on 101 not far from here when he'd driven his week-old BMW into an oncoming chip truck at a combined speed of about 150. It'd been a few years now, but Jess still found it entertaining" (369). The novel affirms Jess's belief in retributive justice a few pages later, as Brock Vond is thwarted by his own side, his program canceled by Reagan just as he is on the verge of kidnapping Prairie. Turning renegade, Brock steals a helicopter, which crashes and leaves him in the hands of Vato and Blood, tow-truck drivers who also serve as the repository for the old myths of the Yurok tribe, which once lived in Vineland. The justice that awaits Brock is divine (although not necessarily Christian), as he is brought to the Ghosts' Trail and taken across the river to Tsorrek, the land of death.

Even the novel's most egregious accident is reinterpreted as part of a larger plan. DL Chastain met her partner Takeshi when she accidentally gave him the Vibrating Palm—one form of the Ninja Death Touch— thinking that he was Brock Vond. The head of the Sisterhood of Kunoichi Attentives, the order of Ninjettes to which DL belongs, manages to stave off Takeshi's death with the aid of a Puncutron Machine. As penance, DL must serve as Takeshi's assistant for a year with the provision that the two never become sexually intimate, an agreement that is rolled over each year when Takeshi and DL return to the Sisterhood for his Puncutron checkup. At the end of the novel, however, the ban on sex is lifted, and DL discovers that she's actually been crazy about Takeshi—a Japanese Robert Redford, according to her mother—for all these years. Sister Rochelle puts the whole story into perspective, claiming that DL's obsession with Brock Vond, "appearing like a cop cruiser in the dark sooner or later down every roadway her life took, had also been afflicting DL's spirit, acting as a major obstacle, this time around, to fulfilling her true karmic project," which turns out to be "the usual journey from point A to point B." And she suggests that perhaps Vond was, in fact, "never any destination at all, only the means of transport, maybe only some ticket, one the conductor even forgot to punch" (382). Sister Rochelle's version of DL and Takeshi's story thus describes a universe that is not only ordered and just but also hospitable to romantic love, another departure from the account offered by *The Crying of Lot 49*. DL and Takeshi's relationship begins with a sexual misadventure but develops over time through friendship and professional partnership, and it stands in stark contrast to the sexual obsession that links Brock Vond and Frenesi Gates.

Pynchon's depiction of this universe makes it clear that violence and death sometimes result from the pursuit of justice, redemption, and love, an insight embodied by the novel's final image: Prairie, sleeping alone in the clearing where she was almost abducted by Brock Vond and to which she returned hoping that he might come again (for reasons that remain ambiguous both to her and to us), finds herself awakened by "a warm and persistent tongue all over her face." It is not Brock, of course, but Desmond, her dog, missing for days, "the spit and image of his grandmother Chloe, roughened by the miles, face full of blue-jay feathers, smiling out of his eyes, wagging his tail, thinking he must be home" (385). Desmond, it seems, has gotten even with the blue jays, who, we remember from the opening pages of the novel, used to steal food from his dish, eventually developing "an attitude" that made them bold enough "to chase cars and pickups for miles down the road and bite anybody who didn't like it" (4). What goes around comes around, thematically and structurally, as the final image of the book returns us to its beginning.

This circularity is, however, a Pynchonian joke because, unlike *The Crying of Lot 49*, *Vineland* is an essentially teleological novel. The quote from Emerson is drawn from the late essay "The Sovereignty of Ethics" (1878), and as we saw in chapter 2, it is governed by the idea of liberal teleology: "The civil history of men might be traced by the successive meliorations as marked in higher moral generalizations;—virtue meaning physical courage, then chastity and temperance, then justice and love;—bargains of kings with peoples of certain rights to certain classes, then of rights to masses,—then at last came the day when, as the historians rightly tell, the nerves of the world were electrified by the proclamation that all men were born free and equal" (187). Toward the end of the essay, Emerson declares that "man does not live by bread alone, but by faith, by admiration, by sympathy," and he predicts that "America shall introduce a pure religion" (202–3).

Vineland demonstrates what this idea might look like in practice. The fact that Pynchon pointedly identifies the source of the passage from Emerson as William James's *The Varieties of Religious Experience* emphasizes the renewed prestige of religious feeling in this novel. In *The Crying of Lot 49*, Pynchon parodies sacred ritual with his invocation of Pentecostal imagery and the language of prophecy, but the characters in *Vineland* display a folksy religiosity that is never satirized. Zoyd and Mucho, for example, conclude their reminiscences by putting on some music: "Mucho went to the stereo and put on *The Best of Sam Cooke*, volumes 1 and 2, and then they sat together and listened, both of them this time, to the sermon, one they knew and felt their hearts comforted by, though outside spread the lampless wastes, the unseen paybacks, the heartless power of the scabland garrison state the green free America of their childhoods even then was turning into" (314). This lyrical and nostalgic evocation of a pastoral America provides a ringing conclusion to Mucho's brief appearance in the novel, and there is not an ironic note in the chord that it strikes.

The most telling index of the extent to which *Vineland* offers a revised vision of the nature of divinity is a passage in which Pynchon rewrites the "odd, religious instant" in which Oedipa Maas compares San Narciso to a printed circuit. Standing at the crest of a slope, Oedipa feels that "a revelation" is "trembl[ing] just past the threshold of her understanding" (1966, 24). The corresponding passage in *Vineland* is the one in which Frenesi Gates realizes that "Reaganomic ax blades" are about to cut off the "time-free zone" that she has occupied and force her to "reenter the clockwork of cause-and-effect." In contrast to Oedipa, Frenesi stands in the aisle of a supermarket and finds herself "entering a moment of undeniable clairvoyance, rare in her life but recognized." Frenesi thinks to herself that "someplace there would be a real ax, or something just as painful, Jasonic, blade-to-meat final—but at the distance she, Flash, and Justin had by now been brought to, it would all be done with keys on alpha numeric keyboards that stood for weightless, invisible chains of electronic presence or absence." Her train of thought leads her to consider the difference between the human and the divine:

> If patterns of ones and zeros were "like" patterns of human lives and deaths, if everything about an individual could be represented by a long string of ones and zeros, then what kind of creature would be represented by a long string of lives and deaths? It would have to be up one level at least—an angel, a minor god, something in a UFO. It would take eight human lives and deaths just to form one character in this being's name—a complete dossier might take up a considerable piece of the history of the world. We are digits in God's computer, she not so much thought as hummed to herself to a sort of standard gospel tune. And the only thing we're good for, to be dead or to be living, is the only thing He sees. What we cry, what we contend for, in our world of toil and blood, it all lies beneath the notice of the hacker we call God. (1990, 90–91)

In *The Crying of Lot 49*, technology has assumed a quasi-divine status, but in *Vineland*, it is pressed into the service of the divine, becoming the metaphor that enables human beings to begin to comprehend the nature of the higher order of divine reality.

Near the end of the novel, Sister Rochelle offers an alternative view of the relation between divinity and humanity, treating Takeshi to "another of her allegories, this time about Hell." She tells him, "When the Earth was still a paradise, long long ago, two great empires, Hell and Heaven, battled for its possession. Hell won and withdrew to an appropriate distance. Soon citizens of the Lower Realm were flocking up to visit Occupied Earth." But once "the novelty wore off, . . . the visitors began to realize that Earth was just like home, same traffic conditions, unpleasant food, deteriorating environment, and so forth." The tourist trade dropped off, the empire recalled its administrators and then its troops, and finally "all of the gateways to Hell were finally lost to sight, surviving only in local tales handed down the generations." The guilt associated with not being good enough for hell transformed these tales until, "over time, Hell became the storied place of sin and penitence." Thus, according to Sister Rochelle, human beings "forgot that its original promise was never punishment but reunion, with the true, long-forgotten metropolis of Earth Unredeemed"

(383–84). Behind Pynchon's reformulation of the relation between the human and the divine, we can find the promise of reunion and redemption, and this promise becomes the end point at which all the narrative lines of *Vineland* finally converge. *Vineland* marks the reinstatement of God in heaven and the return of the miraculous to Pynchon's world.

In Morrison's *Song of Solomon* (1987), the counterweight to the pathologies that arise from the possessive individualism pursued by Macon Dead the younger can be found in the link to folk history embodied by his sister, Pilate. Their naming is ironic, for it is Macon and not his sister who has washed his hands of his family history and his communal roots, embracing instead the dominant culture's narrative of individualism. In an analysis of Morrison's use of folklore in the novel, Joseph T. Skerrett Jr. argues that, "if Morrison's protagonists are always the 'single, separate persons' of American individualism, then the community from which they have become isolated and alienated is always the community of shared beliefs, practices, stories, and histories that is the folk heritage of Afro-Americans" (193). Morrison uses elements of magical realism to demonstrate that the worldview of the Enlightenment simply does not account for the experiences of African Americans. What is wrong with Enlightenment thinking for Morrison is not simply its link to "Scientific Racism" (1987b, 108): it is also limited by its failure to leave room for what Pynchon calls the "miraculous" (1984a, 40). Although Morrison's most overt depiction of the miraculous is found in her revisionist Gothic novel *Beloved*, she first experimented with magical realism in *Sula* (1973): her portrayal of Ajax, who woos Sula in part by letting "butterflies loose in the bedroom" (127), seems like a deliberate reference to García Márquez's *Cien Años de Soledad* (1967), and her account of Sula's death is a surreal moment that recalls the speech of the dead used powerfully by Juan Rulfo in *Pedro Páramo* (1955).[12] In her essay "Rootedness: The Ancestor as Foundation," Morrison describes *Song of Solomon* as an attempt to depict the simultaneous "acceptance of the supernatural and . . . profound rootedness in the real world" that is "indicative of the cosmology, the way in which Black people looked at the world." According to Morrison, "We are a very practical people, very down-to-earth, even shrewd people. But within that practicality we also accepted what I supposed could be called superstition and magic, which is another way of knowing things." Morrison's use of magical realism is, however, linked to her conception of the Enlightenment as the age of scientific racism because she portrays the marginalization of the magical as the direct result of the marginalization of nonwhite peoples: "Superstition and magic . . . [were] discredited only because Black people were discredited therefore what they *knew* was 'discredited'" (1984, 342).

"Milkman" Dead starts out as his father's son, setting off to find a bag of gold that he believes his aunt to have hidden, but he becomes his aunt's protégé instead, discovering that he is in fact engaged in a quest to recover his family's history. The key to this history turns out to be an old folktale about "flying African children." A long-lost relative named Susan Byrd tells Milkman, "Some of those Africans they brought over here as slaves could fly. A lot of them flew back to Africa"—including Milkman's great-grandfather, "Solomon," also known as "Shalimar." When Susan tells him that Solomon "flew off," Milkman believes that she is speaking metaphorically:

> "When you say 'flew off' you mean he ran away, don't you? Escaped?"
>
> "No, I mean flew. Oh, it's just foolishness, you know, but according to the story he wasn't running away. He was flying. He flew. You know, like a bird. Just stood up in the fields one day, ran up some hill, spun around a couple of times, and was lifted up in the air. Went right on back to wherever it was he came from. There's a big double-headed rock over the valley named for him. It like to killed the woman, the wife. I guess you could say 'wife.' Anyway she's supposed to have screamed out loud for days. And there's a ravine near here they call Ryna's Gulch, and sometimes you can hear this funny sound by it that the wind makes. People say it's the wife, Solomon's wife, crying. Her name was Ryna. They say she screamed and screamed, lost her mind completely. You don't hear about women like that anymore, but there used to be more—the kind of woman who couldn't live without a particular man. And when the man left, they lost their minds, or died or something." (1987, 322–23)

Susan Byrd doesn't believe that this kind of intense love really exists, but the novel does because it has already depicted it. Pilate's granddaughter, Hagar, who is not only Milkman's cousin but also his ex-lover, goes mad and then wastes away because Milkman has left her, and her death occurs in the chapter that directly precedes the one in which Milkman hears this story. And, at the very climax of the novel, Milkman will put his faith in the possibility that the first part of the story is true as well. Standing on the precipice where Solomon is said to have made his final leap, about to be assassinated by his friend Guitar, a terrorist who believes that he has been double-crossed, Milkman imitates his ancestor: "He could just make out Guitar's head and shoulders in the dark. 'You want my life' Milkman was not shouting now. 'You need it? Here.' Without wiping away the tears, taking a deep breath, or even bending his knees—he leaped. As fleet and bright as a lodestar he wheeled toward Guitar and it did not matter which one of them would give up his ghost in the killing arms of his brother. For now he knew what Shalimar knew: If you surrendered to the air, you could *ride it*" (337). These are the final words in the novel, and what they signify is the need to break out of existing paradigms of belief and action. Solomon could not simply "escape" from slavery, a fact proven by the attitudes of his grandson, Milkman's father. So he changes the rules and flies away: he thinks, not like a man of reason, but like a magical realist.

The ending of the novel offers a further critique of Enlightenment thinking. Guitar belongs to a revolutionary group called "The Seven Days," which assassinates a white person whenever a black person is killed, not to make a political point, but to keep things even: it is a matter, Guitar tells Milkman, of "Numbers. Balance. Ratio." Guitar believes that what distinguishes his group from either "the Mafia or the Klan" (158) is that it is "reasonable": "I am not, one, having fun; two, trying to gain power or public attention or money or land; three, angry at anybody." For Milkman, this logic is simply evidence that Guitar has become a copy of those whom he is fighting, "doing what the worst of them do" (157). And it is not the way to achieve social change: "None of that shit is going to change how I live or how any other Negro lives. What you're doing is crazy. And something else it's a habit. If you do it enough you can do it to anybody. . . . You can off me" (160–61), a statement that will prove prophetic. Guitar's response indicates how difficult it is to find an alternative to methodological individualism on which the dominant culture is based:

> "We don't off Negroes."
>
> "You hear what you said? *Negroes*. Not Milkman. Not 'No, I can't touch *you*, Milkman,' but 'We don't off Negroes.' Shit man, suppose you all change your parliamentary rules. (161)

Guitar thinks generically here, reducing Milkman to simply the representative of a type, the "Negro." Attempting to put things in a larger perspective that transcends mere individuals, Guitar loses respect for individuality and for the social bond of friendship.

Critics have read *Song of Solomon* as Milkman's struggle to move between two ideological points of view: between the patriarchal, possessive individualism of Macon Dead and the woman-centered, historically oriented communitarianism of Pilate (see, for example, Smith 1987). It is important, however, to remember that Guitar's group represents one way of negotiating between these alternatives: the Seven Days combine rugged masculinity and Enlightenment reason with a communal orientation. This combination reproduces many of the pathologies of the dominant culture that Guitar seeks to resist, and, when he murders Pilate, he also destroys the forms of community that she represents. Milkman represents a different alternative, a way of moving beyond possessive individualism without embracing an Enlightenment rationalism that has proven to be equally corrosive.

We find a similar configuration of characters and ideals at work in *Paradise* (1998), which presents two opposed communities: the town of Ruby, ruled over by the Morgan twins, who are cut from the same ideological cloth as Macon Dead; and the Convent, a woman-centered community that recalls Pilate's home. To the twins, Ruby is "the one all-black town worth the pain," a second-generation town built from the ashes of Haven, a "ghosttown" that had once been "a dreamtown in Oklahoma Territory" (5). Built in opposition both to the white culture and to the other black communities that once shunned its inhabitants, Ruby's communitarianism nevertheless organizes itself around conceptions of racial purity and patriarchal authority. When their experiment in isolationism begins to go awry, the town fathers use the Convent as a scapegoat: like Cholly Breedlove, they vent their frustration through misogynistic violence; like the inhabitants of the Bottom, they turn on women who (like Sula Peace) presume to think independently and who refuse to curb their sexuality. The activist Reverend Misner believes that, for the town father, "Booker T. solutions trumped Du Bois problems every time," but, in the end, the leaders of Ruby adopt a strategy that recalls neither Washington nor Du Bois but Malcolm X and the Seven Days. Their victims, however, are not powerful oppressors but "lively, free, unarmed females" (308).

The "official story" that is told "after the assault on the Convent women" comes in "two editions": "One, that nine men had gone to talk to and persuade the Convent women to leave or mend their ways; there had been a fight; the women took other shapes and disappeared into thin air. And two . . . that five men had gone to evict the women; that four others—the authors—had gone to restrain or stop them; these four were attacked by the women but had succeeded in driving them out, and they took off in their Cadillac; but unfortunately, some of the five had lost their heads and killed the old woman" (296–97). The problem is that, when the undertaker arrives to collect the dead, he finds "no bodies. Nothing. Even the Cadillac was gone" (292). And so Lone Dupres, who knows the truth (or, at least, the nearest thing to a true story that there can be), must watch as "people" changed the story "to make themselves look good": she cannot "prevent altered truth from taking hold in other quarters. If there were no victims the story of the crime was play for anybody's tongue. So Lone shut up and kept what she felt certain of folded in brain: God had given Ruby a second chance" (297). Billie Delia, who once sought refuge at the Convent, finds herself "hop[ing] for a miracle": "that the women were out there, darkly burnished, biding their time, brass-metaling their nails, filing their incisors—but out there" (308). Magical realism functions at the end of *Paradise* as a deus ex machina that paves the way—uneasily—for redemption. Like *Song of Solomon*, *Paradise* ends with a silent conflict that cannot be solved through rational discussion, only through the intervention of the miraculous.

Morrison's novels before *Paradise* suggest that African American communities have a special purchase on the kinds of "discredited" knowledge that magical realism is designed to express. In *Paradise*, however, magical realism grows out of the community of women living in the Convent, a mixed-race community in which the particular racial origins of its members are deliberately obscured by the novel, as if to say that race is present but comparatively insignificant. In this novel, communities that organize themselves around racial identity, whether white or black, produce a bad communitarianism that either perpetuates or replicates the oppressive structures of the dominant culture.

Using magical realism to deemphasize race brings Morrison closer to Pynchon's use of this form as a way of destabilizing our reliance on reason. For both writers, a story based on "numbers," "balance," and "ratio"—like the abstract philosophizing examined in the previous chapter—leaves out the "richer" view that Martha Nussbaum finds in the world of the novel. For Morrison and Pynchon, achieving that richer view requires more than simply the realism of the nineteenth-century novels that Nussbaum admires: it requires the magical realism that resurrects the women of the Convent, that thwarts Brock Vond, that enables the hyperrational Mason to have conversations with his dead wife. For both writers, the invocation of the miraculous is one way of constructing a counternarrative that reveals the limitations and indeed the oppressiveness of the Enlightenment rationalism that looms so large within Emersonian liberalism.

FOUR. Contemplating Community

In the last chapter, I explored some of the ways in which Pynchon's and Morrison's novels dramatize the flaws within the Enlightenment's conception of the individual. This critique of individuality aligns them with communitarian theorists who describe liberalism's conception of the individual as "untenable." Stephen Holmes notes that these theorists find liberalism "dissatisfying . . . because it fails to provide what we yearn for most: fraternity, solidarity, harmony, and most magically, *community*. Communitarians invest this word with redemptive significance. When we hear it, all our critical faculties are meant to fall asleep" (1993, 177). Holmes, however, points out that community may not be all that it is cracked up to be. "What the communitarian antiliberals forget," he argues, "is that society is a dangerous place in which to grow up. It is only through intense social interaction, for example, that human beings acquire their worst follies and fanaticisms: the capacity for intolerance or racism would never flourish in presocial isolation" (179). Even as they explore the limits of negative liberty and Emersonian self-reliance, the novels of Pynchon and Morrison also explore the ways in which failures of community and positive liberty can prove to be equally debilitating.

Both writers demonstrate that racism, one of the corrosive by-products of Western social life, can render the ideal of community useless as an antidote to the negative effects of the negative conception of freedom. Racism, however, is simply one manifestation of a larger cultural pathology, in which intolerance breeds narcissism, not just among individuals (as Christopher Lasch [1979] famously suggested), but among social groups. Many of Morrison's and Pynchon's characters long for community, but, as we shall see in this chapter, their novels vividly dramatize that all communities—and all communitarianisms—are not created equal.

The Bad Society

In *The Good Society* (1991), the follow-up to *Habits of the Heart*, Bellah et al. write that twentieth-century Americans "live through institutions," although they are loathe ever to admit it. Continuing the line of argumentation begun in their earlier study, Bellah et al. contend, "The individualistic assumptions of our culture lead us to believe that we can live as we choose, using the big institutions—the agencies of the state, the companies or organizations we work for, the schools we attend—for our own ends, without being fundamentally influenced by them" (19). Like Michael Sandel, they find Americans to be constrained by a conception of identity that seems to make no provision for a communally constituted self, that prevents them from fully understanding the role that institutions play in both their personal lives and the life of their country. According to Bellah et al., Americans tend to follow the classic liberal view that "institutions ought to be as far as possible neutral mechanisms for individuals to use to attain their separate ends," fearing "that institutions that are not properly limited and neutral may be oppressive. This belief leads us to think of institutions as efficient or inefficient mechanisms, like the Department of Motor Vehicles, that we learn to use for our own purposes, or as malevolent 'bureaucracies' that may crush us under their impersonal wheels" (10). The aim of *The Good Society* is to make the dynamics of institutional life more comprehensible and more acceptable to its readers, to give them a sense that they can bring about institutional change. The alternative, to imagine institutions as "autonomous systems operating according to their own mysterious internal logic, to be fine-tuned only by experts," is, in their view, "to opt for some kind of modern gnosticism that sees the world as controlled by the powers of darkness." Such a view "encourages us to look only to our private survival" (15).

Pynchon's first three novels vividly dramatize what it means to see the word in this way. The "exitlessness," "the absence of surprise to life," that Oedipa Maas laments in *The Crying of Lot 49* is the sign of a coercive culture that enforces conformity by draining its subjects of their individuality and transforming modern life into a series of empty rituals. Bellah et al. argue that it is important for individuals to be able to see "that the work each of us does is something we do *together* and *for each* other as much as by and for ourselves.... Doing work that is challenging and cooperative seems to fulfill a deep human need" (1991, 105). This conception of work is all but impossible in the worlds of Pynchon's early novels. As we saw in the previous chapter, Oedipa Maas's husband, Mucho, confronts the steady erosion of individuality within modern U.S. culture every day that he works as a used-car salesman, watching his customers trade in "motorized, metal extensions of themselves." What he calls "the endless rituals of trade-in" come to symbolize for him the futility of everyday life. He finds himself unable "to accept the way each owner, each shadow, filed in only to exchange a dented, malfunctioning version of himself for another, just as futureless, automotive projection of somebody else's life" (1996, 14).

Mucho's job, however, does not simply make him aware of the erosion of the individuality of others; it also poses a direct threat to his own individuality, as he struggles to prevent himself from being swallowed up by a cultural stereotype that he cannot control:

> For a couple years he'd been a used car salesman and so hyperaware of what *that* profession had come to mean that working hours were exquisite torture to him. Mucho shaved his upper lip every morning three times with, three times against the grain, to remove any remotest breath of a moustache, new blades he drew blood invariably but kept at it; bought all natural-shoulder suits, then went to a tailor to have the lapels made yet more abnormally narrow, on his hair used only water, combing it like Jack Lemmon to throw them further off. (12–13)

Communitarian theorists often argue that individualism prevents people from understanding the extent to which their identities are constituted by social relations such as work. To identify with one's work is enabling if that work seems meaningful and challenging, but what if one's work means nothing? Mucho's nights are plagued by a recurrent nightmare: "It was only that sign in the lot, that's what scared me. In the dream I'd be going about a normal day's business and suddenly, with no warning, there'd be the sign. We were a member of the National Automobile Dealer's Association. N.A.D.A. Just this creaking metal sign that said, nada, nada, against the blue sky. I used to wake up hollering" (144). Not only does Mucho's job mean nothing, but it also confers on him a stereotyped identity—the used-car salesman—that threatens to overwhelm all other aspects of his identity. The combination of his customers' "rituals of trade-in" and his own struggles with the stereotyped image of the used-car salesman leads Mucho to see all individuals as interchangeable, a vision that brings him to the brink of nihilism. Mucho seems to be on the verge of becoming the abstract individual that serves as the basis for individualist philosophy, and he finds it intolerable.

The ending of *The Courier's Tragedy*, in which "about the only character left alive in a stage dense with corpses is the colorless administrator, Gennaro" (75), serves as an emblem for another way in which individuality is crushed by the modern culture of work. Pynchon vividly dramatizes the view that bureaucracies are "malevolent" entities that "may crush us under their impersonal wheels" (Bellah et al. 1991, 10). Administrators and bureaucrats stifle the creativity of men like the inventor Stanley Koteks:

> In school they got brainwashed, like all of us, into believing the Myth of the American Inventor—Morse and his telegraph, Bell and his telephone, Edison and his light bulb. Only one man per invention. Then when they grew up they found they had to sign over all their rights to a monster like Yoyodyne; got stuck on some "project" or "task force" or "team" and started being ground into anonymity. Nobody wanted them to invent—only perform their little role in a design ritual, already set down for them in some procedures handbook. (88)

The corporations that employ these inventors stress the value of "teamwork," but for Koteks "teamwork" is nothing but "a way to avoid responsibility . . . a symptom of the gutlessness of the whole society" (85). Readers of *V.* will recognize Yoyodyne Corporation as the company for which Kurt Mondaugen is working when Herbert Stencil encounters him. Yoyodyne had been the tiny Chiclitz Toy Company, until its founder, Bloody Chiclitz, learned from a group of schoolchildren that gyroscopes are not only toys but also crucial pieces of equipment for ships, airplanes, and missiles. Chiclitz renames the rapidly growing company after an engineer tells him that "dyne" is a unit of force: "To symbolize the humble beginnings of the Chiclitz empire and to get the idea of force, enterprise, engineering skills and rugged individualism in there too, Chiclitz christened the company Yoyodyne." Now a large corporation with "more government contracts than it really knew what to do with" (1963, 227), Yoyodyne follows the prototypical evolutionary pattern of a business within a culture of corporate capitalism: begun by an individual entrepreneur, it soon grows into a large entrenched bureaucracy that is hostile to individual initiative and inventiveness. The only way to maintain your individuality in the face of such pressure to conform is to drop out of the system and become a "nut" like John Nefastis—or Mucho Mass.

Late in *The Crying of Lot 49*, Oedipa finds that Mucho has taken to using hallucinogenic drugs supplied by her psychiatrist, Dr. Hilarius, whose experiments are designed to enable their subjects to find "the bridge inward" (17). Mucho has undergone a transformation: once the interchangeable, abstract, Rawlsian individual, he seems to have become the Emersonian democratic individual that George Kateb describes—or, rather, a proleptic parody of Kateb's democratic individual. The drugs cure Mucho's nightmares and give him what appears (to him) to be both amplified sensory awareness and heightened communal sensitivity: he explains to Oedipa that he takes the drugs because "you hear and see things, even smell them, taste like you never could. Because the world is so abundant. No end to it, baby. You're an antenna, sending your pattern out across a million lives a night, and they're your lives too" (143–44).

Mucho has become a parody of the narrator of Walt Whitman's "Song of Myself," who declares, "I am large . . . I contain multitudes" (1855 version, line 1316). His boss complains that Mucho "enters a staff meeting and the room is suddenly full of people, you know? He's a walking assembly of man" (140). The narrator of "Song of Myself" begins as a narcissist who figuratively makes love to himself:

> I believe in you my soul . . . the other I am must not abase itself to you,
> And you must not be abased to the other.
>
> Loafe with me on the grass . . . loose the stop from your throat
> Not words, not music or rhyme I want . . . not custom or lecture, not even the best,
> Only the lull I like, the hum of your valved voice.
>
> I mind how we lay in June, such a transparent morning;
> You settled your head athwart my hips and gently turned over upon me,
> And parted the shirt from my bosom-bone, and plunged your tongue to my barestript heart,
> And reached till you felt my beard, and reached till you held my feet.
>   (lines 73–81)

For Whitman's narrator, this experience turns out to be a revelation of connectedness; in the next stanza, Whitman writes:

> Swiftly arose and spread around me the peace and joy and knowledge
> that pass all the art and argument of the earth;
> And I know that the hand of God is the elderhand of my own,
> And I know that the spirit of God is the eldest brother of my own,
> And that all the men ever born are also my brothers. . . . and the
> women my sisters and lovers. (lines 82–85)

Mucho's hallucinogenic drugs give him a "vision of consensus" that approximates the Whitmanian experience: " 'Whenever I put the headset on now,' he'd continued, 'I really do understand what I find there. When those kids sing "She loves you" yeah well, you know, she does, she's any number of people, all over the world, back through time, different colors, sizes, ages, shapes, distances from death, but she loves. And the "you" is everybody. And herself. Oedipa, the human voice, you know, it's a flipping miracle' " (143). From Oedipa's point of view, however, Mucho's connectedness is a sham: "My husband, on LSD, gropes like a child further and further into the rooms and endless rooms of the elaborate candy house of himself" (153). Nor does Mucho's self-exploration confer the benefits of Emersonian self-reliance that Kateb might predict. Instead of developing his individuality in order to become a "whole man" like Emerson's American Scholar, Mucho "is losing his identity," according to Funch, becoming "less himself and more generic" (140). Neither representative like the Emersonian self nor truly expansive like the Whitmanian self, Mucho remains a stripped-down, abstract, Rawlsian self—an all-too-common least common denominator. Mucho's narcissistic ontological state becomes a version of the alienation that communitarian thinkers predict.

A culture that breeds narcissism undermines the foundations of such important forms of connectedness as friendship, romantic love, marriage, and family life. Oedipa realizes that she has lost Mucho, that, as he ventures further and further into "the candy house of himself," he is moving "away, hopelessly away, from what has passed, I was hoping forever, for love" (153). The culture's hostility toward romantic love is embodied in the novel by the Inamorati Anonymous (IA), a society of self-described "isolates" whose belief that love is "the worst addiction of all" serves as an ironic parody of Oedipa's professed self-reliance. "The whole idea is to get where you don't need it," says one member of the IA. "I was lucky. I kicked it young. But there are sixty-year-old men, believe it or not, and women even older, who wake up in the night screaming" (112–13). Inamorati Anonymous was founded by a corporate executive who found himself first "automated out of a job" and then betrayed by his wife. The erosion of romantic love represents the erosion of the foundation on which marriage bonds are built, leading to the breakdown of domesticity and family life. Oedipa and Mucho are childless, and, in the second chapter, we learn that Mucho is in trouble with his boss at the radio station for failing to create an acceptable on-air persona: instead of sounding "a young father" or a "big brother," Mucho, it seems, comes across as "horny." Later, we learn that he has a penchant for picking up seventeen-year-olds at record hops. Oedipa's lover, Metzger, also turns out to be "one of these Humbert Humbert cats" (147) when he runs off with a fifteen-year-old. Even when it is not torn apart by such sexual proclivities, family life seems to involve a comic contentiousness, exemplified by the slapstick scene of family strife that Oedipa encounters when she visits the Bortz household: "Maxine's in bed," says one of the Bortz children at the door. "She threw one of Daddy's beer bottles at Charles and it went through the window and Mama spanked her good. If she was mine I'd drown her" (150). The happiest family depicted in the novel seems to be the family of resistance fighters depicted in Metzger's film—Baby Igor, his father, and their dog—and they *do* drown.

In short, there are no happy familial relations in *The Crying of Lot 49*, and the novel suggests in passing that children are not untouched by the pervasive atmosphere of conspiracy.[1] During her night of wandering in San Francisco, Oedipa finds a group of children who bear an uncomfortable resemblance to the outcasts who communicate via the W.A.S.T.E. system:

> In Golden Gate Park she came on a circle of children in their nightclothes, who told her they were dreaming the gathering. But that the dream was really no different from being awake, because in the mornings when they got up they felt tired, as if they'd been up most of the night. When their mothers thought they were out playing they were really curled in cupboards of neighbors' houses, in platforms up in trees, in secretly hollowed nests inside hedges, sleeping, making up for these hours. The night was empty of all terror for them, they had inside their circle an imaginary fire, and needed nothing but their own unpenetrated sense of community. They knew about the post horn. (118)

To achieve the "unpenetrated sense of community" that renders them self-sufficient, these children must create an alternative to family life, if necessary by defining themselves negatively against the world of adulthood. Ironically, Oedipa's search for the Tristero has made her look like a parent. Grace Bortz is surprised to find that Oedipa does not have any children: "There's a certain harassed style . . . you get to recognize. I thought only kids caused it. I guess not" (150). This comparison between the effects of child-rearing and the effects of the Tristero is a small point, one of the novel's in-jokes, but it does reinforce the idea that the same forces that deform individuality are also deforming another element in the official story of individualism—the family.

Far more typical than the "unpenetrated sense of community" that the children in the park achieve is the strategy for survival that preserves groups like the Inamorati Anonymous, the ultra-right-wing Peter Pinguid Society, the ultra-left-wing Conjuración de los Insurgentes Anarquistas, and the inventors' underground. Regarding themselves as collections of individuals, such groups define themselves against a social structure that threatens individuality. *The Crying of Lot 49* dramatizes the fruition of Tocqueville's warnings about the valorization of individualism. What Oedipa finds as she digs into the mystery of the Tristero is a version of the withdrawal from public life that Tocqueville foresaw as the result of unchecked individualism. Tocqueville described individualism as "a calm and considered feeling which disposes each citizen to isolate himself from the mass of his fellows and withdraw into the circle of his family and friends; with this little society formed to his taste, he gladly leaves the greater society to look after himself" (1959, 506). What Oedipa finds looks similar: "For here were God knew how many citizens, deliberately choosing not to communicate by U.S. Mail. It was not an act of treason, not possibly even of defiance. But it was a calculated withdrawal, from the life of the Republic, from its machinery. Whatever else was being denied them out of hate, indifference to the power of their vote, loopholes, simple ignorance, this withdrawal was their own, unpublicized, private" (124). Tocqueville claimed that, although "individualism at first only dams the spring of public virtues, . . . in the long run it attacks and destroys all the others too and finally merges in egoism." Democracy and equality exacerbate individualism because they encourage citizens to "form the habit of thinking of themselves in isolation and imagine that their whole destiny is in their own hands." As a result, Tocqueville argued, "each man is forever thrown back on himself alone, and there is danger that he may be shut up in the solitude of his own heart" (1969, 506–8)—a fate that envelops not only each member of the Inamorati Anonymous but also Mucho Maas and perhaps even Oedipa herself.

There is, however, a crucial difference between the scenario that Tocqueville imagined and the world that Pynchon depicts, for while Tocqueville regarded this destructive atomization of society as the natural result of individualism, Pynchon portrays this withdrawal from the life of the Republic as a last-ditch effort to prevent the destruction of individualism and the consequent loss of individuality, family, and community. To succeed, such an effort requires a viable system of communication to prevent this "private withdrawal" from degenerating into solipsism. The novel, however, consistently dramatizes the failure of even simple and ordinary forms of communication, suggesting the impossibility of creating viable forms of community. Oedipa finds herself unable to talk to Mucho about certain things: contemplating his affairs with underage girls, and remembering that at seventeen she had been "ready to laugh at almost anything," she finds herself "overcome," not by hostility, but by "a tenderness she'd never go quite to the back of lest she get bogged. It kept her from asking him any more questions. Like all their inabilities to communicate, this too had a virtuous motive" (46). Oedipa's conversations with Pierce were marked by his apparently constant vocal impersonations, and her seduction by (or of) Metzger is a slapstick comedy in which she falls "asleep once or twice," finally awakening "to find herself getting laid; she'd come in on a sexual crescendo in progress, like a cut to a scene where the camera's already moving" (42). When Metzger runs off with a nymphet, he leaves her a note in which there is "no word to recall that Oedipa and Metzger had ever been more than co-executors" (148). The failure to communicate extends even to those underground movements that attempt to circumvent the established channels of communication. The members of the Peter Pinguid Society use the Yoyodyne interoffice mail less to communicate with one another than to perform symbolic acts of resistance to the government's postal monopoly; the letters that they send one another are virtually empty of content: "*Dear Mike, it said, how are you? Just thought I'd drop you a note. How's your book coming? Guess that's all for now. See you at The Scope*" (53). And the W.A.S.T.E. system itself is haphazard and unreliable, its messages ambiguous. Oedipa notices that Jesús Arrabal has in his possession "an ancient rolled copy of the anarcho-syndicalist paper *Regeneración*":

> The date was 1904 and there was no stamp next to the cancellation, only the handstruck image of the post horn.
> "They arrive," said Arrabal. "Have they been in the mails that long? Has my name been substituted for that of a member who's died? Has

it really taken sixty years? Is it a reprint? Idle questions, I am a foot-soldier. The higher levels have their reasons." (121)

"Communication is the key" (105), says John Nefastis, describing the mechanism of his Nefastis Machine, which serves only to reinforce the dubious status of communication in the novel: Oedipa can find no proof that its operations are anything but hallucination.

In a world in which the process of signification is breaking down everywhere, in which nothing—not God, not nature, not society, not the self—has any stable meaning, the only way to be "inside, safe" and thus simulate the benefits of community is to pick your own metaphor and your own paranoia. This strategy is validated by the language of the novel, which elevates paranoid narcissism into a literary style. Paranoia operates like metaphor: both processes create connections between seemingly unrelated phenomena. Pynchon's paranoid style revolves around wit, not simply because it is full of puns and jokes, but rather because it depicts, as well as deploys, Johnson's definition of wit as a "*discordia concors;* a combination of dissimilar images, or discovery of occult resemblances in things apparently unlike" (348). Wit, which Johnson also described as the violent yoking together of heterogeneous ideas, becomes the essential narrative principle behind *The Crying of Lot 49*. Pynchon often uses this technique to indicate the collision of cultures, highbrow into lowbrow, traditional into contemporary. Sometimes he employs similes that would have made Chandler proud: remembering her relationship with Inverarity, Oedipa recalls that "she had noticed the absence of an intensity, as if watching a movie just perceptibly out of focus, that the projectionist refused to fix" (29). At other times, he creates metaphors, such as the "printed circuit" (8) or "the mainliner L. A." (26), that are startlingly apt. At still other times, however, he includes idiosyncratic details that fracture narrative decorum or upset the flow of the prose: in the midst of an elaborate comparison of Oedipa's situation to that of Rapunzel, Pynchon writes: "When it turned out to be Pierce she'd happily pulled out the pins and curlers and down it tumbled in its whispering, dainty avalanche, only when Pierce had got maybe halfway up, her lovely hair turned, through some sinister sorcery, into a great unanchored wig, and down he fell, on his ass. But dauntless, perhaps using one of his many credit cards for a shim, he'd slipped the lock on her tower door and come up the conchlike stairs, which, had true guile come more naturally to him, he'd have done to begin with" (20). The indecorousness of "the pins and curlers," the vulgarity of the word *ass*, and the incongruity of Pierce's use of his credit card all serve not only to update but also to mock the story of Rapunzel. Pynchon's use of detail in this passage creates comedy but also maintains the reader's uncertainty about which details are significant and which extraneous, thereby establishing an analogy between the reader's experience of the text and Oedipa's experience of her reality.

But this yoking together of heterogeneous ideas is more than simply a narrative technique: it is also the only hope—however faint—for the attainment of meaning and truth in the novel. The process is given a variety of different names in the novel—*revelation, miracle, coincidence, hallucination, paranoia, entropy, metaphor*—each of which implies a different relation between cause and effect. Several of these names are brought into contact with one another through the Nefastis Machine, which links together "two distinct kinds" of entropy, one "having to do with heat-engines, the other having to do with communication." Oedipa learns that the "equation for one, back in the '30s, looked a lot like the equation for the other. It was a coincidence. The two fields were entirely unconnected, except at one point: Maxwell's Demon." Seeking to make Oedipa understand the meaning of all this, Nefastis finally says, "Entropy is a figure of speech, then, . . . a metaphor. It connects the world of thermodynamics to the world of information flow. The Machine uses both. The Demon makes the metaphor not only verbally graceful, but also objectively true" (106). In other words, what begins as "coincidence" is then expressed by a "metaphor" that is then literalized into reality—at least for Nefastis and his followers.

Oedipa has another name for this phenomenon—*hallucination*—but behind her dismissal of Nefastis lies disappointment. She calls Nefastis's beliefs hallucinations, then immediately thinks to herself, "How wonderful they might be to share. For fifteen minutes more she tried; repeating, if you are there, whatever you are, show yourself to me, I need you to show yourself" (107). The experience with Nefastis indicates that Oedipa still believes that she can draw a line between hallucination and true revelation, but later, when she encounters the old sailor, she finds that the lines separating the concepts *hallucination, revelation,* and *metaphor* are not so easily drawn:

> She knew then, because she held him, that he suffered DT's. Behind the initials was a metaphor, a delirium tremens, a trembling unfurrowing of the mind's plowshare. The saint whose water can light lamps, the clairvoyant whose lapse in recall is the breath of God, the

> true paranoid for whom all is organized in spheres joyful or threatening about the central pulse of himself, the dreamer whose puns probe ancient fetid shafts and tunnels of truth all act in the same special relevance to the word, or whatever it is the word is there, buffering, to protect us from. The act of metaphor then was a thrust at truth and a lie, depending on where you were: inside, safe, or outside lost. (128–29)

Metaphor yokes together not only dissimilar images but also "truth" and "lie." By substituting one concept for another, metaphor creates statements that are literally false (Los Angeles is a city, not a drug addict) but that capture an aspect of truth that is lost in ordinary description. In addition, as Oedipa recognizes at the end of this passage, metaphor functions as a litmus test for membership in a particular interpretive community: if you understand it, then you are "inside, safe"; if not, "outside, lost."

The Crying of Lot 49 thus debunks the official narrative of individualism by revealing narcissism in place of individuality and paranoia in answer to Emerson's call for self-reliance. In such a culture, communication is constantly thwarted, family bonds are ineffectual, and communities and institutions become threatening. Pynchon's novel confirms the communitarian diagnosis of the ills of individualism, but it also dramatizes the hopeless inadequacy of the communitarian prescription for social healing.

The View from the Bottom

Critics of individualism often point to African American communities as examples of alternative formulations of the relation between individual and community. For example, in The New Individualists (1991), Paul Leinberger and Bruce Tucker argue that, in a number of American subcultures, "the indigenous psychology of self is more fluid, more inclusive, and recognizes that the self exists as part of various social networks, rather than as an independent entity somehow apart," and they find models of this "more ensembled individualism" both "in much African-American culture and in the culture of many American women" (35). As a theoretical analogue to this view, critical legal theorists like Peter Gabel seek to move away from a discourse about rights to a discourse about need, away from a negative and toward a positive conception of liberty. But Patricia Williams finds that Gabel's "language of circumstantially defined need, of informality, of solidarity, overcoming distance, sounded dangerously like the language of oppression to someone like me who was looking for freedom through the establishment of identity, the formulation of an autonomous social self" (1991, 148).

Creating such an autonomous social self is the dream of most of Morrison's characters as well, and more than simply white culture stands in the way of its realization: sometimes family and community, rather than supporting and empowering the self, stand in the way of its fulfillment. Morrison's first novel, *The Bluest Eye*, depicts a young girl's descent into madness as a result of pathological familial relations; in *Sula*, she explores this theme more fully, adding a dramatization of communal will into the mix. *Sula* depicts a neighborhood that is both an African American community and a woman's subculture, and it shares with Pynchon's early novels a skepticism about the viability of communitarian modes of social organization.

Sula explores the narrative of individualism from the standpoint of African American women. Although the first major character presented to us in the opening pages of *Sula* is Shadrack, a black man who served in World War I, men remain at the periphery of the narrative, unable or unwilling to serve as responsible husbands and fathers. The novel registers the fact that black men face a difficult situation in America, but it has little sympathy or time to spare for that subject because its primary interest is in the far more difficult situation faced by black women, who not only are abandoned by their husbands and fathers but also suffer from two types of repression—racism and sexism. Despite its title, the novel investigates the subject position of the African American woman, not by using a restricted narrative point of view, or even by concentrating on a single protagonist, but instead by focusing on the friendship of two women and the history of the community in which they were raised, a black neighborhood called the Bottom, which lies in the hills on the outskirts of the small Ohio town of Medallion. Nel Wright and Sula Peace "were two throats and one eye" (1973, 147), but they choose divergent paths: Nel marries and immerses herself in the life of the Bottom; Sula, however, leaves for ten years, going to college, then wandering rootless from city to city, and finally returning to the Bottom, where she soon becomes an outcast, perceived as a threat to the community's traditional practices and mores.

In addition, the novel presents other strong female characters while relegating its men to social and narrative obscurity. These dominating women are all mothers who, despite their divergent ideas about marriage and heterosexual relationships, serve as the backbone of their community. *Sula* becomes an account of the history of this matriarchal community from its legendary origins to its final dissolution; the novel opens with a prologue set in the present, but its subsequent chapters take us into the past, each bearing the label of the year in which its events take place. Morrison thus explores the dynamics of a community forced by the contingencies of race to define itself, and its ideas of family and male-female relationships, against the grain of the official narrative of U.S. individualism. And, in the process, the novel presents a startling discovery: that such a community must occasionally receive a challenge—a jolt of energy—from the self-reliant, Emersonian individual.

The abrogation of familial responsibilities by the Bottom's black men forces the community to become a matriarchy in order to survive. The first dominating matriarch to whom we are introduced in Sula is Nel's mother, Helene Wright. Born the daughter of a Creole whore, Helene's life is regulated by her desire to achieve and then maintain respectability and social position. Even more formidable is Sula's grandmother, Eva Peace, "the creator and sovereign" (30) of the enormous house at No. 7 Carpenter's Road, who, as a young abandoned wife, decided to find a solution to her poverty, disappearing for eighteen months, returning to the Bottom "with two crutches, a new black pocketbook, and one leg"—and enough money to build the house on Carpenter's Road. As the years pass, Eva becomes a figure of legend in the community, and strange tales circulate about the loss of her leg:

> Unless Eva herself introduced the subject, no one ever spoke of her disability; they pretended to ignore it, unless, in some mood of fancy, she began some fearful story about it—generally to entertain children. How the leg got up by itself one day and walked on off. How she hobbled after it but it ran too fast. Or how she had a corn on her toe and it just grew and grew and grew until her whole foot was a corn and then it traveled on up her leg and wouldn't stop growing until she put a red rag at the top but by that time it was already at her knee.
>
> Somebody said Eva stuck it under a train and made them pay off. Another said she sold it to a hospital for $10,000—at which Mr. Reed opened his eyes and asked, "Nigger gal legs goin' for $10,000 a *piece*?" as though he could understand $10,000 a *pair*—but for *one*? (pp. 30–31)

Eva's actions outstrip those of her biblical namesake: with no Adam in sight, Eva makes some sort of shady bargain that enables her, not only to provide for her family, but also to prosper.[2] She appropriates Adam's privilege of naming, not only bestowing nicknames that stick with her children and her white boarder (whom she labels *Tar Baby*) but also naming the three orphans whom she adopts in a way that puts limits on the development of their identities: she calls each one *dewey* (with a lowercase d), and, despite the fact that they have different heights and skin colors, they come to seem undifferentiated and interchangeable, not only to others but also to themselves.

Eva's authoritative manner reinforces her mythic stature. Treating her many "gentlemen callers" as equals, Eva "test[s] and argue[s] with her men, leaving them feeling as though they had been in combat with a worthy, if amiable, foe" (42–43). As a mother she is far from conventional, allowing her children to grow up "stealthily," under her "distant eye, and prey to her idiosyncrasies" (41). Seemingly fearless, she is willing to sacrifice not only her leg but her life for her children: seeing Hannah burning to death in the field next to the house, Eva jumps, without a fear or a second thought, out of her second-story window and then attempts to crawl toward her daughter in a vain attempt to put out the flames. A true matriarch, she concerns herself with the perpetuation of her community, boarding newlywed couples in her rambling house and offering them advice, although it is advice that makes it clear that Eva supports a conventional concept of marital relations and regrets the ineffectiveness of the patriarchal order:

> With other people's affairs Eva was equally prejudiced about men. She fussed interminably with the brides of the newly wed couples for not getting their men's supper ready on time; about how to launder shirts, press them, etc. "Yo' man be here direct'lin. Ain't it 'bout time you got busy?"
>
> "Aw, Miss Eva. It'll be ready. We just having spaghetti."
>
> "Again?" Eva's eyebrows fluted up and the newlywed pressed her lips together in shame. (42)

Eva wants her men to act like men, a desire that leads to her most shocking and arrogant act: the execution of her only son, who is hopelessly addicted to heroin. Holding him in her arms, she lets "her memory spin, loop and fall" and cries. Then she douses him with kerosene and sets him on fire. A year later, Eva tells Hannah that she killed Plum because "he wanted to crawl back" into her womb: "I would have done it, would have let him if I'd've had the room but a big man can't be a baby all wrapped up inside his mamma no more; he suffocate. I done everything I could to make him leave me and go on and live and be a man but he wouldn't and I had to keep him out so I just thought of a way he could die like a man not all scrunched up inside my womb, but like a man" (72). Eva gives life, and she takes it. She is punished for her presumption, as Hannah burns to death very shortly after Eva explains her reasons for killing Plum, forcing Eva to "smell the familiar odor of cooked flesh" (77) and to contemplate "the perfection of the judgment against her" (78). But, like Faulkner's Dilsey, Eva endures: she outlives the Bottom, and, at ninety years old, despite the onset of senility, she can still steer Nel into the heartbreaking moment of self-understanding that concludes the novel.

Eva's attitudes about marriage and masculinity reinforce the impression that the Bottom is a matriarchy by default, its men disempowered less by their women or their community than by the white-dominated culture around them that refuses to accord them the dignity promised by individualism. The erosion of patriarchy is thus, not a sign of greater equality and social progress, but rather a sign of the Bottom's exclusion from the dominant ideology of American culture. The potential social gains made possible by the erosion of patriarchy in the Bottom are offset by the fact that those who live in the neighborhood suffer from constant racial oppression. The Bottom's identity as a community is defined negatively, through contrast with the white community that lives in the valley below. As we have already seen, the very name *Bottom*, which comes from what the narrator calls "a nigger joke" (6), symbolizes the basic injustice on which the community was founded, namely, the dispossession of African Americans.

For most of the novel, the black community's attitude toward this fundamental inequality is simply a tacit and docile acceptance of the fact that they represent "the Bottom" of the hierarchy of order that is heaven and earth. After the funeral of Chicken Little, a young boy who is accidentally drowned while playing with Sula and Nel, the narrator describes the community's feelings of grief: "When they thought of all that life and death locked into that little closed coffin they danced and screamed, not to protest God's will but to acknowledge and confirm once more their conviction that the only way to avoid the Hand of God is to get in it" (65–66). Evil is considered to be a natural and unavoidable part of the order of things:

> In their world, aberrations were as much a part of nature as grace. It was not for them to expel or annihilate it. They would no more run Sula out of town than they would kill the robins that brought her back, for in their secret awareness of Him, He was not the God of three faces they sang about. They knew quite well that He had four, and that the fourth explained Sula. They had lived with various forms of evil all

their days, and it wasn't that they believed God would take care of them. It was rather that they knew God had a brother and that brother hadn't spared God's son, so why should he spare them? (117–18)

The black community's acceptance of adversity and affliction recalls the sufferings of Job:

> What was taken by outsiders to be slackness, slovenliness or even generosity was in fact a full recognition of the legitimacy of forces other than good ones. They did not believe doctors could heal—for them, none ever had done so. They did not believe that death was accidental—life might be, but death was deliberate. They did not believe Nature was ever askew—only inconvenient. Plague and drought were as "natural" as springtime.... The purpose of evil was to survive it and they determined (without ever knowing they had made up their minds to do it) to survive floods, white people, tuberculosis, famine and ignorance. (90)

The people of the Bottom believe in the ordered nature of the universe, but this passage indicates that they have come to classify socially generated phenomena such as the priority of "white people" and the existence of "ignorance" along with such natural afflictions as floods, tuberculosis, and famine. The behavior of white people becomes for the Bottom simply a part of the evil of the universe, which cannot be solved through violence: "There was no creature so ungodly as to make them destroy it. They could kill easily if provoked to anger, but not by design, which explained why they could not 'mob kill' anyone. To do so was not only unnatural, it was undignified. The presence of evil was something to be first recognized, then dealt with, survived, outwitted, triumphed over" (118). This reference to the practice of lynching suggests that the violence with which white culture treats blacks is evidence of the moral inferiority of whites. In contrast, the blacks behave with a dignity that attests to their moral superiority and more highly civilized nature: "They knew anger well but not despair, and they didn't stone sinners for the same reason they didn't commit suicide—it was beneath them" (90). The final irony of the "nigger joke" is the fact that "every day" the black folks "could literally look down on the white folks" (5) in a reversal of typical black-white relations, but the novel suggests that, in the universe of morals at least, the Bottom believes in the superiority of its position.

Such an affirmation of moral superiority does not, however, dispose of the troubling suggestion that the community's pacifist approach to the problem of evil may result in a passive acceptance of the repression generated by white society. To see white people as an affliction akin to famine and flood is to naturalize humanly generated evil and to buy into white culture's use of the Bible to rationalize its scorn of blacks. The bargeman who discovers the body of the drowned Chicken Little thinks to himself, "When . . . will those people ever be anything but animals, fit for nothing but substitutes for mules, only mules didn't kill each other the way niggers did," and he finds himself "bemused by God's curse and the terrible burden his own kind had of elevating Ham's sons" (63). Helene Wright's religious fervor carries weight only within her own community; it cannot protect her from the scorn of a white person, even one as low on the social ladder as a railroad conductor. Implicit in the "nigger joke" is the suggestion that whites have manipulated Christian teaching in order to rationalize the inequality of institutional arrangements: it is, after all, the master's invocation of God's sight that proves to be the convincing piece of his argument to the slave.

The communal practices and social structures of the Bottom arise in reaction to white culture but not in opposition to it. It is matriarchal, but most of its matriarchs lament the passing of the patriarchs. Despite the continuing, residual prestige of superstitious belief, the Bottom is nonetheless a community that values a Christian conception of order inherited from the dominant culture. The Bottom is not therefore an alternative culture in Raymond Williams's sense of the term: it is simply an impoverished version of the dominant culture, the culture of the white American.[3] The novel suggests that to radicalize the Bottom into an oppositional culture requires the agency of an individual who can challenge the community's ossified structures.

The novel presents two such figures, self-reliant, unencumbered selves who represent a challenge both to the Bottom and to American culture. One of them is Shadrack, a man drafted and then discarded by the dominant culture. Each year, on the third day of January, he leads the celebration of "National Suicide Day." Shadrack hopes to allay the fear generated by the unexpectedness of death by devoting one day a year to it so that "everybody could get it out of the way and the rest of the year would be safe and free." On "the first, or Charter, National Suicide Day in 1920," Shadrack "walked through the Bottom down Carpenter's Road with a cowbell and a hangman's rope calling the people together. Telling them that this was their only chance to kill themselves or each other" (14–15). The town is frightened:

"They knew Shadrack was crazy but that did not mean that he didn't have any sense, or, even more important, that he had no power." During the rest of the year, Shadrack is generally "drunk, loud, obscene, funny and outrageous," but he respects the inviolability of the individual: "He never touched anybody, never fought, never caressed." The people of the Bottom come to accept Shadrack, once they understand "the boundaries and nature of his madness," because they can "fit him . . . into the scheme of things." Shadrack's holiday is "absorbed . . . into their thoughts, into their languages, into their lives," and it becomes a part of the public discourse of the Bottom, a point of reference used even in a sermon by the Reverend Deal (15–16). What Shadrack's holiday expresses is an extreme version of the desire for order that is a defining characteristic of the Bottom's communal life. Moreover, his madness stands as an emblem of white oppression: like all of them, Shadrack is a victim. Shadrack's madness thus momentarily unsettles the order of life in the Bottom, but, ultimately, it reinforces the neighborhood's ingrained sense of its identity. For most of the novel, Shadrack stands as a symbol of futility rather than protest.

It is Sula Peace who offers the most serious challenge to the communal ways of the Bottom. When she returns to the neighborhood, she bears all the hallmarks of the Emersonian self. Emerson's call for nonconformity, his disdain for that "foolish consistency" that hobbles "little minds," and his celebration of process all manifest themselves in what the narrator calls Sula's "experimental life" (118). Emerson declares, "I would write on the lintels of the door-post, Whim. I hope it is somewhat better than whim at last, but we cannot spend the day in explanation" ("Self-Reliance"; 1836, 262). Discovering both that "a lover was not a comrade and could never be—for a woman" and that no woman "would ever be that version of herself which she sought to reach out to and touch with an ungloved hand," Sula finds that she can turn to no one but herself: "There was only her own mood and whim, and if that was all there was, she decided to turn the naked hand toward it, discover it and let others become as intimate with their own selves as she was" (121; emphasis added).

The fact that she is a woman makes her enactment of the precepts of Emersonianism a challenge to Emerson himself, who rarely explicitly includes women in his descriptions of self-reliance. If Sula's demand for equal access to self-reliance represents a challenge to Emersonianism to live up to its own logic, to the Bottom it represents a stark defiance of the community's traditions. The Bottom breeds strong women, but it breeds them to fill a particular role, that of mother. Almost as soon as Sula walks in the door of No. 7 Carpenter's Road, her grandmother Eva tells her to get married, but Sula proclaims, "I don't want to make somebody else. I want to make myself" (92). In the Bottom, such ambitions are the prerogative of men only: women cannot be rootless. Nel tells Sula, "You *can't* do it all. You a woman and a colored woman at that. You can't act like a man. You can't be walking around all independent-like, doing whatever you like, taking what you want, leaving what you don't." Sula tells Nel that she is repeating herself by calling her "a woman and colored. Ain't that the same as being a man?" Women in the Bottom (and, by implication, in all black communities) have assumed the man's role as the head of the household. Nel replies, "I don't think so and you wouldn't either if you had children," to which Sula retorts, "Then I really would act like what you call a man. Every man I ever knew left his children" (142). Sula's experience of family life as conducted by Eva and Hannah Peace has left her with nothing but scorn for the institution.

To Eva, Sula's desire to concentrate on making herself instead of babies is simply "selfish," for Eva believes that a woman "got no business floatin' around without no man" (92)—at least not by choice. Eva and Hannah were women without men, but only because their husbands either left or died. Sula decides to go Eva and Hannah one better, by *choosing* to explore to the fullest the benefits of that manless independence: "Eva's arrogance and Hannah's self-indulgence merged in her and, with a twist that was all her own imagination, she lived out her days exploring her own thoughts and emotions, giving them full reign, feeling no obligation to please anybody unless their pleasure pleased her" (118). Nel tells Sula that men are "worth keeping," but Sula replies, "They ain't worth more than me." Sula sleeps with Nel's husband, Jude, simply because "there was some space in front of me, behind me, in my head. Some space. And Jude filled it up. That's all. He just filled up the space" (144). Sula expects to be able to share Jude with Nel as they "had always shared the affection of other people: compared how a boy kissed, what line he used with one and then the other." She realizes too late that marriage has changed Nel and set limits on what is acceptable within the bounds of friendship: "Having had no intimate knowledge of marriage, having lived in a house with women who thought all men available, and selected from among them with a care only for their tastes, [Sula] was ill prepared for the possessiveness of the one person she felt close to." Like her mother, Sula has sexual intercourse with many of the men in the Bottom, but, unlike Hannah, Sula displays no generosity or affection to her lovers: "the fury she created in the women of the town was incredible—for she would lay their husbands once and then no more. Hannah had been a nuisance, but she was complimenting the women, in a way, by wanting their husbands. Sula was trying them out and discarding them without any excuse the men could swallow. So the women, to justify their own judgment, cherished their men more, soothed the pride and vanity Sula had bruised" (115). For Sula, casual sex is not an opportunity to commune with a fellow human being or even enjoy physical pleasure; it is instead an opportunity to commune with herself: rarely able to remember the name of a man she has just slept with, Sula cannot wait for him "to turn away and settle into a wet skim of satisfaction and light disgust" so that she can enjoy "the postcoital privateness in which she met herself, welcomed herself, and joined herself in matchless harmony" (123). Sex allows Sula not only to reaffirm her belief that men "ain't worth more than me" but also to assert her superiority: these men, whose names she does not even remember, expose their vanity and ignorance to Sula in the act of making love to her.

Sula's conscious decision to concentrate on making herself is an affront not only to Eva but also to the community as a whole because it represents a "scorn for the role" of motherhood (153), a role that is crucial to the Bottom's communal life. Sula has equal disdain for the role of the obedient offspring who cares for her elders. Her decision to put her grandmother into a rest home is a blatant rejection of the Bottom's traditions, and it initiates Sula's transformation into a pariah. Sula's behavior recalls the question that Emerson claims to have asked "a valued advisor": "What have I to do with the sacredness of tradition if I live wholly from within?" When warned by his older friend that his "impulses may be from below," Emerson claims to have replied, "They do not seem to me to be such; but if I am the Devil's child, I will live then from the Devil" ("Self-Reliance"; 1836, 262). Sula conducts a similar conversation with Eva:

> "Don't talk to me about no burning. You watched your own mamma. You crazy roach! You the one should have been burnt!"
> "But I ain't. Got that? I ain't. Any more fires in this house, I'm lighting them!"
> "Hellfire don't need lighting and it's already burning in you...."
> "Whatever's burning in me is mine!"
> "Amen!"
> "And I'll split this town in two and everything in it before I'll let you put it out." (93)

Determined to preserve her individuality, Sula enacts a brutal version of Emerson's declaration in "Self-Reliance" "I shun father and mother and wife and brother, when my genius calls me" (1836, 262). Sula's rejection of her grandmother is her second act of shunning: the first occurred years earlier when Sula watched "her own mamma burn up" without lifting a finger to help (78), still bitter from the experience of overhearing Hannah say to a friend, "I love Sula. I just don't like her" (57). Her mother's words had "taught her there was no other that you could count on," a lesson reinforced by Nel's behavior over the years: by Nel's inability to understand Sula's self-mutilation, her decision to get married, and, most crucially, her refusal to "get over" the fact that Sula slept with Jude.[4]

As a child, Nel seemingly aspired to the state of self-reliance that Sula would eventually achieve. Horrified by her mother's humiliatingly cheerful acceptance of the white conductor's scorn, Nel returns home from New Orleans and makes a discovery: "'I'm me,' she whispered. 'Me.'" This sudden encounter with the fact of her individuality is immediately linked to a shunning of father and mother: "'I'm me. I'm not their daughter. I'm not Nel. I'm me. Me.'" Momentarily assuming the right to rename herself, she experiences a feeling of empowerment:

> Each time she said the word *me* there was a gathering in her like power, like joy, like fear. Back in bed with her discovery, she stared out the window at the dark leaves of the horse chestnut.
> "Me," she murmured. And then, sinking deeper into the quilts, "I want . . . I want to be . . . wonderful. Oh, Jesus, make me wonderful." (28–29)

Nel's final prayer already indicates the loss of her empowerment: relying on "Jesus" to make her "wonderful," Nel thus diminishes her ability to be self-reliant. The narrator immediately tells us, "It was the last as well as the first time she was ever to leave Medallion." The trip does give Nel "the strength to cultivate a friend in spite of her mother"—Sula, on whose mother Helene Wright frowns (29). But, as time passes, Jesus will indeed transform Nel, through the agency of the devout Helene, who succeeds in her project of driving "her daughter's imagination underground" (18). Later in the novel, Sula will think to herself, "Now Nel was one of them" (119).

The novel suggests, in fact, that Nel and Sula are similar but crucially different even in childhood. Before they met, Nel and Sula were both "solitary little girls whose loneliness was so profound it intoxicated them and sent them stumbling into Technicolored visions that always included a presence, a someone, who, quite like the dreamer, shared the delight of the dream" (51). Their dreams are versions of the familiar story of the knight in shining armor, which becomes for Morrison (as for Pynchon) a parable about individualism. Rather than reversing the signification of the story as Pynchon does in sending Oedipa Maas the captive maiden out on a quest, Morrison splits the roles between her two female protagonists. Nel imagines herself as the maiden waiting for the knight:

> When Nel, an only child, sat on the steps of her back porch surrounded by the high silence of her mother's incredibly orderly house, feeling the neatness pointing at her back, she studied the poplars and fell easily into a picture of herself lying on a flowered bed, tangled in her own hair, waiting for some fiery prince. He approached but never quite arrived. But always, watching the dream along with her, were some smiling sympathetic eyes. Someone as interested as she herself in the flow of her imagined hair, the thickness of the mattress of flowers, the voile sleeves that closed below her elbows in gold-threaded cuffs. (51)

Nel's dream includes both a knight and a companion, and like the novel itself, the passage ultimately proves to be about her relationship with the companion rather than with the knight. In the dream, Nel appears as a passive, receptive figure, stereotypically female. Despite the fact that Morrison introduces Sula's dream by stressing its similarity to Nel's, the dream is rather different, placing Sula in the position of the knight on horseback: "Similarly, Sula, also an only child, but wedged into a household of throbbing disorder constantly awry with things, people, voices and the slamming of doors, spent hours in the attic behind a roll of linoleum galloping through her own mind on a gray-and-white horse tasting sugar and smelling roses in full view of someone who shared both the taste and the speed" (51–52). Like Oedipa, Sula assumes the role of the questing rider, but, in contrast to both Oedipa and Nel, she never figures herself as the captive maiden. Indeed, there is no captive maiden in her dream, as the triangular situation of Nel's dream collapses into a single relationship between adventurous individuals. The fact that Sula is "galloping through her own mind" further reinforces the idea of her confident self-reliance.

On her deathbed, Sula chastises Nel with words that echo those that Nel used as a child to express her sense of self-discovery. Sula may be dying, but she believes that Nel and "every colored woman in this country" are dying, too: "Just like me. But the difference is they dying like a stump. Me, I'm going down like one of those redwoods. I sure did live in this world." When Nel asks her what she has to show for it, Sula replies, "Show? To who? Girl, I got my mind. And what goes on in it. Which is to say, I got me" (143). Sula remains a nonconformist to the very end and dies believing that she has preserved her individuality.

The Emersonian ethos does not, however, represent a panacea for Morrison or even a viable conception of the self. As much as Sula resembles a self-reliant Emersonian, she lacks a crucial ingredient, which proves, ironically, to be a sense of self. Morrison identifies two crucial, formative moments in Sula's life: the discovery that her mother loves but does not like her and the accidental drowning of Chicken Little, for which Sula feels responsible. "The first experience taught her there was no other that you could count on; the second that there was no self to count on either." As a result, Sula "had no center, no speck around which to grow." Her behavior seems to embody Emerson's belief that "a foolish consistency is the hobgoblin of little minds," but it grows out of a very un-Emersonian lack of self-esteem: "She was completely free of ambition, with no affection for money, property or things, no greed, no desire to command attention or compliments—no ego. For that reason she felt no compulsion to verify herself—be consistent with herself" (119). What looks like boldness in Sula may instead be a form of desperation. Seeking to protect Nel from four white hooligans, Sula performs an act of self-mutilation:

> Her aim was determined but inaccurate. She slashed off only the tip of her finger. The four boys stared open-mouthed at the wound and the scrap of flesh, like a button mushroom, curling in the cherry blood that ran into the corners of the slate.
>
> Sula raised her eyes to them. Her voice was quiet. "If I can do that to myself, what you suppose I'll do to you?" (55)

Years later, when Sula remembers this act on her deathbed, her thoughts indicate that it is Nel and not herself whom she considers to be strong and self-reliant: "Nel, she remembered, always thrived on a crisis. The closed place in the water; Hannah's funeral. Nel was the best. When Sula imitated her, or tried to, those long years ago, it always ended up in some action noteworthy not for its coolness but mostly for its being bizarre. The one time she tried to protect Nel, she had cut off her own finger tip and earned not Nel's gratitude but her disgust. From then on she had let her emotions dictate her behavior" (141).

Despite her self-reliant facade, Sula seems occasionally to yearn for a form of self-fulfillment that depends on relationships with others. Her brief affair with Ajax gives her a taste of the kind of lover's possessiveness that she once blamed Nel for feeling. This possessiveness is a communally instilled feeling that is at odds with self-reliance: what attracts Ajax to Sula originally is that she seems to be the "only other woman he knew" (aside from his mother) "whose life was her own, who could deal with life efficiently, and who was not interested in nailing him" (127); when he discovers signs of Sula's growing attachment to him, he realizes that she will ultimately become like "all of her sisters before her" (133) and leaves her soon afterward. These moments, when the underside of Sula's self-reliance bursts into the open, occur only in private. Sula's public face consistently displays arrogance and independence, and, even after she thinks to herself that "Nel was the best," she cannot keep herself from putting on this brash, self-reliant face and arguing with Nel shortly thereafter. Yet, in the moment after the death of her body, Sula's spirit thinks about Nel: " 'Well, I'll be damned,' she thought, 'it didn't even hurt. Wait'll I tell Nel' " (149).

The novel suggests that a complete individual must be a synthesis of Nel, who seeks her identity within the bonds of community, and Sula, who seeks it within herself—a synthesis, in other words, of what communitarian theorists refer to as *unencumbered* and *situated* selves. This lesson is lost on the inhabitants of the Bottom, who can find no redeeming features in Sula's challenge to their ways.[5]

What the Bottom fails to realize, however, is that Sula's presence has served as a catalyst for the renewal of the community's familial and communal bonds: "Their conviction of Sula's evil changed them in accountable yet mysterious ways. Once the source of their personal misfortune was identified, they had leave to protect and love one another. They began to cherish their husbands and wives, protect their children, repair their homes and in general band together against the devil in their midst" (117–18). Sula's death removes this reinvigorating challenge to the community, which soon reverts to its old ways:

> The tension was gone and so was the reason for the effort they made. Without her mockery, affection for others sank into flaccid disrepair. Daughters who had complained bitterly about the responsibilities of taking care of their aged mothers-in-law had altered when Sula locked Eva away, and they began cleaning those old women's spittoons with-

out a murmur. Now that Sula was dead and done with, they returned to a steeping resentment of the burdens of old people. Wives uncoddled their husbands, there seemed no further need to reinforce their vanity. And even those Negroes who had moved down from Canada to Medallion, who remarked every chance they got that they had never been slaves, felt a loosening of the reactionary compassion for Southern-born blacks that Sula had inspired in them. They returned to their original claims of superiority. (154)

Unaware of the extent to which Sula's presence had generated harmony and consensus in their community, the women and men of the Bottom expect to see the dawning of "a brighter day" (151). Instead, a freezing rain covers the entire neighborhood with ice, killing crops and causing sickness. Spiritually and materially, the Bottom sinks further and further into poverty and depression. For the first time since its charter celebration, the sense of protest behind National Suicide Day is renewed, and a parade of Bottom dwellers follow Shadrack to the river, acting "as though there really was hope. The same hope that kept them picking beans for other farmers; kept them from finally leaving as they talked of doing; kept them knee-deep in other people's dirt; kept them excited about other people's wars; kept them solicitous of white people's children; kept them convinced that some magic 'government' was going to lift them up, out and away from that dirt, those beans, those wars" (160). Such hope, dependent as it is on the good will of the powerful, is nothing but a form of self-deception that keeps the Bottom where it is—at the bottom of society. Sula set herself against this deadening form of hope, which, with her death, turns deadly. As we have already seen, Shadrack's followers vent their rage on the uncompleted tunnel that has come to symbolize their exclusion from economic hope; their act of protest is ineffectual and self-destructive. National Suicide Day, predictably enough, is a suicide day only for the Bottom.

Sula depicts the powerfully formative roles that family, community, and cultural context play in the making of an individual. Oppressed by racism, sexism, and a poverty perpetuated by inequality of opportunity, African American communities like the Bottom are transformed into poor copies of the dominant culture. Social injustice sets individuality into a contentious and oppositional relation to family and community, and as a result, each of these vital aspects of social life—individuality, family, and community—begins to decay. In the Bottom, respect for tradition is translated into simple conformity, which becomes as deadening in Morrison's work as it is in Emerson's. Conformity transforms the bonds of family and community into empty rituals without content; it conceives of individuality merely as a threat to communal stability rather than as a potential source of communal renewal. As a result, the Bottom can only demonize Sula, without ever recognizing that she offers the community a chance to revivify its traditions and ensure its survival.

From San Narciso to Vineland

The fact that *Vineland* marked a departure from the pessimism of its predecessors did not go unnoticed by its first reviewers. Edward Mendelson argued in the *New Republic* that *Vineland* represents a change in both narrative style and conceptual framework. Calling the style of *Vineland* "less flashy" than that of *Gravity's Rainbow*, Mendelson claimed that the new novel's "style is more densely integrated with its emotions and less hesitant to speak in the voices of feeling" (42). Pynchon, it seems, has taken his own advice: in the introduction to his collection of early stories, *Slow Learner* (1984), he claimed that his early work had ignored the fact that the fiction "that moved and pleased me . . . was precisely that which had been made luminous, undeniably authentic by having been found and taken up, always at cost, from deeper and more shared levels of the life we all really live" (1984b, 21). Mendelson argued that the depiction of "the relations between parents and children in the book, relations often tangential to the main plot, intermittently make *Vineland* 'luminous, undeniably authentic' and give it a warmth that the intellectual exoticism of his earlier work excluded" (1990, 42). With the stylistic thaw comes a conceptual warming, an increasing optimism about American culture and about individualism. Writing in the *New York Times Book Review*, Salman Rushdie, a writer whose work continually advances strong critiques of authoritarian politics, called *Vineland* a "major political novel about what America has been doing to itself, to its children, all these many years." Rushdie claimed that *Vineland* contains "something new to report" on the Pynchon front, "some faint possibility of redemption, some fleeting hints of happiness and grace," which grow out of the novel's suggestion that "community," "individuality," and "family" might serve as "counterweight[s] to power." According to Rushdie, community, individuality, and family "are the values the Nixon-Reagan era stole from the 60's and warped, aiming them back at America as weapons of control. They are values that *Vineland* seeks to recapture, by remembering what they meant before the dirt got thrown all over them" (1990, 36–37).⁶ The mordant poststructuralist critique of individualism implicit in the earlier novels is replaced in *Vineland* by a more optimistic communitarian critique that accounts for the novel's stylistic differences from its predecessors.⁷

Vineland is Pynchon's most openly political novel. In the introduction to *The Vineland Papers* (1994), the first collection of critical essays devoted to the novel, Geoffrey Green noted that, "previously, when Pynchon had addressed paranoid visions of political activity, the locale had been either generally or historically defined: readers were able to approach Pynchon's vision as a fictional one—even as the fiction emphasized themes that epitomized our own deepest fears and dreams. But *Vineland* was set in 1984, in Reagan's America: in a time and place familiar to readers and about which most readers had particular political views" (Green, Greiner, and McCaffery, ix). In the eleven years that had elapsed since the publication of *Gravity's Rainbow* in 1983, a shift had occurred in American politics, from the atmosphere of mistrust that followed the Nixon presidency, to the so-called malaise of the Carter administration, to the "Morning in America" optimism of the Reagan years. Aptly enough, the year 1984 marked the height of Reagan-era optimism.

What had been described as a "culture of narcissism" during the Carter years was redescribed during the Reagan era as a culture of "individualism." Christopher Lasch's best-seller *The Culture of Narcissism* (1979) argued that "the logic of individualism" had degenerated into "the extreme of a war of all against all, the pursuit of happiness to the dead end of a narcissistic preoccupation with the self" (21): individualism, according to Lasch, was destroying America's sense of community. In Reagan's rhetoric, however, individualism became the source of community in America. Where Lasch described a Lockean culture become Hobbesian, Reagan's rhetoric described a Lockean culture with communitarian characteristics. Michael Sandel wrote in 1988 that "Reagan's genius" was "to bring together in a single voice two contending strands in American conservatism. The first is individualistic, libertarian, and laissez-faire, the second communal, traditionalist and Moral Majoritarian." In keeping with his communitarian point of view and his hostility toward individualism, Sandel claimed that, "for all of Reagan's talk of individual liberty and market solutions, the most potent part of his appeal was his evocation of communal values—of family and neighborhood, religion and patriotism" (1988, 21). Sandel, however, had gotten it backward: what was potent about Reagan's discourse was its ability to incorporate potentially oppositional communal ideals into its description of individualism. Reagan's rhetoric did not simply juxtapose individualist and communitarian values: it deployed a teleology that began with individualism but always ended with family, community, and nation.

In other words, Reagan's rhetoric offered up Emersonian liberalism in its simplest and most compelling form. In his first inaugural address, Reagan claimed that Americans had "prospered as no other people on earth" because they had "unleashed the energy and individual genius of man to a greater extent than has ever been done before. Freedom and the dignity of the individual have been more available and assured here than in any other place on earth" (1989, 64–65). At the Republican Party convention in 1984, Reagan described "the dream conceived by our Founding Fathers" as the achievement of "the ultimate in individual freedom consistent with an orderly society" (1989, 212–13), and his rhetoric sought to identify his party's platform with the pursuit of that dream: "America is presented with the clearest political choice of half a century. . . . The choices this year are not just between two different personalities, or between two political parties. They are between two different visions of the future, two fundamentally different ways of governing—their government of pessimism, fear and limits, or ours of hope, confidence, and growth. Their government sees people only as members of groups. Ours serves all the people of America as individuals" (1989, 200–201). This rhetoric equates seeing people as "members of groups" with "pessimism, fear and limits." Individualism, on the other hand, embodies "hope, confidence, and growth."

Reagan had become an almost mythic figure for many Americans, the self-styled embodiment of a tradition of rugged individualism who was nevertheless also perceived as a kind of grandfather to the nation, usually jovial, occasionally stern, a patriarch who told stories about good and evil that always ended with an unambiguous moral.[8] Garry Wills would write three years later that Reagan "believes the individualist myths that help him to play his communal role. He is the sincerest claimant to a heritage that never existed, a perfect blend of an authentic America he grew up in and of that America's own fables about its past" (1987, 94). The success of Reagan's deployment of the national narrative of individualism baffled many academics, including those who convened at the conference "Reconstructing Individualism" at Stanford University in early 1984. In the introduction to the volume collecting papers from the conference, the editors found themselves compelled to admit that, "in America, the post-structuralist critique of individuality has had only a feeble impact on the persistently individualist imagery of our institutions and popular culture. In the political, economic, and artistic spheres of public life, these images have remained unshaken by the theoretical trauma that has led to the subtleties of post-structuralist theory" (Heller and Wellbery, 12–13). Emphasizing the failure of poststructuralism to undermine the ideological persuasiveness of individualism, Heller and Wellbery set themselves the task of "reflecting anew on the status of the individual in our contemporary world" in order to begin the process of discovering "an alternative conceptualization of the experience of subjectivity, enriched by the chastening experiences of the last century" (2). The new direction that Pynchon takes in *Vineland* marks, I think, a similar attempt to reflect anew.

Frenesi's affair with Brock Vond represents the betrayal of, not one, but two oppositional traditions: leftist radicalism and matriarchal feminism. Pynchon uses Frenesi's genealogy to set the radicalism of the 1960s into a much longer American tradition. Her grandfather Jess Traverse was a "heroic Wobbly" who dedicated his life to organizing loggers in the area around Vineland; his wife, the former Eula Becker, "liked to say in later years" that he had introduced her to her conscience. Together, they shared the "dream of One Big Union," of "the commonwealth of toil that is to be," which entailed "getting used to an idea of 'together' that included at least one of them being in jail in any given year." After Jess was crippled by an "accident" prearranged by one Crocker "Bud" Scantling on behalf of the Vineland Employers' Association, their daughter Sasha left home to find work as an organizer, eventually marrying a gaffer named Hubbell Gates and becoming deeply involved in the politics of leftist Hollywood during the McCarthy era. In this family, it is the women—Eula and Sasha—who prove to be the most enduring. Jess is crippled by the tree that crushes his legs during a local baseball game, and the accident enables Eula to arrive "at last at the condition of cold, perfected fury she had been growing into, as she now understood, all these years." Eula finds herself remembering "the first time she was shot at, by Pinkertons in a camp up along the Mad River, more clearly than the birth of her first child, who was Sasha" (76). The fact that both Eula and Sasha have undergone the experience of being shot at by "vigilante squads and hired goons" forms an integral part of the mother-daughter bond (77).

Sasha's daughter, Frenesi, finds herself unable to continue either tradition because of her fatal attraction for Brock Vond, but Zoyd proves himself to be an admirable replacement. What is ultimately at stake in the rivalry between Brock Vond and Zoyd Wheeler is a battle between two forms of communitarianism: one coercive, majoritarian, and bad; the other voluntary, pluralist, and good. Unlike Pynchon's earlier novels, in which bad karma and disorder run unchecked, *Vineland* reinstates the idea of an ordered universe through its emphasis on the possibility of beneficent forms of community.

Although the novel seems to be building toward Frenesi's reunion with Prairie, Pynchon leaves the moment in which they meet understated, even anticlimactic, subsumed in the more generalized reunion of an extended family so large it seems more like a community:

> The girl followed them to a beer and soda cooler beneath an oak tree, where they would sit and hang out for hours, spinning and catching strands of memory, perilously reconnecting—as all around them the profusion of aunts, uncles, cousins, and cousins' kids and so on, themselves each with a story weirder than the last, creatively improved over the years, came and went, waving corncobs in the air, dribbling soda on their shirts, swaying or dancing to the music of Billy Barf and the Vomitones, while the fragrance of barbecue smoke came drifting down from the pits where Traverse and Becker men stood in a line, a dozen of them, in matching white chef's hats, behind fires smoking with dripped fat, tending great cuts of beef executed by assault rifle and chain-sawed on the spot in some raid off a steep pasture between here and Montana, beside some moonless dirt road, dressed out, wrapped ready for fire. A squad of kids stood by with squirt bottles full of secret marinades and sauces, which they shot from time to time as the meat went turning, and the magical coatings clung, flowed, fell, smoked, rose, seared. (368–69)

This detailed description of the preparation and subsequent sharing of food suggests a primitive and ritualistic affirmation of communal bonds. Unlike the various rituals of *The Crying of Lot 49*, which are depicted as threats to individuality, the Traverse-Becker reunions nurture both communal bonds and individual identity. The meal forms "the heart of this gathering meant to honor the bond between Eula Becker and Jess Traverse, that lay beneath, defined, and made sense of them all, distributed from Marin to Seattle, Coos Bay to downtown Butte, choker setters and choppers, dynamiters of fish, shingle weavers and street-corner spellbinders, old and beaten at, young and brand-new" (369). In a revision of the biblical figuration of the descendants of Jesse, this family tree, which rises and spreads its branches at the end of *Vineland*, grows out of the bond between Jess and

Eula. It thus serves as a testament to the nurturing powers of both romantic love and marriage. The bond "that makes sense of them all," however, is, not only the bond of marriage, but also a shared "indenture to an idea" (76), a commitment to an alternative, communitarian idea of America. Eula, Jess, and most of their progeny are examples of situated selves, whose individual identities are formed by work, social commitment, and family life. The fierce family loyalty of the Traverses and the Beckers provides an alternative to the authoritarian, patriarchal idea of a "national family" that Brock Vond and Ronald Reagan seek to impose. Vond's and Reagan's national family represents a form of bad communitarianism because it seeks to crush rather than nurture individuality and to do so in the name of preserving individual freedom.

Pynchon's use of the name *Vineland* suggests the possibility of an alternate, non-Columbian, non-Puritan genealogy for America because it is an echo of *Vinland*, the name that Leif Erikson gave to the continent. True to its description in an 1851 survey map, Vineland proves to be "A Harbor of Refuge to Vessels that may have suffered on their way North from the strong headwinds that prevail along this coast from May to October" (316). Although the still lovelorn Zoyd came with Prairie to Vineland hoping that one day Frenesi might show up at one of the reunions, as time passes he discovers that his life has meaning because of his relationship with his daughter: "After a while Zoyd was allowed into the Traverse-Becker annual reunions, as long as he brought Prairie, who at about the age of three or four got sick one Vineland winter, and looked up at him with dull hot eyes, snot crusted on her face, hair in a snarl, and croaked, 'Dad? Am I ever gonna get bett-or?' pronouncing it like Mr. Spock, and he had his belated moment of welcome to the planet Earth, in which he knew, dismayingly, that he would, would have to, do anything to keep this dear small life from harm" (321). As Zoyd watches Prairie's face become more and more like those of her relatives at the Traverse-Becker reunions, he begins to "understand that this had been the place to bring her and himself after all," realizing that "he must have chosen right for a change, that time they'd come through the slides and storms to put in here, to harbor in Vineland, Vineland the Good" (pp. 321–22).

Pynchon, however, recognizes the precariousness of the haven that is Vineland, and the novel makes it clear that the battle to lay claim to the values of individuality, family, and community (not to mention idealism, justice, and truth) is far from over. In the time that Zoyd and Prairie have lived there, Vineland has been discovered not only by "idealistic flower children looking to live in harmony with the Earth" but also by the Tube (in the form of cable television companies) and by real estate developers who will one day transform the area into "a Eureka–Crescent City–Vineland megalopolis" (317). For now, however, it is a haven that protects Zoyd and Prairie from Brock Vond, although just barely: Brock manages to decimate Zoyd's house and misses getting his hands on Prairie by inches. Even more disturbing is the fact that Prairie almost succumbs to the Vond mystique, returning to the clearing where he almost snatched her to call into the night, "You can come back.... It's OK, rilly. Come on, come in. I don't care. Take me anyplace you want" (384). But Vond is gone for good, and Pynchon has already provided us with the barest of glimpses into a future in which Zoyd and Prairie are still a loving father-daughter combo (374–75).

In *The Crying of Lot 49*, Pynchon turned a pessimistic eye on the official narrative of U.S. individualism, demonstrating the different ways in which it is attacked by a modern culture that transforms individualism into paranoia and individuality into narcissism, thereby eroding the viability of both family and community. In *Vineland*, however, Pynchon offers a different kind of critique of individualism, finding renewed hope in the communitarian belief that familial and communal bonds play a constituting role in the formation of individual identity. *Vineland* seeks to wrest the ideals of family and community away from the Reaganite political rhetoric that links them to individualism. It proposes an alternative vision of America: vital, chaotic, and nurturing, if not exactly idealized (lots of entropy and still too much Tube). Pynchon suggests that the transformation of the "America coded in Pierce's testament" into "Vineland the Good" will begin only when we find a way to develop a communitarianism that will foster respect for individuality, autonomy, and self-expression, the ideals that the national narrative of individualism has always held up but has yet to uphold.

Communal Difference, Communal Sameness

Morrison's sixth novel, *Jazz* (1992), finds an emblem for the interpenetration of self, community, tradition, and renewal in the formal requirements and social history of jazz music. Jazz remains American culture's most distinctive contribution to music history; it is also a distinctly African American form, although African Americans are not the only ones who play it.[9] During the 1920s, white jazz artists like Paul Whiteman, the so-called King of Jazz, sought to appropriate jazz, to Europeanize it: according to Kathy Ogren, "Whiteman's popular music became so closely identified with jazz that many Americans had no knowledge of its Afro-American origins" (159). It was Louis Armstrong who rescued jazz from the white man: the series of records that Armstrong recorded at Okeh Studios, which came to be known as the "Hot Fives and Hot Sevens," were, according to James Lincoln Collier, "landmarks in jazz history, causing great excitement among jazz players and jazz fans, and they turned jazz in its course" (146). Jazz is an emblem of the unavoidable centrality of African American culture within American culture as a whole, but it also attests to African American culture's ability to resist, to its refusal to be wholly appropriated or incorporated by the wider culture.

In addition to this feature of its social history, jazz offers a compelling suggestion about what a revitalized Emersonian liberalism could be like. Like classic Emersonianism, it values the dynamics of process, harnessing them as improvisation, yet it teaches the lesson that Wynton Marsalis learned from Louis Armstrong: "the communal conception of improvisation" that underlay Armstrong's assertion that "early New Orleans music is the foundation of jazz music and the closer you get to playing that way, the closer you are to jazz" (quoted in Breitwieser, 57–58). What jazz presents is a pluralist vision, in which individual voices can be consonant even if they seem to be at melodic cross-purposes. At the same time, each individual voice is representative: a solo means nothing without the context of its accompaniment, and in the very best jazz, even a single solo note embodies the totality in which it sounds. Jazz is a model for the pluralism that Emerson ultimately cannot bring himself to embrace.

Jazz serves as the point of departure for Morrison's critical study *Playing in the Dark*, which is devoted in part to offering a counternarrative to the official story of U.S. individualism. Recounting her reading of Marie Cardinal's autobiography *The Words to Say It*, Morrison describes "Cardinal's project" as one of "document[ing] her madness, her therapy, and the complicated process of healing in language as exact and as evocative as possible in order to make both her experience and her understanding of it accessible to a stranger" (1992c, v). For Morrison, the decisive moment of Cardinal's account occurs when she describes her first anxiety attack, which occurs when she is listening to Armstrong:

> Armstrong was going to improvise with his trumpet, to build a whole composition in which each note would be important and would contain within itself the essence of the whole. I was not disappointed: the

atmosphere warmed up very fast. The scaffolding and flying buttresses of the jazz instruments supported Armstrong's trumpet, creating spaces which were adequate enough for it to climb higher, establish itself, and take off again. The sounds of the trumpet sometimes piled up together, fusing a new musical base, a sort of matrix which gave birth to one precise, unique note, tracing a sound whose path was almost painful, so absolutely necessary had its equilibrium and duration become; it tore at the nerves of those who followed it. (quoted in Morrison 1992c, vi–vii)

The effect on Cardinal is dramatic: the music produces not only Gothic cathedrals of sound but also pain that tears at the nerves, and it sends her "[running] into the street like someone possessed" (vii). Cardinal is a French woman born in Algeria—"a colonialist, a white child, loving and loved by Arabs" (ix)—and Morrison finds herself wondering "whether the cultural associations of jazz were as important to Cardinal's 'possession' as were its intellectual foundations." She tells us that she added Cardinal's anecdote to a "file" of "instances" in which "black people ignite[d] critical moments of discovery or change or emphasis in literature not written by them" (viii). Surely, however, both elements are significant for Morrison: Cardinal's story not only points out the power of African American artistic traditions but also suggests that they might serve as the model for a reconstituted communal culture. Armstrong's jazz, Cardinal seems to say, renders concepts that could be at cross-purposes—individual versus whole, improvisation versus composition, music versus architecture—consonant with one another.

Extrapolating from Morrison's account of her interest in Cardinal's story, we can see another way in which jazz might serve as an inspirational model. For, in the structure of call-and-response that is so essential to jazz music, lies a vision of what social responsibility might be in a culture of individualism. Hayden Carruth writes that

in my listening to most early jazz I hear far more resemblance to the call-and-response pattern of black (and many other) folk traditions than to European counterpoint. The lead instrument, usually trumpet, plays a phrase, to which the other instruments, trombone, clarinet, rhythm, etc. give answers. These may be and usually are somewhat overlapped, fitted together in very complex movements. But one does not listen vertically, one listens sequentially. And this skipping back and forth among the instruments as they call and respond irregularly against the fundamental beat, not at all the rhythmically fixed chordal polyphony of Bach, is what gives jazz its particularity, authenticity, and immanent cultural autonomy among all the world's musics. (72)

In jazz, answering the call of another not only serves the community but also sets the stage for individual achievement. One player's lead is taken by another, who revises it and gives it an individual stamp, before passing on, while the piece as a whole moves forward all the while. Jazz is both highly individual and highly collaborative.

There is a telling moment in *Gravity's Rainbow* when Tyrone Slothrop receives a dose of truth serum and spews forth a wild fantasy involving a blues harp, Malcolm X, and Charlie "Yardbird" Parker, with a bit of stereotypical African American dialect thrown in (1973, 61–62). Jazz is a suggestive model for Pynchon as well as for Morrison. In the introduction to *Slow Learner*, Pynchon cites "the wide availability of recorded jazz" in the 1950s as a formative influence, a counterweight to "the undeniable power of tradition." (1984b, 7). Self-deprecatingly, Pynchon recalls, "Like others, I spent a lot of time in jazz clubs, nursing the two-beer minimum. I put on hornrimmed sunglasses at night. I went to parties in lofts where girls wore strange attire" (8). *V.* pokes fun at such parties, which form an integral part of the life of the Whole Sick Crew, but it takes its jazz seriously. The novel makes a subtle link between individualism and jazz through the figure of Dahoud, the gargantuan African American sailor who says that "life is the most precious possession you have": Dahoud's name, after all, recalls a famous jazz piece from the 1950s, "Daahoud," which was written by the trumpeter Clifford Brown.[10]

But the most vivid embodiment of the possibilities of jazz is the sax player McClintic Sphere. In contrast to supposed artists like Slab with his sculptures of cheese danishes and his "Catatonic Expressionism" (1963, 297), Sphere is the real thing, an innovator who challenges his audiences: "Inside McClintic Sphere was swinging his ass off. . . . He blew a hand-carved ivory alto saxophone with a 4½ reed and the sound was like nothing any of them had heard before." Sphere's band is spare—just his alto sax, bass, drums and "a natural horn in F"—and there is something rugged about its sound: "Horn and alto together favored sixths and minor fourths and when this happened it was like a knife fight or a tug of war: the sound was consonant but as if cross-purposes were in the air" (59). Sphere's solos, however, are "something else," a wholly different plane of individualism: "There were people around, mostly those who wrote for Downbeat magazine or the liners of LP records, who seemed to feel he played disregarding chord changes completely. They talked a great deal about soul and the intellectual and the rising rhythms of African nationalism. It was a new conception, they said, and some of them said: Bird Lives" (59–60). Refuting the suggestion that McClintic Sphere is merely a "parody" of Ornette Coleman, William Lhamon describes Pynchon's Sphere as "an affectionate rendering compacting details from Coleman and other jazz musicians, writers, and legends to create a complex tonal picture" and argues that "Sphere's aesthetic"—with its consonance of cross-purposes—"is Pynchon's" (230–31). But although Pynchon's style, with its elaborate puns and its pastiche of different narrative modalities, resembles a form of word jazz, as a thematic element jazz ultimately plays a minor role in the imaginative logic of Pynchon's texts. McClintic Sphere remains a peripheral character who quietly drops from view; he represents a possibility for redemption that remains to be fully explored.

Morrison's novels explore the possibilities of jazz more fully than Pynchon's do, but jazz is still no panacea for Morrison. It proves to be a troublesome model with some disturbing implications, as if Morrison were committed to representing both the power and the pain that Cardinal locates in the experience of listening to Armstrong's jazz. F. Scott Fitzgerald once noted that, in its "progress toward respectability," the word jazz "has meant first sex, then dancing, then music" (1931, 16), and Morrison's *Jazz* brings out all three of these meanings. Morrison has described *Jazz* as a continuation of the project begun in *Beloved* because it depicts the joys and costs of having the freedom to seek out your own lover or mate. For African Americans, she argues, possessing this simple freedom represents a great step forward: most slaves were treated as livestock to be bred for profit or as concubines to be used for pleasure, or both (Morrison 1992a). This description is, however, a misleadingly benign account of *Jazz*, which also represents a rewriting of *The Bluest Eye*.[11] Joe and Violet Trace are migrant workers who fall in love, marry, and (like the Breedloves) move north in an attempt to escape the poverty and racism of the South. Their marriage falters after Joe begins an obsessive affair with a teenager named Dorcas; when she attempts to leave him, Joe follows Dorcas to a party and shoots her during a dance. What captivates Joe most about his relationship with Dorcas is the fact that he chose her as his lover, a fact that transfigures him and makes him feel like a virgin:

> Your first time. And mine, in a manner of speaking. For which, and I will say it again, I would strut out of the Garden, strut! as long as you held on to my hand, girl. Dorcas, girl, your first time and mine. I *chose* you. Nobody gave you to me. Nobody said that's the one for you. I picked you out. Wrong time, yep, and doing wrong by my wife. But the picking out, the choosing. Don't ever think I feel for you, or feel over you. I didn't fall in love, I rose in it. I saw you and made up my mind. My mind. (1992b, 134–35)

Joe's affair with Dorcas is thus depicted as an assertion of freedom and autonomy, an assertion of individuality apart from (even in rebellion against) the bonds of marriage. The reference to the Garden in this interior monologue indicates that Joe knows that he is tasting forbidden fruit, that he is "doing wrong," but, like a true unencumbered self, he is content to be the author of his own moral meanings. Once his desires are thwarted, however, Joe's feelings become pathological, and individualism claims another female victim.

Joe Trace belongs to a line of male characters in Morrison's fiction who establish their masculinity by dominating, degrading, and even destroying women, a line that begins with Cholly Breedlove of *The Bluest Eye*. Despite her antipatriarchal stance in public interviews, Morrison remains surprisingly indulgent toward the behavior of African American men, not because their philandering undermines patriarchy by destroying the traditional family, but because she admires self-reliance and autonomy even in debased form. Denied the fruits of economic individualism, most of the African American men that Morrison depicts find that the only individualism open to them is a form of rugged individualism that emphasizes masculinity and aloofness. Yet Morrison is unwilling to see this stance as purely negative: there is a certain awe, for example, in her description of Cholly Breedlove as "free. Dangerously free. Free to feel whatever he felt—fear, guilt, shame love, grief, pity" (1970, 159). The narrator of the novel calls it a "godlike state" (160), and Morrison herself, speaking about Cholly Breedlove in an interview, applies the word that figures so largely in Emerson's "Self-Reliance," *whim*: "By the time he met Pauline he was able to do whatever his whims suggested and it's that kind of absence of control I wanted" (Stepto 1979, 19). Morrison describes both Cholly and Sula's Ajax in terms similar to those that political theorists use to describe the unencumbered self: they "make up themselves. . . . They allowed themselves to be whomever they were" (20). Calling these men "adventuresome" (20),

Morrison acknowledges that sociologists describe the fact that black men "do not stay home and take care of their children ... as a major failing" but admits that she has always found this itinerant nature to be "one of the most attractive features about black male life." Sensing that this view might be seen as irresponsible, Morrison confesses, "I guess I'm not supposed to say that," but she refuses to back down: "The fact that they would split in a minute just delights me. It's part of that whole business of breaking ground, doing the other thing. They would leave, do something else" (26). Morrison, in other words, seems to find self-reliance, autonomy, and rugged individualism exhilarating, not just in black women like Sula, for whom it represents a departure from the norm, but also in black men, for whom it often represents a justification for violence.

Vineland's vision of a community of individuated yet situated selves bound together by nonpatriarchal familial relations seems even more evanescently utopian when set next to the dynamics of individual, family, and community that exist in Morrison's novels. Embedded into Morrison's texts are contradictory moments that demonstrate how difficult it is to strip negative liberty of its negative associations, moments such as the description of Cholly Breedlove as "free" and "god-like," or Sethe's final reliance on Paul D to show her that she is her own "best thing," or the degeneration of self-reliance into murder in *Jazz* and *Paradise*.

What both *Jazz* and *Paradise* dramatize powerfully is the necessity of situating individualism within a pluralist framework that fosters mutual respect between individuals. The freedom that Cholly Breedlove and Joe Trace experience is powerful and seductive but ultimately anarchic: it must be tempered by a respect for the dignity of others. These characters are never taught the lessons that can be gleaned from Morrison's reading of Cardinal's memoir. *Jazz* has something to teach us about the difference that difference makes. Morrison insists that the difference between African American culture and mainstream white culture can enable the former to act as a catalyst for new experiences and insights. That is the "cultural" lesson. The "intellectual" lesson, however, is also important: jazz teaches us that we must not fetishize difference to the point of ignoring the ways in which we are like others, despite differences in race, class, or gender. A jazz ensemble is a collection of soloists working together, with each individual solo dependent on the musical context from which it arises. Individuals like Cholly and Joe realize only a fraction of the potential inherent in the idea of freedom because their freedom is predicated on a refusal to empathize with others.

In thus privileging jazz as a model of cultural interaction, Morrison is revising the official narrative of U.S. individualism, with its shift from negative to positive liberty, by emphasizing that community is viable only if it is based in respect for individuality. A community's attitude toward other communities is important, but so is its attitude toward its own members. Constructing communal identity around external difference (difference from other communities) and internal sameness (homogeneity of membership) creates a form of bad communitarianism that eventually proves to be debilitating. Pluralist communities that respect difference—both external and internal—foster a healthier, cosmopolitan form of communitarianism that is compatible with the goals of Emersonian liberalism.

Morrison continues her exploration of these cultural dynamics in *Paradise*, which, like Pynchon's *Vineland*, offers two models of communitarianism—one good, one bad—formed in the shadow of the national narrative of individualism. Founded by a group of African American war veterans and their families in 1949, the all-black town of Ruby, Oklahoma, seems at first to be a communitarian's paradise. Motivated by a politics of the common good and of civic virtue, Ruby is a town that "neither had nor needed a jail. No criminals had ever come from [this] town. And the one or two people who acted up, humiliated their families or threatened the town's view of itself were taken good care of" (1998, 8). Ruby is a religious town, with a firm standard of moral behavior made possible by the town's homogeneity. Michael Sandel notes that "communitarians would be more likely than liberals to allow a town to ban pornographic bookstores, on the grounds that pornography offends its way of life and the values that sustain it" (1984a, 17). Communitarians, in other words, can agree on a standard of moral behavior that promotes civic virtue, and they place that standard and that virtue ahead of the individual's rights of self-expression. Ruby functions in precisely this way, and it is deeply suspicious of the collection of independent women living in the abandoned convent on the outskirts of town, women whose more liberal ideas about sexuality seem to present a challenge to the moral standards of the town.

"Liberals often argue," writes Sandel "that a politics of the common good, drawing as it must on particular loyalties, obligations, and traditions, opens the way to prejudice and intolerance. . . . Communitarians reply, rightly in my view, that intolerance flourishes most where forms of life are dislocated, roots unsettled, traditions undone" (1984a, 17). The families of Ruby *have* been dislocated; they have uprooted themselves from the town of Haven, which their forefathers founded, because its ideals have been corrupted. But they know the value of roots and traditions: in addition to moving their families, the men of Ruby disassemble the communal oven that had once served as the center of town life in Haven and take it with them: "An Oven. Round as a head, deep as desire. Living in or near their wagons, boiling meal in the open, cutting sod and mesquite for shelter, the Old Fathers did that first: put most of their strength into constructing the huge, flawlessly designed Oven that both nourished them and monumentalized what they had done" (7). In the early days of Haven, the oven was a place where "unembellished stories were told and retold" (14), where "Haven people . . . stayed to gossip, complain, roar with laughter and drink walking coffee in the shade of the eaves. And any child in earshot was subject to being ordered to fan flies, haul wood, clean the worktable or beat the earth with a tamping block" (15). Emblazoned with a stern religious motto—"Beware the Furrow of His Brow"—the oven embodies the values around which Ruby has constructed itself.

One of these values is patriarchy. In making the oven the center of town life, the citizens of Ruby have taken a symbol of privacy, domesticity, and womanhood and transformed it into something public, communal, and masculine. They have taken the hearth out of the home and put it in the town square. They have inscribed it with a motto and given it an official history. But, like the town fathers in Hawthorne's *The Scarlet Letter*, they discover that the appropriation of public symbols cannot be fully controlled. The virulent arguments over the exact wording and meaning of the motto on the oven are a sign of how desperate the town fathers are to control the town's official narrative: they conceive of the oven as a place for conversation but not debate, a place to share accepted narratives but not to propose new counternarratives.

The arguments over the motto on the oven are symptomatic of the town's central ideological problem: Ruby is a town founded in fear, the same fear that led to the development of the concept of negative liberty in the first place. What the men of Ruby want is freedom from constraint; they seek to create for themselves a sphere of immunity that can protect them and their families from the unwarranted incursions of others. They conceive of the world outside in terms that recall Pynchon's entropic nightmares:

> Ten generations had known what lay Out There: space, once beckoning and free, became unmonitored and seething; became a void where random and organized evil erupted when and where it chose—behind

any standing tree, behind the door of any house, humble or grand. Out There where your children were sport, your women quarry, and where your very person could be annulled; where congregations carried arms to church and ropes coiled in every saddle. Out There where every cluster of whitemen looked like a posse, being alone was being dead. But lessons had been learned and relearned in the last three generations about how to protect a town. (16)

This fear turns Ruby into a place of prejudice and intolerance. Victimized themselves by racial prejudice and discrimination, "neither the founders of Haven nor their descendants could tolerate anybody but themselves," and their communitarian ideals implicitly include a set of prejudices based on skin color that are the reverse of those of white America. The unofficial town historian, Pat Best, knows this. Of the fifteen families that founded Ruby, nine had helped found Haven, and "their names [are] legend" (190). Pat refers to these "intact nine families" as "8-R. An abbreviation for eight-rock, a deep deep level in the coal mines." The members of these families are "blue-black people, tall and graceful, whose clear wide eyes gave no sign of what they really felt about those who weren't 8-rock like them" (193). Their late nineteenth-century ancestors had discovered that their dark skin color was "their misfortune's misfortune, . . . the one and only feature that distinguished them from their Negro peers. . . . [T]hey knew there was a difference in the minds of whites, but it had not struck them before that it was of consequence, serious consequences, to Negroes themselves. . . . The sign of racial purity they had taken for granted had become a stain" (193–94). As a result, Ruby operates according to a "blood rule [that] nobody admitted existed" (195), a rule that makes racial purity a badge of honor instead of a stain—and that makes Ruby a negative image of the culture that it abhors.

Ruby manifests another aspect of communitarian culture that makes liberals uncomfortable: it is resolutely patriarchal and operates according to a traditionally restrictive conception of family life. Feminist thinkers have noted that communitarians like Jean Bethke Elshtain, Elizabeth Fox-Genovese, Christopher Lasch, and Alasdair MacIntyre tend to evince a nostalgia for prefeminist conceptions of families and communities. Too often, the communitarian critique of individualism seems willing, if not eager, to forsake the gains made by the women's movement under the aegis of equal rights in favor of greater emphasis on communal obligation and responsibility.[12] The communitarian consensus of Ruby is founded on a similar nostalgia, and when the communitarian consensus fails to cohere, the town fathers search for a scapegoat. The Convent becomes the inevitable target:

> Outrages that had been accumulating all along took shape as evidence. A mother was knocked down the stairs by her cold-eyed daughter. Four damaged infants were born in one family. Daughters refused to get out of bed. Brides disappeared on their honeymoons. Two brothers shot each other on New Years Day. Trips to Demby for VD shots common. And what went on at the Oven these days was not to be believed.... The proof they had been collecting ... could not be denied: the one thing that connected all these catastrophes was the Convent. And in the Convent were those women. (11)

The men of Ruby pride themselves on the fact that "there wasn't a slack or sloven woman anywhere in town"; Ruby is a place where women are protected, where a woman doesn't have to worry about being thought of as "prey," where a woman is free to "stroll as slowly as she liked, think of food preparations, war, of family things, or lift her eyes to stars and think of nothing at all" (8). This is a patriarch's view of woman's freedom; the women of the Convent—each in her own way a victim of patriarchal oppression—have other ideas about freedom.

Billie Delia, who thinks of Ruby as "a backward noplace ruled by men whose power to control was out of control and who had the nerve to say who could live and who not and where," calls the women of the Convent "lively, free, unarmed females" who were guilty of "mutiny" in the eyes of Ruby's men (308). These are "not women locked safely away from men; but worse, women who chose themselves for company, which is to say not a convent but a coven" (276). The men, however, are at least partially correct: the Convent does represent a challenge to the mores of Ruby. For Ruby is "a sleepy town with three churches within one mile of one another but nothing to serve a traveler" (12); it is a town that prides itself on its religious rectitude but has no interest in providing succor to any but its own. In contrast, even after it is no longer a missionary school for the purpose of Christianizing and domesticating Arapaho Indian girls, the Convent is all about helping the lost and cast out. Consolata, the spiritual leader of the Convent, remembers how "over the past eight years they had come.... Each one asking permission to linger a few days but never actually leaving. Now and then one or another packed a scruffy little bag, said goodbye and seemed to disappear for a while—but only a while. They always came back to stay on, living like mice in a house no one, not even the tax collector, wanted" (222). Consolata has a mystical healing gift—she calls it "stepping in"—and she brings the women of the Convent together through storytelling and "loud dreaming" in which they share one another's tales (264). It is a form of spirituality based on empathy, and it heals the women: they are "no longer haunted" (266).

But, as Morrison's narrator points out, they are "hunted" (266). The bad communitarianism of Ruby hunts down and kills the good communitarianism of the Convent. At the novel's end, there is redemption and regeneration, but only through the intervention of magical realism. Ruby is given a second chance. The Reverend Misner, never truly accepted by the nine families, contemplates Ruby's folly:

> Whether they be the first or the last, representing the oldest black families or the newest, the best of the tradition or the most pathetic, they had ended up betraying it all. They think they have outfoxed the whiteman when in fact they imitate him. They think they are protecting their wives and children, when in fact they are maiming them. And when the maimed children ask for help, they look elsewhere for the cause. Born out of an old hatred, one that began when one kind of black man scorned another kind and that kind took the hatred to another level, their selfishness had trashed two hundred years of suffering and triumph in a moment of such pomposity and error and callousness it froze the mind. Unbridled by Scripture, deafened by the roar of its own history, Ruby, it seemed to him, was an unnecessary failure. How exquisitely human was the wish for permanent happiness, and how thin human imagination became trying to achieve it. Soon Ruby will be like any other country town: the young thinking of elsewhere; the old full of regret. The sermons will be eloquent but fewer and fewer will pay attention or connect them to everyday life. How can they hold it together, he wondered, this hard-won heaven defined only by the absence of the unsaved, the unworthy and the strange? Who will protect them from their leaders? (306)

This unusually expository passage leaves little room for doubt about what has gone wrong in Ruby. Seeking to free themselves from white oppression, the inhabitants of Ruby create a community that is equally oppressive. What had made both Haven and Ruby living, vibrant communities was the abundant exchange of stories: they were places where "unembellished stories were told and retold" (14). Implicit in this passage is an

Emersonian perspective: as long as the cultures of these towns remained fluid and dynamic, they flourished. With the attempt to make happiness "permanent," however, came a failure of the "imagination": the transformation of multiple "unembellished" stories into a single "official story" told each year in the annual Christmas pageant. What saves the women of the Convent is their ability to tell stories to one another, to share each other's dreams and pain, to make use of their imaginations. Our last view of Ruby, in the penultimate section of the novel's final chapter, shows us Billie Delia, "hop[ing] for a miracle" (308). Her imagination is alive, and where there is imagination, there is the hope of breaking any impasse that human beings can create.

CONCLUSION. Beyond Individualism

One of the things that the novels of Morrison and Pynchon dramatize so vividly is the fact that communitarian critiques of U.S. individualism are often too negative about negative liberty. In their zeal to reconceptualize the basis of individual identity, communitarian theorists sometimes forsake the real conceptual advances that have been made by liberal theory because of its assumption of the importance of individual rights. As the twenty-first century begins, it is hard to look at the front page of the *New York Times* on any given day and not feel that negative liberty and the tradition of rights-based individualism that it underwrites represent one of the major achievements of human culture, a conceptual leap forward yet to be made by many societies around the world. From Europe, Asia, Africa, and both of the Americas come chilling stories of the depredations wrought by those who have no respect for, perhaps no belief in the existence of, the rights of others. The kinds of outrages that Pynchon and Morrison describe in their novels occur every day in our supposedly enlightened era: in places like the Balkans, Haiti, Rwanda, Somalia, and the inner cities of the United States, men and women live in conditions that approximate a Hobbesian state of nature, in which the strong prey upon the weak with impunity and without remorse.

Meanwhile, in societies that have chosen an anti-individualist course guided by Communist doctrine or religious fundamentalism, the claims of the individual are so subordinated to the claims of the group that individuals have no rights and nonconformists are punished with Draconian severity. As George Kateb reminds us, rights-based individualism is "a strange idea," an idea that is "untypical of past human experience" (1992, 241); indeed, it is so new an idea that even many self-proclaimed democracies have yet to comprehend its meaning fully.[1] When Kateb asks us to think about individualism, he emphasizes its idealist manifestations, portraying for us what that anonymous author in the *Democratic Review* described in "The Course of Civilization" (1839) as "an individualism more elevated, moral and refined" (209). U.S. culture has not yet achieved such an individualism. What we learn from reading Morrison and Pynchon is that such an individualism may not be possible, and, even if it is, it will never be achieved until U.S. culture faces up to the flaws that exist both within its conception of freedom and within its institutionalization of that conception.

This process of self-interrogation should begin with those early uses of the term *individualism*. When we read, for example, that the "history of humanity is the record of a grand march . . . at all times tending to one point—the ultimate perfection of man," when we read that "the course of civilization is the progress of man from a state of savage individualism to that of an individualism more elevated, moral and refined," we miss something if we do not see that the humanist ideals propounded by these statements rest on both patriarchal and racist logic. The United States in 1839 did not let its women vote, and it justified its policy of Indian Removal by claiming that the native inhabitants of this continent were "savages" who must inevitably submit to the elevated, moral, and refined values of white civilization. A year earlier, Emerson, protesting the removal of the Cherokees in his "Letter to Martin Van Buren," feels sympathetic to the Cherokees because he has "witnessed the painful endeavors of these red men to redeem their own race from the doom of eternal inferiority, and to borrow and domesticate in the tribe the inventions and customs of the Caucasian race" (1838, 2). The "immortal question" that Emerson asks Van Buren is "whether justice shall be done by the race of civilized to the race of savage man; whether all the attributes of reason, of civility, of justice, and even of mercy, shall be put off by the American People" (4). The answers given, then and now, are disheartening: no, justice was not done; yes, the American people disavowed reason, civility, justice, and mercy. Morrison's and Pynchon's novels show us that little has changed in the century and a half since Emerson asked his "immortal question."

The United States is still far from fully realizing the promises contained in its founding documents. When we read that the Declaration of Independence has "universal appeal" because it sets forth "a philosophy of human rights" that can be "applied not only to Americans, but to peoples everywhere" (Bailyn et al., 190), we should take our cue from Toni Morrison and focus our attention on the fact that these principles have not yet been applied to all Americans. The principles of individualism set out in the Declaration may have universal appeal and applicability, but they arose out of a culture that was unwilling to apply them universally. That unwillingness has remained a part of the logic of U.S. individualism, a subtext of its official story. And, because that unwillingness has been largely implicit, it may prove to be very difficult to take that next step toward an individualism that is "elevated, moral and refined." Remember the words of that first reviewer of the second volume of *Democracy in America*: " 'Individualism' has its immutable laws [which] when allowed to operate without let or hindrance . . . must, in the end, assimilate the species, and evolve all the glorious phenomena of original and eternal ORDER;—that order which exists in man himself, and alone vivifies and sustains him" ("Catholicism," 333). In the years since the Declaration of Independence was signed, U.S. culture has removed many of the legal barriers to the free operation of individualism, but the barriers that remain are hidden in the recesses of U.S. ideology, given deep cover by the accommodating universality of the culture's rhetoric of freedom.

The persistence of racism, sexism, homophobia, and other forms of discrimination is a nettlesome but nonetheless obvious way in which individualism has not been "allowed to operate without let or hindrance." It is when we try and fail to find remedies for these persistent problems that we run up against what may be the most insidious barrier to the realization of the full potential of individualism as an ideology: our overreliance on methodologically individualist modes of thought. Emerson, Rawls, and Kateb all demonstrate the power of methodological individualism as a tool with which to craft philosophical idealism, to derive principles of justice for an ideal liberal society, or to make a case for the inviolability of the individual. But too many intractable problems that exist in U.S. culture today prove resistant to methodologically individualist solutions.

How, for example, can we break the cycle of discrimination, poverty, misogyny, violence, and cultural dispossession that Toni Morrison's novels so vividly portray? In the preface, I discussed the way in which one remedy—affirmative action—has been discredited by opponents who make use of methodologically individualist logic. Another example of the horror with which many Americans react to nonindividualist solutions to the problems of discrimination can be found in the virulent opposition to the nomination of Lani Guinier for the position of assistant attorney general, Civil Rights Division, in 1993. Guinier's work on civil rights is devoted to the assessment of the fairness of voting systems, and it poses the question of whether the systems that are in place in the United States tend to produce permanent, locked-in winners and losers on the basis of race. In *The Tyranny of the Majority* (1994), Guinier argues that individuals have a "right . . . to participate in politics" and that this right is "best realized in association with other individuals, i.e., as a group" (125). The creation of winner-take-all districts on the basis of geography assumes that one person will be able to represent a district because the members of such a district share overriding common interests on the basis of geography. But in a society where individuals tend to vote according to overriding collective self-interest based on race rather than geography, perpetual minorities within a district will never have adequate representation. She finds that liberal individualism handicaps our ability to think about the fairness of geographically based, winner-take-all districting in a racially divided society: "Proponents of the philosophy of individualism attempt to use the one-person, one-vote principle to locate voting in the status of individual or constituent. They rely on the fact that every individual has the opportunity to cast a potentially winning vote or to be represented vicariously by one who does. This approach camouflages the group nature of voting by emphasizing the personal aspects of representation" (126). The aim of the alternative voting systems that Guinier has investigated is to create "equal opportunity to *influence* legislative outcomes regardless of race" (14), but in order to achieve a system that is truly race blind, she recognizes that we must be race conscious for the time being in order to create the conditions of fairness that would have existed in a nondiscriminatory society. In aiming to protect minorities from the tyranny of the majority, Guinier's work belongs to a tradition of U.S. political thought that was pioneered by James Madison. The willingness of not only right-wing political pundits but also the media and the public to brand her a "quota queen" without even listening to her arguments demonstrates how averse U.S. culture is to nonindividualist ways of thinking, particularly when admitting the failure of methodological individualism also involves admitting the presence of racism, sexism, and other forms of discrimination based on qualities shared by entire groups. The lesson illustrated by the Guinier episode has less to do with the viability of her arguments than with the violence with which her ideas were dismissed. The

United States is not yet willing to let its public figures openly renounce methodological individualism.

What we need now is not "compensatory justice," which involves compensating minority groups for suffering due to past harm, but "distributive justice," which involves assuring that arrangements are made to eradicate injustice in the present. Distributive justice means that members of groups that have been discriminated against have a claim to the advantages, benefits, and standing to which they would have been entitled in a society that was always nondiscriminatory; it also means that no one is entitled to advantages, benefits, and standing that would not have been acquired without discrimination (Fiscus, 8–14). The validity of various forms of distributive justice can be derived through methodological individualism: Rawls does it when he formulates the difference principle. But it seems likely that distributive justice will not be achieved until U.S. ideology experiences a transformation that enables it to consider alternatives to methodological individualism when thinking about social issues.

Such a transformation might not only help us to find remedies for discrimination but also help us to resolve social conflicts that appear unsolvable when viewed from an individualist perspective. As Ronald Dworkin has suggested, individual rights are best viewed as "political trumps held by individuals. Individuals have rights when, for some reason, a collective goal is not a sufficient justification for imposing some loss or injury upon them" (1978, xi). Any good bridge player knows that trumps must be used judiciously, but Americans today trot out rights as their opening move without regard to consequences. So proponents of abortion rights open with the fundamental right to privacy that assures the inviolability of the individual, opponents of abortion rights counter with the fundamental right to life of the individual, the two trumps nullify one another, and the two sides have no common ground for discussion. Our theories of individual rights simply do not offer the resources necessary to resolve the issue of abortion.

Similar stalemates are often quickly reached in disputes involving the First Amendment. The press covering a controversial trial demands full access to every shred of evidence, arguing that "the public has a right to know," setting this right ahead of the individual's (and ultimately the public's) right to a fair trial. The public's desire to know must be measured against the public's need for a fair judicial system, but methodological individualism provides no way to take such a measurement and thus to balance one collective desire against another. Similarly, speech codes at universities are struck down as unconstitutional, but such codes would be unnecessary if students were not culturally encouraged to use rights first and ask questions later. Rights need to be handled with caution and invoked sparingly, but we lack a fully developed discourse of responsibility that could serve as an owner's manual for the rights bearer.

We have come, in short, to a cultural impasse, and we will not advance until we come to terms with the following paradox: that we must give up the rigid methodological individualism that characterizes our thinking on so many social and cultural issues if we are ever to achieve the values and goals that Emersonian liberalism and its popular variants were designed to foster.

In the first chapter, I described two groups of democratic theorists who have sought to break this impasse by "defend[ing] the gains of the democratic revolution and acknowledg[ing] the constitutive role of liberalism in the emergence of a pluralistic democracy, while trying to redress the negative consequences of individualism" (Mouffe 1992, 5). My readings of Pynchon and Morrison make it difficult for me to have much faith in the approach taken by Habermas and his followers because it rests so heavily on foundations of reason and civility. Both Morrison and Pynchon belong to a tradition of writers who have used the genre of Gothic fiction to question the Enlightenment's emphasis on reason as the value on which to found a culture. Like the Gothic writers whom Pynchon cites in his article on Luddism (1984a) (Charles Brockden Brown and Edgar Allan Poe), Pynchon and Morrison show us the power of the irrational within human culture; moreover, they demonstrate how deep the human desire is for what Pynchon calls "the miraculous."[2] In their novels, reason fails more often than it succeeds, and as a result, the worlds that they portray are worlds that are characterized by conflict and violence.

Mouffe cautions, however, that we must be careful lest we retreat too far from what is valuable within the liberal tradition. The desire to be able to render moral judgment that lies behind both the universalism and the rationalism of the Enlightenment must not be abandoned altogether in the favor of cultural relativism and absolute pluralism. As Mouffe notes, there are certain distinctions—between "the public and the private, the separation of Church and State, and of civil and religious law"—that are the "basic achievements of the democratic revolution" and that "are what make the existence of pluralism possible. One cannot therefore call these distinctions into question in the name of pluralism" (1993, 132). To put it another way, pluralism cannot tolerate antipluralism: it cannot include any fundamentalism that rejects the basic premises of pluralism. Mouffe asks, "How are we to make the distinction between those values and customs in our 'public morality' that are specific to Christianity and which we therefore cannot justly impose on everyone in what has become objectively a multi-ethnic and multi-cultural society, and those values and customs that are an expression of principles without which pluralist democracy could not continue to exist?" (132). How, in short, can we keep from slipping into a cultural relativism that paralyzes us?

Ironically, it is precisely this sort of cultural relativism that has kept critics from examining Morrison and Pynchon in tandem. They are thought to be writing from such different subject positions that their texts must have little in common. But, as I have argued, one of the things that these two novelists demonstrate is that we must find a middle ground between the extremes of individualism and communitarianism. We can, in fact, apply this insight to our practices of reading as well. The movement in twentieth-century criticism from New Critical to multicultural paradigms can be mapped onto the liberal-communitarian debate.

We might say that, from its emergence as a discipline through the era of the New Criticism, literary criticism was ruled by an individualist model of literary production, in which critics and authors alike conceived of literary genius as a function of what Keats called *negative capability*, an author's ability to create transcendent art by projecting himself out of the particular biases and interests of his or her personal situation. Conceived in these terms, the imaginative act bears a striking resemblance to the thought experiment that John Rawls devises in order to discern principles of justice for a liberal society: both the artist and the Rawlsian individual must attain an Archimedean standpoint from which to survey the world. In contrast, critics who write about late twentieth-century U.S. fiction tend to work with a communitarian model of authorial production: they assume that authors are situated selves whose authorial identities are constituted by the historical juncture, the sociocultural position, and the moment within literary history into which they are born. This stance represents a retreat from the more radical critique of the "Rawlsian" model offered by the poststructuralist criticism that grew out of the work of such theorists as Roland Barthes, Michel Foucault, and Jacques Derrida. Following Barthes, critics who adopted this model proclaimed "the death of the author" and treated texts, not as the result of an author's design or intention, but rather as nothing but "a tissue of quotations drawn from the innumerable centres of culture" (Barthes, 146). In contrast, critics who adopt the "communitarian" model—particularly those who study texts in relation to "identity politics"—believe in the importance of authors and in the relevance of an author's biography to the study of his or her text. Yet, too often, instead of producing the kind of subtle consideration of author, text, and context called for by theorists of aesthetic reception such as Hans Robert Jauss, these "communitarian" critics end up creating merely a variant of the poststructuralist model: instead of remaining a situated self, the author is transmuted into a radically situated self, wholly the product of social relations, incapable of exercising negative capability. In short, what I believe that the novels of Morrison and Pynchon suggest to us is that we need to find a way to break through two different impasses: between individualism and communitarianism in the field of liberal political theory and between New Criticism and multiculturalism in the field of literary criticism.

I suggested that Pynchon and Morrison each explore what might be termed *good* and *bad* forms of communitarianism. I believe that a similar logic can be applied to the practice of multiculturalism. "Bad" multiculturalism fosters a cultural relativism that can be debilitating because it prevents us from being able to render judgments about oppressive practices within other cultures.[3] In contrast, "good" multiculturalism creates new paradigms for understanding the complex interrelations among different subject positions. For example, many of the critics currently seeking to revise the academy's conception of "American literature" in the light of multiculturalism find a useful conceptual tool in the idea of the *borderlands*, which has replaced the *frontier* as the dominant site within American studies. In the introduction to the collection *Cultures of United States Imperialism* (1993), Amy Kaplan calls for a "multicultural critique of American ethnocentrism" that links the "internal categories of gender, race, and ethnicity to the global dynamics of empire-building." The goal of this critique is to deconstruct "the binary opposition of the foreign and the domestic," an opposition reinforced within American studies by the field's early obsession with the idea of "the frontier" in the aftermath of Henry Nash Smith's landmark study *Virgin Land* (1950). Describing "the Frontier" as "a major conceptual site in American studies," Kaplan notes that it has "undergone revision from the vacant space of the wilderness to a bloody battlefield of conflict and conquest, and more recently to a site of contacts, encounters, and collisions that produce new hybrid cultures." In Kaplan's view, all these accounts are limited by their reliance on "a model of center and periphery, which confront one another most often in a one-way imposition of power." Kaplan finds an alternative model in the field of Chicano studies, which "has begun to redress the conceptual limits of the frontier, by displacing it with the site of 'the borderlands.'" What appeals to Kaplan about the model of the borderlands is its emphasis on the "multidimensional and transterritorial"; for Chicano theorists, the borderlands "not only lie at the geographic and political margins of national identity but as often traverse the center of the metropolis. . . . The borderlands thus transform the traditional notion of the frontier from the primitive margins of civilization to a decentered cosmopolitanism" (16–17).

What Kaplan means here by *decentered cosmopolitanism* is, I think, a cosmopolitanism that emphasizes its pluralist rather than its universalist aspects. It is important to note, however, that *cosmopolitan pluralism* is not the same as what Werner Sollors describes as *pure pluralism*. As we saw in chapter 2, David Hollinger "distinguish[es] between a universalist will to find common ground from a cosmopolitan will to engage human diversity" (84). At the same time, however, he also makes a distinction between pluralism and cosmopolitanism, arguing that "pluralism and cosmopolitanism have often been united in the common cause of promoting tolerance and diversity" and therefore "have not always been distinguished as sharply as I believe today's circumstances demand" (85). According to Hollinger, a pluralist conception of multiculturalism "respects inherited boundaries and locates individuals within one or another of a series of ethno-racial groups to be protected and preserved" (3). Multiculturalism, in other words, divides "American culture" into a variety of separate "American cultures": it transforms what we thought was a single identity into a multiplicity of separate identities. If this stress on divisions, however, is pushed too far—into the realm of "pure pluralism"—it becomes merely divisive and leads us to the impasse of cultural relativism.

In my view, "good" multiculturalism stresses a cosmopolitan conception of pluralism: it instills a respect for difference, not out of the fear that often characterizes "pure pluralism," but rather out of respect and intellectual curiosity. It emphasizes diversity over division. It allows us to build on the pluralism that Chantal Mouffe identifies as the most valuable contribution made by traditional liberalism to democratic theory without allowing that pluralism to be a dangerous caricature of itself.

This shift toward cosmopolitan pluralism has already received a kind of philosophical blessing from Richard Rorty, who has tempered the support for ethnocentrism that characterized his writings during the 1980s in order to embrace a cosmopolitanism that might one day bring about a "planetary community" bound by its respect for "human rights" (1998a, 178). In his essay "Justice as a Larger Loyalty" Rorty offers a critique that is consonant with Morrison's and Pynchon's dramatizations of the failures of Enlightenment rationalism. Arguing that, in order to construct a "global moral community" based on a respect for human rights we must "peel apart Enlightenment liberalism from Enlightenment rationalism" (1998b, 57), Rorty suggests that "the rhetoric we Westerners use in trying to get everybody to be more like us would be improved if we were more frankly ethnocentric and less professedly universalist" (56). Rorty concludes "that getting rid of rationalistic rhetoric would permit the West to approach the non-West in the role of someone with an instructive story to tell, rather than in the role of someone purporting to be making better use of a universal human capacity" (57). In other words, once we begin to recognize the ethnocentrism that has always lurked behind our professed universalism, we "might better be able to construct . . . a global moral community" (57), to achieve the kind of "cosmopolitan utopias" that rationalist philosophers like Kant have prophesied (1998a, 173).

Multiculturalists who remains skittish about this shift toward a cosmopolitanism that is capable of postulating laws of culture and regulating human behavior would do well to consider their stance toward the condition of slavery, which is after all the condition that the concept of rights is designed to combat. Do we want to embrace a multiculturalism that prevents us from being able to condemn slavery wherever and whenever it occurs on the grounds that we have no right to judge the culture of another? If reading Morrison's and Pynchon's novels teaches us anything, it teaches us that the answer to this question must be no. Rather than worrying about a slippery slope that will lead us from the position of being able to make moral judgments about other cultures to a position of dominating other cultures, perhaps we should begin at the bottom of the slope: starting with the idea of that ultimate domination—slavery—that we can all agree to condemn, we can slowly work our way up to the ideal of a set of cultural laws that hold in all human orders, guided on our journey by the appreciation for diversity inherent in cosmopolitanism.

On 15 November 1763, Mason and Dixon arrived in Philadelphia to begin the project of drawing their boundary line—Philadelphia, the heart of the American Enlightenment, where the Declaration of Independence would be signed a little less than thirteen years later. The drawing of the line takes them west, almost to Ohio, a territory that will one day serve as the site of freedom for the ex-slaves in Morrison's *Beloved* and as the site of a different kind of oppression for the protagonists of her novel *Sula*. The passage from Enlightenment to slavery is one of the central motifs in *Mason & Dixon* as well as in Pynchon's career as a whole, which moves from postmodern critique in *V.* to the multicultural critique implicit in his account of the drawing of the boundary line. Mason and Dixon hew their way toward Ohio; with *Mason & Dixon*, which depicts a world of imperialism in which slavery is ubiquitous, Pynchon makes his closest approach yet to Morrison's territory. Together, these two writers help us to expose the flaws within the national narrative that U.S. culture has woven around its conception of individual freedom and to imagine a new cosmopolitanism able to promote the ideals of self-autonomy and self-expression *and* to expose and defeat slavery and oppression wherever they exist. Morrison and Pynchon thus point the way to a new way of conceiving individual and communal identity that will enable us to reject the old, Bad History and begin to write anew.

NOTES

PREFACE

1. This quote was presented as representative in *Time* magazine, which claimed, "Many voters were clearly casting their ballots for Ronald Reagan the man, not for the Republican Party" (Thomas 45).
2. Although it does not discuss Reaganism directly, Christopher Newfield's *The Emerson Effect* makes a compelling case for a symbiotic relation between liberal and authoritarian impulses in Emerson's conception of individualism. Newfield uses the term "*corporate individualism* . . . to describe the desired outcome of Emerson's liberalism: the enhancement of freedom through the loss of both private and public control" (5). In Newfield's account, Emerson's writing helps to produce a middle-class culture of submission and deference.
3. Fiscus adopts "what might be called a group perspective on the law rather than restricting himself to what might be called the individual perspective" (xi). He characterizes his central argument as the combination of "a claim of distributive justice with a stipulated assumption about equality at birth and with deductive reasoning about subsequent departures from that equality" (15).
4. The editors of the volume *Is Multiculturalism Bad For Women?* offer this definition: "Multiculturalism, according to one especially compelling formulation, is the radical idea that people in other cultures, foreign and domestic, are human beings, too—moral equals, entitled to equal respect and concern, not to be discounted or treated as a subordinate caste. Thus understood, multiculturalism condemns intolerance of other ways of life, finds the human in what might seem Other, and encourages cultural diversity." They note, however, that, "on closer inspection, multiculturalism resists easy reconciliation with egalitarian convictions. After all, some cultures do not accept, even as theory, the principle that people are owed equal respect and concern (of course, no culture fully practices the principle). Moreover, tensions with decent treatment for women seem especially acute. In

some contemporary cultures we see practices—including differential nutrition and health care, unequal rights of ownership, assembly, and political participation, unequal vulnerability to violence, and the denial of educational opportunities—that appear to fly in the face of the idea that women are entitled to be treated as equals" (Okin et al., 4).

5 For example, in the *Columbia Literary History of the United States* (1988), edited by Emory Elliott, Pynchon is mentioned in essays entitled "Culture, Power, and Society" and "Self-Reflexive Fiction," but Morrison is not; Morrison appears in an essay entitled "The Literature of Radical Statement," but Pynchon does not. Both authors are cited in an essay entitled "Neorealist Fiction," but Pynchon is listed with Barth, Vonnegut, Hawkes, and Coover as an author of "metatexts," while Morrison is classified in contradistinction as a "neorealist"; a similar distinction is made in "The Fictions of the Present," where Pynchon is described as a postmodernist and Morrison as a neorealist, although the essay does imply that both are authors of "political" fiction. Pynchon and Morrison emerge as two of the most major figures in "Postmodern Fictions, 1970–1990," Wendy Steiner's contribution to the vol. 7 of the new *Cambridge History of American Literature*, but Pynchon is analyzed in a section about experimental fiction entitled "Fables of the Fetish," while Morrison is included in "Women's Fiction: The Rewriting of History." Steiner does note that women writers share with postmodernists the desire "to test the boundaries between fiction and fact, between private and public fantasies" (1999, 500). The division is even more pronounced in Elliott's *Columbia History of the American Novel* (1991): Morrison is mentioned in "Society and Identity" and discussed at length in "Postmodern Realism," while Pynchon is analyzed in both "Postmodern Fiction" and "The Avant-Garde." The one essayist who does mention Pynchon and Morrison together (describing them in "Postmodern Culture" as "contemporary masters" along with Russell Banks and Joyce Carol Oates [1991, 520]) is the exception who proves the rule: Cornel West is not a literary critic proper but rather a professor of divinity and Afro-American studies at Harvard.

6 The first chapter of Pynchon's *V.* (1963) bears an intriguing subtitle—"In which Benny Profane, a schlemihl and human yo-yo, gets to an apocheir"—that is typeset to approximate a V formation and uses a heterogeneous yoking of incongruous words to cast a playful nod at the venerable tradition of the bildungsroman; the first two pages of Morrison's *The Bluest Eye* also manipulate typography as they invoke and then distort a child's "Dick-and-Jane" story by presenting it three times—the first time with loose leading and proper punctuation, the second time with tight leading and no punctuation, the third time with all the words smashed together into one long sequence of letters—suggesting the development of hysteria or delirium and thus also the utter uselessness of this story as a description of African American childhood.

ONE. Narrating Individualism

1 Compare, for example, Morrison's remarks to formulations offered by Priscilla Wald and Lauren Berlant. In *Constituting Americans*, Wald explores the ways in which five authors—Frederick Douglass, Herman Melville, Harriet Wilson, W. E. B. Du Bois, and Gertrude Stein—"came, in their works, [to offer] analyses of the official stories through which a nation—'a people'—spoke itself into existence." According to Wald, "Official stories are narratives that surface in the rhetoric of nationalist movements and initiatives—legal,

political, and literary—such as John Marshall's legislation of Indian Removal, Abraham Lincoln's program for a consolidated Union, and the efforts of literary Young America and the *Democratic Review* to shape an American literature. Official stories constitute Americans. I use the term 'official' because of the authority they command, articulated, as they are, in relation to the rights and privileges of individuals. They determine the status of an individual in the community" (2). In *The Anatomy of National Fantasy*, Lauren Berlant writes that "law dominates the field of citizenship, constructing technical definitions of the citizen's rights, duties, and obligations. But the National Symbolic also aims to link regulation to desire, harnessing affect to political life through the production of 'national fantasy.' By 'fantasy' I mean to designate how national culture becomes local—through the images, narratives, monuments, and sites that circulate through personal/collective consciousness" (1991, 5). Morrison's description of official stories shares with Wald's and Berlant's formulations an understanding of the ways in which these stories or fantasies serve nationalist ends; I will suggest, however, that Morrison and Pynchon both understand official stories as a component of all ideologies—not simply the national—and therefore see official stories at work even in communities that set themselves against the grain of nationalism.

2 For an analysis of the dynamics of individualism in one arena of popular culture, see Patell 1993.

3 The strategies of critical reading that Morrison deploys in *Playing in the Dark* (1992c) are likewise those of a cultural critic; she understands literature to be indelibly marked by its cultural context. She understands, too, what theorists of reception aesthetics have long pointed out: that the way in which we read literature is often based on "assumptions conventionally accepted among literary historians and critics and circulated as 'knowledge' " (4). In other words, if narrative serves as a principal conduit for the transmission of cultural knowledge, that process of transmission is often mediated by professional readers whose acts of literary criticism can either amplify or mute the challenges to the dominant culture posed by literary works. It is the argument of *Playing in the Dark* that Americanist literary criticism has tended to perpetuate the official story that American culture tells about itself by stressing characteristics that ostensibly have nothing to do with the fact of race or the oppression of African Americans: "individualism, masculinity, social engagement versus historical isolation; acute and ambiguous moral problematics; the thematics of innocence coupled with an obsession with figurations of death and hell" (5). *Playing in the Dark* was significant less for the originality of its critical arguments than for the cultural persona of its author: here was a Pulitzer Prize–winning novelist aligning herself with a revisionist trend in American studies that sought, as Donald Pease puts it, to "restore . . . the relations between cultural and political materials denied by previous Americanists" and "to link repressed sociopolitical contexts *within* literary works to the sociopolitical issues *external* to the academic field" (32).

4 According to Shklar, fiction is "best at seeing politics as a scenario of subtle interactions" (1984, 231).

5 For an example of a political philosopher who brings together both these strains of critique, see the work of William Connolly.

6 Let me present one suggestive example, which comes from a letter to the editor of the *Atlantic*, in response to a piece by Claude M. Steele entitled "Race and the Schooling of

Black Americans." The author of the letter argues that "most black students want very much to enter the mainstream of American society, but some black opinion-makers keep telling them that they belong to a different stream—and they tend to believe it." What the author himself believes is this: "It is time to stop insisting to black students that they are different. It is time to let them get on with their studies and with living as individuals in society, like everyone else" (R. Smith, 8). Willfully ignoring the fact that blacks have always been made to feel "different"—less by "black opinion-makers" than by everybody else (in other words, by American culture as a whole)—this view implies both that discrimination is illusory, a psychological hurdle that African Americans must learn to conquer, and that American culture is ready and willing to accept African Americans as fully equal individuals, two ideas that are still demonstrably false in late twentieth-century America. Moreover, this view is symptomatic in equating legal equality with cultural sameness, thereby suggesting that cultural difference and American individualism are incompatible ideas. In other words, to be an individual in America is not to be different but to conform, to be part of the "mainstream," to be just like "everybody else." I am indebted to Stanley Fish for bringing this exchange to my attention.

7 See Benjamin Constant's "The Liberty of the Ancients Compared with that of the Moderns" (Constant, 309–28). Isaiah Berlin admired Constant's essay and called it "one of the best I know on this topic" (Jahanbegloo, 42).

8 For a detailed discussion of political individualism, see Lukes, 79–87.

9 Berlin develops the argument in greater detail on pp. 133–54.

10 For a recent defense of positive liberty, see Skinner, who makes a distinction between positive liberty and republican views of liberty. In my terms, republicanism as Skinner describes it is a form of positive liberty.

11 The link between American individualism and American nationalism was first explored in Arieli. Three studies of nineteenth-century American individualism written during the 1980s offer crucial extensions and revisions of Arieli's work: Brown, Dimock, and Jehlen. These studies focus primarily on the American cultural imagination as it is expressed in literary texts, and they offer close textual readings within a new historicist framework. For a more traditional set of analyses of nineteenth-century American individualism, grounded in the historian's point of view rather than the literary critic's, see Curry and Goodheart, *American Chameleon*, which includes an essay by Arieli.

12 See, in particular, Bailyn, chap. 2; Wood, chap. 2; and Pocock 1975, chap. 13. Pocock has gone so far as to call the idea of a dominant Lockeanism in American thought a "myth" (1980, 462).

13 Hartz's thesis of a dominant Lockean consensus in American political thought has recently been defended by James P. Young and Joshua Foa Dienstag, both of whom, however, call for certain revisions. Young argues that Hartz underestimated the communal influences of both Puritanism and republicanism; the United States was not born Lockean, according to Young, but grew into it gradually, a thesis that puts him in agreement with Bellah et al. 1985. Dienstag, on the other hand, seeks to discover a communitarian impulse within Locke himself, taking issue with the "republican" analyses offered by Bailyn, Wood, and Pocock, he argues that "the language of 'virtue' and 'slavery,' which was pervasive at the time of the founding, and which many have been eager to take as evidence for the influence of civic humanism, in fact has a perfectly plain

Lockean provenance." He is less convinced, however, that the fact that "a Lockean sympathy once existed across a wide range of American political thinkers" means "that such a situation obtains today" (497).

14 See Ferguson, 472. In *American Dream: An Immigrant's Quest* (1986), Angelo Pellegrini describes Jefferson's transposition of Locke's formulation as a decisive moment in American culture. It is important to note that in identifying this aspect of Jeffersonian thought as representative of American culture as a whole, Pellegrini is himself deploying Jefferson's rhetorical strategy. In other words, both Jefferson, with his substitution, and Pellegrini, with his description, make use of a strategy of idealization. After all, for many Americans, both in Jefferson's time and in ours, the pursuit of property has been a crucial component of the pursuit of happiness. Indeed, it might be said that, when one strips away the idealized rhetoric of liberty and equality from revolutionary discourse, what remains is a decided aversion toward the payment of taxes, an aversion that flourishes, stronger than ever, more than two hundred years later. Gans argues that, for the average American, taxation provides one of the most concrete experiences of the abridgment of negative liberty, and he cites the desire for lower taxes as a cornerstone of late twentieth-century American individualism (25–28).

15 It is interesting to note that the process of idealization that I am describing can be found in the very text that the OED credits with containing the earliest use of the term *American dream*, James Truslow Adams's one-volume history of the United States, *The Epic of America* (1931), which describes the "American dream" as "the greatest contribution we have as yet made to the thought and welfare of the world" (viii), America's "distinctive and unique gift to mankind" (404). Adams defines *the American dream* as "that dream of a land in which life should be better and richer and fuller for every man, with opportunity for each according to his ability or achievement" (404). Arguing that the American dream "has been present from the start" (viii) and that it is based on a democratic conception of equality that makes it "difficult . . . for the European classes to interpret adequately" (404), Adams acknowledges the material basis of the dream but describes it as fundamentally idealistic:

> It is not a dream of motor cars and high wages merely, but a dream of a social order in which each man and each woman shall be able to attain to the fullest stature of which they are innately capable, and be recognized by others for what they are, regardless of the fortuitous circumstances of birth or position. . . .
>
> No, the American dream that has lured tens of millions of all nations to our shores in the past century has not been a dream of merely material plenty, though that has doubtless counted heavily. It has been much more than that. It has been a dream of being able to grow to fullest development as man and woman, unhampered by the barriers which had slowly been erected in older civilizations, unrepressed by social orders which had developed for the benefit of classes rather than for the simple being of any and every class. And that dream has been realized more fully in actual life here than anywhere else, though very imperfectly even among ourselves. (404–5)

The use of the word *merely* in this passage demonstrates the extent to which material values must form the basis of any accurate description of the American dream: "motor cars," "high wages," and "material plenty" are the obvious and universally acknowledged characteristics of the American dream; what the European upper classes and those

Americans who "have grown weary and mistrustful of it" fail to grasp is its *ultimately* idealistic nature. This passage is, in fact, a rhetorical argument about the nature of the American dream that deploys the word *merely* to shift attention toward those aspects of the dream that are not materialistic but idealistic.

Compare Lauren Berlant's description of "the fantasy of the American Dream." Berlant describes the dream as

> a popular form of political optimism, [which] fuses private fortune with that of the nation: it promises that if you invest your energies in work and family-making, the nation will secure the broader social and economic conditions in which your labor can gain value and your life can be lived with dignity. It is a story that addresses the fear of being stuck or reduced to a type, a redemptive story pinning its hope on class mobility. Yet this promise is voiced in the language of unconflicted personhood: to be American in this view, would be to inhabit a secure space liberated from identities and structures that seem to constrain what a person can do in history. For this paradoxical feeling to persist, such that a citizen of the Dream can feel firmly placed in a zone of protected value while on the move in an arc of social mobility, the vulnerability of personal existence to the instability of capitalism and the concretely unequal forms and norms of national life must be suppressed, minimized, or made to seem exceptional, not general to the population. This sets the stage for a national people imagining itself national only insofar as it feels unmarked by the effects of these national contradictions. (4)

Berlant's description of the American dream recapitulates, in different language, the national narrative that I have been describing. The citizen who exists "in a zone of protected value" is the abstract individual garbed in negative liberty, whose "personhood" is "unconflicted" because contingencies of history and context have been pared away. Berlant's description shows us how the cultural mythology of the American dream relies on idealization; we might view it as the flip side of the description offered by Pellegrini (see n. 14 above).

16 In *Domestic Individualism*, Gillian Brown explores the ways in which the discourses of individualism and domesticity are interdependent in nineteenth-century American culture, and she argues that "nineteenth-century American individualism takes on its peculiarly 'individualistic' properties as domesticity inflects it with values of interiority, privacy, and psychology" (1).

17 According to Gans, two popular television programs of the late 1970s and early 1980s—"Dallas" and "Dynasty"—"touch [a] chord in middle American individualism because of their essentially familial conception of the contemporary economy. Although the major protagonists of both dramas are heads of international corporations, their companies are run as family businesses in which decisions are based on interfamilial dynamics" (55). Gans also points out that "the strength of nationalist emotion during wartime and the intensity of hate toward the enemy may be partly explained by familistic qualities projected onto the nation at war" (63).

18 Compare Berlant: "There is no logic to a national form but, rather, many simultaneously 'literal' and 'metaphorical' meanings, stated and unstated" (5).

The fact that slavery is sanctioned by Locke's *Two Treatises* as well as by many other early theorists of natural rights may well have helped to make the contradiction between liberty and slavery palatable during the revolutionary and antebellum periods (McDonald, 51). Locke takes it for granted that slavery was a facet of social organization authorized by the Bible, and he argues that a human life can be forfeited and thus become subject to enslavement through the commission of an act punishable by death (284) or by being taken captive in a "just War" (322). Some American social theorists would find further justification in the fact that the republics of ancient Greece, the very crucible of democracy, had been based on slavery. (See, for example, the comments of Charles Pinckney [cited in McDonald 1985, 51] and Thomas Dew [cited in Arieli 1964, 300].) Southern intellectuals would eventually develop a philosophical defense of slavery in which the existence of freedom and the institutions that protect it were predicated on the existence of slavery. For example, John C. Calhoun could claim in 1838 that "Many in the South once believed that [slavery] was a moral and political evil. That folly and delusion are gone. We see it now in its true light, and regard it as the most safe and stable basis for free institutions in the world. It is impossible with us that the conflict can take place between labor and capital, which makes it so difficult to establish and maintain free institutions in all wealthy and highly civilized nations where such institutions as ours do not exist" (quoted in Arieli 1964, 300). Calhoun openly rationalizes what good Lockeans would be ashamed to admit: that the existence of negative liberty for some depends on the negation of liberty for others.

There is a further historical link between liberty and slavery, although it is more phenomenological than philosophical. It seems likely that the existence of slavery in the American colonies served as a constant reminder of the value and sweetness of freedom. Edmund Morgan speculates that the republican zeal that gripped colonial Virginia can be attributed, at least in part, to the existence of slavery: "The presence of men and women who were, in law at least, almost totally subject to the will of other men gave to those in control of them an immediate experience of what it could mean to be at the mercy of a tyrant." Virginians like Washington, Jefferson, Monroe, and Madison "may have had a special appreciation of the freedom dear to republicans," Morgan suggests, "because they saw every day what life without it could be like" (376). Small farmers identified with plantation owners because "neither was a slave" and "both were equal in not being slaves" (381). Patterson corroborates Morgan's analysis by arguing that, in almost all large-scale slaveholding societies, the "poorest free person took pride in the fact that he was not a slave. By sharing in the collective honor of the master class, all free persons legitimized the principle of honor and thereby recognized the members of the master class as those most adorned with honor and glory" (99). The abolition of slavery in the United States did not eliminate the culture's need for a subservient group of people, and thus a de facto caste system emerged, based, as slavery had been, on the supposed superiority of whites.

On the other hand, the contradiction between the rhetoric of liberty and the practice of slavery was a matter of controversy even during the revolutionary and early Republican eras. Slavery was a favorite trope among those who wrote in support of the American revolutionary cause. In his *Letters from a Farmer in Pennsylvania*, for example, John Dickinson wrote that "*those who are taxed without their own consent expressed by themselves or their representatives are slaves. We are taxed without our consent expressed by ourselves or our representatives. We are therefore—*SLAVES" (quoted in Bailyn, 232–33). In a similar vein, Thomas Paine (quoting from the text of Parliament's 1766 Declaratory Act) argued that "Britain, with an army to enforce her tyranny, has declared that she has a right (*not only to* TAX) but to 'BIND us in ALL CASES WHATSOEVER'; and if *being bound in that manner is not slavery, then is there no such thing as slavery upon earth*" (41).

Such vehement bursts of rhetoric were typical, but those who voiced them were often loathe to make the connection between their alleged oppression at the hands of the British "tyrant" and their own practice of enslaving Africans. By the time Jefferson penned the first draft of the Declaration of Independence, however, the contradiction between the American colonists' demands for liberty and their refusal to grant it to their slaves had become a major issue among colonial pamphleteers. For example, in his pamphlet *Strictures upon the Declaration of the Congress at Philadelphia*, Thomas Hutchinson criticized the colonists for professing to cherish equality and liberty while depriving "more than an hundred thousand Africans of their rights to liberty and *the pursuit of happiness*, and in some degree to their lives" (quoted in Bailyn, 246). Jefferson's original draft of the Declaration included a paragraph that listed the practice of African slavery as one of the offenses committed by the British crown: "He has waged cruel war against human nature itself, violating it's [sic] most sacred rights of life and liberty in the persons of a distant people who never offended him, captivating & carrying them into slavery in another hemisphere, or to incur miserable death" (22). In his *Autobiography*, Jefferson laments that the paragraph condemning the enslavement of Africans "was struck out in complaisance to South Carolina and Georgia, who had never attempted to restrain the importation of slaves, and who on the contrary still wished to continue it," adding, "Our northern brethren also . . . felt a little tender under those censures: for tho' their people have very few slaves themselves yet they had been pretty considerable carriers of them to others" (18). Encoded into the nation's founding moment, this disjunction between theory and practice would continue to mar American culture long after the actual institution of slavery was abolished.

19 I discuss the Rawlsian model in detail in chap. 2.

20 These novels are marked by what Timothy Melley has usefully termed *agency panic*, "an intense anxiety about an apparent loss of autonomy or self-control—the conviction that one's actions are being controlled by someone else, that one has been 'constructed' by powerful external agents." Melley adds that "in addition to these primary anxieties about individual autonomy, agency panic usually involves a secondary sense that controlling organizations are themselves agents—rational, motivated entities with the will and the means to carry out complex plans" (12–13). For Melley, "the importance of agency panic lies in the way it attempts to conserve a long-standing model of personhood—a view of the individual as a rational, motivated agent with a protected interior core of beliefs, desires, and memories" (14), and he suggests that paranoia—both the kind analyzed by Richard Hofstadter and the kind dramatized by Pynchon's novels—"is a defense of—perhaps even a component of—liberal individualism" (25).

TWO. Idealizing Individualism

1 Tellingly, Connolly is frequently described as a "postmodernist" political philosopher, and his critiques of both individualism and liberalism are in line with those dramatized

by the two postmodern novelists who are my subject here (see, in particular, Connolly 1991, 64–93).

2. For an analysis of the reception of Emerson's lectures, see Cayton, 598–620.

3. For an analysis of Emerson's confrontation with socialism and its decisive effect on his attitudes toward both "individuality" and "individualism," see Bercovitch, 1993. Bercovitch seeks to draw a distinction between Emerson and "the Jacksonian ideologues," who "defend individualism as a social, economic, and political system"; he argues that, for Emerson, "individualism centers first and last on the independent self" (313). What I am arguing here, however, is that (despite his loathing for Andrew Jackson) Emerson's conception of individualism still represents a social system—idealized, even utopian, but a system nonetheless.

4. As a twenty-one-year-old, Emerson had written in his journal that "the highest species of reasoning upon divine subjects is rather the fruit of a sort of moral imagination, than of the 'Reasoning Machines' such as Locke & Clarke & David Hume" (18 April 1824; 1982, 45).

5. Compare Bercovitch 1978, 183: "Many earlier laissez-faire theorists had recognized that open competition and upward mobility could endanger the very enterprise that nourished those values. Thus John Locke urged voluntary submission to authority in order to safeguard rights of property—including the property of the self—and thus in 1776 Adam Smith offered a rationale for self-interest that stressed the mutuality of independence and interdependence. Emerson, who counted Smith's *Wealth of Nations* a 'book of wisdom,' found in America the perfect symbol of that mutuality." See also Bercovitch 1993, 313–14: Emerson's "writings from *Nature* (1836) through *Essays: First Series* (1841) develop a utopian vision of the self which transforms earlier concepts of autonomy (Descartes's cogito, Locke's self-possessive individualism) into a self-emptying mode of visionary possession."

6. In a journal entry dated January 1844, Emerson wrote, "Kant, it seems, searched the Metaphysics of the Selfreverence which is the favourite position of modern ethics, & demonstrated to the Consciousness that itself alone exists" (1982, 320). Emerson, however, received his Kant secondhand, by reading the work of Samuel Taylor Coleridge. According to Stephen Whicher, "The Coleridge who influenced Emerson was not the author of 'The Ancient Mariner' and 'Kubla Khan' but the eclectic philosopher of *Biographia Literaria* (1817) and the Anglican homilist of *The Statesman's Manual* (1816), *The Friend* (1818), and the *Aids to Reflection* (1825). He conveyed to Emerson some of the key insights of Kant and the post-Kantians mixed with enough Platonism and piety to make them palatable" (Emerson 1957, 471). For a reading of Emerson's writings as at least a partial "rejoinder" to Kant, see Cavell 1981, 121–38.

7. For an account of entrepreneurship in seventeenth-century New England, see Martin.

8. Larry J. Reynolds suggests that the idea that Emerson's formulation of an "ideal union" in an "actual individualism" is a sign of "Emerson's commitment to the mystical way, which explains why he thought union with others could only be achieved through union with the divine. When he writes that 'the union is only perfect, when all the uniters are isolated,' this is precisely the argument of the monastic tradition, which he, Thoreau, Fuller, and other transcendentalists subscribed to, as often as they could, when not caught up against their wills, in reform issues" (personal communication, 3 June 1999).

9. For F. O. Matthiessen, Emerson's "inveterate habit of stating things in opposites" is merely a stylistic "reaction" against "the formal logic of the eighteenth century." Matthiessen insists that behind "the multiplicity of [Emerson's] conflicting statements" there is an essential "wholeness of character," which it is the critic's task to excavate (3). In his magisterial study *An Uneasy Solitude: Individual and Society in the Work of Ralph Waldo Emerson* (1964), Maurice Gonnaud writes that "a French mind, however open or unprejudiced it may be, is hardly ever comfortable with Emerson's thought: fragmentary in the extreme, weak in structure even when striving for order, fertile in contradictions, in second thoughts, in non sequiturs, and so indifferent to logical rigor as to seem positively unsound." Emerson, Gonnaud tells us, is no Pascal; therefore, "one has to try to read Emerson with a virgin mind, so to speak—following the movement of his thought, experiencing the alternation of his inward tides—if one wants to catch the original quality of the work" (xxi).

10. Here I am arguing implicitly against an interpretation of Emerson generally put forward by those like Stanley Cavell and Richard Poirier who want to align him with American pragmatist philosophy. For example, in *The Renewal of Literature*, Poirier writes, "Emerson, the father of American pragmatism, practiced what William James was to preach, that a pragmatist turns his back resolutely and once for all upon a lot of inveterate habits dear to professional philosophers. He turns away from abstraction and insufficiency, from verbal solutions, from bad *a priori* reasons, from fixed principles, closed systems, and pretended absolutes and origins. He turns toward concreteness and adequacy, toward facts, toward action, toward power" (17).

11. There are, of course, limits to Emerson's "feminism." A few sentences later, he writes that legislation would not be necessary if women could somehow experience a "rejuvenescence," for "as soon as you have a sound & beautiful woman, a figure in the style of the Antique Juno, Diana, Pallas, Venus, & the Graces, all falls into place, the men are magnetised, heaven opens, & no lawyer need be called in to prepare a clause, for woman moulds the lawgiver." For discussions of the ways in which Emerson and his contemporaries exclude women from their thinking and writing about self-reliance, see Leverenz.

12. The lecture has never been published, and the manuscript is presumed to be lost, but the notes on which it was based survive in Emerson's journal (see Gonnaud, 223–24; and Gougeon, 37–40).

13. Albert J. von Frank takes issue with this formulation of Emerson's attitude to the inferiority of other races. Suggesting that it is "unfair" to "lump Emerson with malevolent racists," von Frank argues that the "inferiority" that Emerson refers to reflects "the cultural primitiveness vis-à-vis European societies—and says nothing about intrinsic capacities" (personal communication, 10 May 1999). He suggests that when Emerson refers to "races of savages," he is "as likely referring to the Germanic tribes as anything else" and using a definition of race similar to the one cited in an 1847 edition of *Webster's*: "the lineage of a family, or continued series of descendants from a parent who is called a stock." I find this reading plausible for the quotation that includes the phrase *race of savages*, but Emerson's use of the term in the following passage seems to be much more plausibly linked to the twentieth-century concept of race than to the idea of a tribe: "When at last in a race, a new principle appears, an idea;—that conserves it; ideas only

save races. If the black man is feeble, and not important to the existing races not on a parity with the best race, the black man must serve, and be exterminated."

I find Barbara Packer's assessment of Emerson's attitudes toward race more compelling: "Slavery," she suggests, "is ultimately a political question, a question of rights, and though it takes Emerson some time to see it that way, once he does, it's not a question upon which he is even ambivalent. But race is another matter—a huge, hideous cauldron of irrational prejudices, disgusts, fears, contempts, and fears of pollution. Emerson is at the mercy of all these violent feelings, just as all his contemporaries were, and like them he can neither acknowledge them, become aware of them, or escape them. Black people disgust him, give him what he himself called 'colorphobia.' He doesn't want to see them, be near them, have them as neighbors or fellow citizens. Yet by 1844 he is fully committed to a political program that will have the effect of freeing up millions of black people to invade his peaceful territory. Is it any wonder that his public pronouncements are so ambivalent, so hesitant, so full of hidden meanings?" (personal communication, 6 August 1999).

For more positive assessments of Emerson's attitudes toward both race and antislavery, see Gougeon 1990 and von Frank 1999. Von Frank takes issue with John Carlos Rowe's contention that "Emersonian transcendentalism and political activism in mid-nineteenth-century America were inherently incompatible" (Rowe 1997, 21). Von Frank sees no distinction between Emerson's transcendentalist writings and his "political writings"; for example, he writes, "Emerson believed that the 'better life' promised by reform had to have reference (and indeed did have reference when properly understood) to his underlying Unitarian/Transcendental construction of 'life' as an empowering spiritual progress" (403). If what I am tracing here may be labeled *the cost of Emersonian abstraction*, then von Frank's essay may be seen as its opposite number, an account of *the benefits of Emersonian abstraction*.

14 Packer writes further: "I don't think Emerson could ever get a handle on his own feelings about race, because they were too strong, too ugly, too out-of-control for him ever to handle, much less understand. He would have needed both a Freudian understanding of the unconscious and an anthropologist's sense of how human beings code groups as part of a social structure that turns on irreconcilable oppositions. He didn't have those things, or even an approach to them. What he had was a belief in the sanctity of the individual and in the universality of the Moral Law. It turns out that one can indeed arrive at an antislavery position out of such tenets, but only by triangulation. 'I loathe, detest, and fear you, but I am willing to concede that you may be human, and that, therefore, you are entitled to the same rights as people whose humanity is not in question. Besides, attempting to hold you in bondage clearly leads to the moral corruption of the whole white race, and therefore is a *sign* that slavery is against the Moral Law, although from a purely intellectual standpoint it might be defended as the natural domination of the weak by the strong.' If I had to put Emerson's antislavery position in a nutshell, that would be how I would phrase it." As my analysis above suggests, I disagree that Emerson lacked a way of approaching the anthropologist's "sense of how human beings code groups as part of a social structure that turns on irreconcilable oppositions." I think that he intuited this insight without ever being able to formulate it fully.

15 I am indebted to Larry J. Reynolds for bringing this letter to my attention.

16 Albert J. von Frank has suggested to me that there is a problem with taking "The Sovereignty of Ethics" to be emblematic in this way because the essay "is a pastiche put together in Emerson's dotage by J. E. Cabot" and therefore "there is no second author twenty years distant from the first" (personal communication, 10 May 1999). In a note preceding the 1883 Riverside Edition of *Lectures and Biographical Sketches*, the volume in which "Sovereignty" appears, Cabot writes that the essay was one of those that "I got ready for [Emerson's] use in readings to his friends or a limited public. He had given up the regular practice of lecturing, but would sometimes, upon special request, read a paper that had been prepared for him from his manuscripts in the manner described in the Preface to Letters and Social Aims,—some former lecture serving as a nucleus for a new" (3).

Moreover, "Sovereignty" was one of the papers that Emerson afterward allowed to be printed. In notes written for the Centenary Edition in 1904, Edward Emerson writes that "the material for this essay, which was printed in the *North American Review* of May 1878, was drawn from several lectures, especially 'Morals,' given at Freeman Place Chapel in 1859, 'The Essential Principles of Religion,' before Theodore Parker's Society at the Music Hall in 1862, 'The Rule of Life' and 'Natural Religion' at Horticultural Hall respectively in 1867 and 1869, and possibly from others. Mr. Cabot made the best mosaic that he could, and it received Mr. Emerson's approval, but as he said in his prefatory note to *Letters and Social Aims*, with regard to 'Immortality,' it contains passages written at periods far apart from one another" (Emerson 1903–4, 549).

Edward Emerson's failure to mention the source in question here—the 1855 "Lecture on Slavery"—may not be a deliberate omission, but it certainly reinforces the image of an Emerson devoted primarily to abstract philosophy rather than the political issues of his day. Should we hold Emerson responsible as author for the contents of "The Sovereignty of Ethics" even if it was put together for him by another hand? I think the fact that Emerson allowed the essay to be printed during his lifetime suggests that he was willing to take responsibility for its contents. Moreover, the essay was certainly regarded by its readers as a piece of Emerson's writing: William James quotes the essay in *The Varieties of Religious Experience* and in his 1903 "Address at the Centenary of Ralph Waldo Emerson" (38, 1122).

17 During the 1960s, Rawls published five more journal articles that continued the public elaboration of his theory: "Constitutional Liberty" (1963), "The Sense of Justice" (1963), "Distributive Justice" (1967), "Distributive Justice: Some Addenda" (1968) and "The Justification of Civil Disobedience" (1969)—all now collected in Rawls 1999a. Privately, Rawls circulated three different drafts of the manuscript of *A Theory of Justice* among professors and students of philosophy.

18 "The priority of right is a central feature of Kant's ethics" (1971, 31n; 1999c, 28n), according to Rawls, who refers his reader both to *The Critique of Practical Reason* and to the essay "On the Common Saying: 'This May Be True in Theory, but It Does Not Apply in Practice.'" In the latter piece, Kant writes that "the whole concept of an external right is derived entirely from the concept of *freedom* in the mutual external relations of human beings, and has nothing to do with the end which all men have by nature (i.e. the aim of achieving happiness) or with the recognized means of attaining this end. And thus the

latter end must on no account interfere as a determinant with the laws governing external right" (73). Kant asserts that the civil state "is based on the following principles: 1. The *freedom* of every member of society as a *human being*. 2. The *equality* of each with all the others as a *subject* 3. The *independence* of each member of a commonwealth as a *citizen*." These principles, according to Kant, "are not so much laws given by an already established state, as laws by which a state can alone be established in accordance with the pure rational principles of external human right" (74).

19 Michael Sandel and others have criticized this conception of justice as being merely "procedural." Sandel argues that this reliance on procedure has led to the erosion of any hope for "a public philosophy of common purposes." The twentieth-century "procedural republic," he argues, has "made its peace with concentrated power," and its practices are marked by "two broad tendencies foreshadowed by its philosophy: first, a tendency to crowd out democratic possibilities; second, a tendency to undercut the kind of community on which it nonetheless depends" (1984b, 93; see also Sandel 1982, 108–9, 125–27). Similarly, Roberto Unger writes in *Knowledge and Politics* that liberal theorists attempt to design "a procedure for lawmaking to which any man, no matter what his values, would have reason to agree" but generally fail to realize that every regime, no matter how committed to neutrality, inevitably "prefers some values over others" (1975, 54, 86–87). Finally, William Connolly argues that "current liberalism cannot be defined merely through its commitment to freedom, rights, dissent, and justice. It must be understood, as well, through the institutional arrangements it endorses" (1987, 83). Liberalism thus "bifurcated" by its commitments to both "liberty" and "practicality" (83) leads to "a technocratic conception of politics" (84).

20 Thomas Nagel argues that Rawls provides "a way of treating the basic problems of social choice, for which no generally recognized methods of precise solution exist, through the proxy of a specially constructed parallel problem of individual choice, which can be solved by the more reliable intuitions and decision procedures of rational prudence" (1).

21 For his initial explanation of "the priority problem," see Rawls 1971, 40–45. See also "The Basic Liberties and Their Priority," in Rawls 1993, 289–371, where he further develops his justification for the assignment of priority to certain basic liberties in response to criticisms offered by H. L. A. Hart in "Rawls on Liberty and Its Priority."

22 See also Sandel 1982, 93–95. In what seems like an attempt to disarm this criticism, the second edition of *A Theory of Justice* offers a revised version of the passage that Sandel quotes. In the 1971 edition, Rawls writes: "The social system is not an interchangeable order beyond human control but a pattern of human action. In justice as fairness men agree to share one another's fate. In designing institutions they undertake to avail themselves of the accidents of nature and social circumstance only when doing so is for the common benefit" (102). The revised edition weakens the suggestion that justice as fairness depends on unacknowledged forms of community by omitting the dramatic sentence about shared fate: "The social system is not an interchangeable order beyond human control but a pattern of human action. In justice as fairness men agree to avail themselves of the accidents of nature and social circumstance only when doing so is for the common benefit" (1999b, 88).

23 The basic argument of this essay is presented in revised form in Rawls 1993, 3–46.

24 Rawls defines *a well-ordered society* as "one designed to advance the good of its members

and effectively regulated by a public conception of justice" (1971, 453) (see generally Rawls 1971, 4–6, 453–62; and Rawls 1993, 35–40).

25 Bellah et al. actually use the term *mythic individualism*, but their definition of that term corresponds to my use of the term *rugged individualism*.

26 See also the critiques of MacIntyre and Lasch in Holmes 1993, 88–140.

27 In the second edition of *Liberalism and the Limits of Justice*, Sandel takes issue with these descriptions of his work, suggesting that it should in fact be distinguished from the work of MacIntyre, Taylor, and Walzer. "The debate," he writes, "is sometimes cast as an argument between those who prize individual liberty and those who think the values of the community or the will of the majority should always prevail, or between those who believe in universal human rights and those who insist there is no way to judge the values that inform different cultures and traditions. Insofar as 'communitarianism' is another name for majoritarianism, or for the idea that rights should rest on the values that predominate in any given community at any given time, it is not a view I would defend" (1998, ix–x).

28 In taking Emerson seriously as a philosopher, Kateb takes a position outside the mainstream of American philosophers. Leo Marx refers to Kateb as part of a group of "eccentric philosophers and political theorists" who have "rediscovered the power and pertinence of Emersonian individualism" (p. 36). For a very different consideration of Emerson and Rawls, see Cavell 1990, 33–63, 101–26.

29 The need for greater mutuality is one of four recurring criticisms of liberal society that Kateb detects within the work of such communitarian thinkers as "Benjamin Barber, Sheldon Wolin, John Schaar, Alasdair MacIntyre, Christopher Lasch, Michael Sandel, Charles Taylor, and Michael Walzer (some of the time)." The other three criticisms are a lack of togetherness, which breeds loneliness and alienation; a lack of discipline, which leads to selfishness; and the fostering of a narcissism that "imprisons people in their individual identities and thus denies them the release into something larger than themselves, while weakening their will to make the inevitable patriotic sacrifices that a hostile world unexpectedly but regularly calls for" (1992, 223–24).

30 Calling *soul* a "key term" that "frequently occurs in 'Song of Myself' and in all of Whitman's work," Kateb notes that Whitman uses the word in both a religious and a secular sense. "In its religious meaning," writes Kateb, the term *soul* represents "unique and unalterable individual identity; one's genius or 'eidolon' "; he quickly adds, however, that "the Whitman that matters" to him is "the one who believes in the secular soul, not the one who fancies he believes in the religious soul (toward which he does sometimes turn a skeptical glance)" (1992, 245).

31 Interestingly, the career of the philosopher Roberto Unger seems to have followed the opposite trajectory. The Unger of *Knowledge and Politics* (1975) is extremely compatible with the communitarian conservatism of MacIntyre and Sandel; indeed, Stephen Holmes describes his former colleague Sandel as "the best-known disciple of MacIntyre and Unger" (1993, 177). But the later Unger of the trilogy *Politics, A Work in Constructive Social Theory* swerves away to become compatible with Emerson (and, indeed, Nietzsche). Instead of faulting liberalism for being excessively individualistic, the Unger of *Politics* faults it for being too restrained, not individualistic enough; he now favors what he calls *superliberalism*, which has much in common with the "self-reliance" advocated by Emer-

son. It also shares many of the defects of Emerson's universalism. Holmes argues that "Unger's superliberalism... has the same relation to liberalism as Nietzsche's superman has to ordinary men and women" (173).

THREE. Unenlightened Enlightenment

1. *Playing in the Dark* is clearly influenced by the work of Orlando Patterson, whose study *Slavery and Social Death* (1982) formed a part of Morrison's research for *Beloved* (see Morrison 1992a).
2. *The Narrative of the Life of Frederick Douglass* demonstrates that the experience of selling one's labor for a wage could also have the effect of making the slave understand both the basic injustice of slavery and the dynamics of freedom in a market economy. Frederick Douglass comes to understand the economic nature of his social death when he reflects bitterly that his ability to earn a wage does not render him capable of keeping it:

    I was now getting... one dollar and fifty cents per day. I contracted for it; I earned it; it was paid to me; it was rightfully my own; yet, upon each returning Saturday night, I was compelled to deliver every cent of that money to Master Hugh. And why? Not because he earned it,—not because he had any hand in earning it,—not because I owed it to him—nor because he possessed the slightest shadow of a right to it; but solely because he had the power to compel me to give it up. The right of the grim-visaged pirate upon the high seas is exactly the same. (133)

    By viewing Master Hugh's actions as theft, Douglass asserts that even a slave has the right to possess property; moreover, Douglass suggests that his master knows in his heart that he is violating his slave's natural rights and therefore assuages his guilt by giving Douglass a few cents a week as encouragement. "The fact that he gave me any part of my wages," writes Douglass, "was proof, to my mind, that he believed me entitled to the whole of them.... I feared that the giving me a few cents would ease his conscience, and make him feel himself to be a pretty honorable sort of robber" (137). Later, Douglass convinces his master to allow him to hire out his time and to keep what he earns, on the condition that he pay Master Hugh three dollars a week for the privilege and an additional three dollars for board, clothing, and tools.

    Douglass's experiences as a wage earner give him a taste of life as a free man, and he begins to understand freedom in economic terms as well: "It was a step toward freedom to be allowed to bear the responsibilities of a freedman, and I was determined to hold on upon it. I bent myself to the work of making money. I was ready to work at night as well as day, and by the most untiring perseverance and industry, I made enough to meet my expenses, and lay up a little money every week" (139). As Houston Baker argues, Douglass's discovery that "slave skills and labor yield surplus value" acts as "a spur to individualistic, economic enterprise" (51). Constrained as it is by "responsibilities," "expenses," and "anxieties," the economic freedom that Douglass describes sounds more like the drudgery described in working-class novels than the economic freedom celebrated by American entrepreneurs, but it proves to be a crucial step toward self-proprietorship. This process continues when, after his escape to the North, Douglass gets married. According to Baker, "Douglass's certificate of marriage, which he transcribes in full, signifies that the black man has *repossessed* himself in a manner that enables him to enter the type of relationship disrupted, or foreclosed, by the economics of slavery" (48). We can extend this assertion by suggesting that Douglass's marriage represents a double declaration of right: it affirms both his right to be a contracting agent and thus a member of civil society and his right to choose his own mate and raise a family (and it is the violation of this second right that is so compellingly dramatized in Morrison's *Beloved*).

For Douglass, the process of achieving self-possession is ultimately completed when, after publishing his *Narrative* and fleeing to England, he is able to raise sufficient funds from book sales, lecture fees, and donations to purchase his freedom. For the nineteenth-century slave, Locke's concept of person as property was no theoretical concept employed to derive individual rights: it was, instead, a bitter actuality. The economics of slavery forced Douglass to become, first, a possessive individualist—far more literally so than your typical Lockean—and, finally, an entrepreneur.

3   Timothy Melley describes this alignment of human and machine as "the novel's machinery of mathematical personation." According to Melley, "To be a person in *Gravity's Rainbow* means to recognize, continually and with great nervousness, that your 'personality' might not be yours, that it constitutes and is constituted by global control structures, and that as it moves in and out of your body, it marks certain lines of discursive production and regulation and moves information through immense but invisible networks" (106).

4   In the scene to which I am referring, Ellison's narrator comes upon a crowd of people watching an old African American couple being evicted from their Harlem apartment. He literally stumbles across what looks like "a lot of junk waiting to be hauled away" but is at first unable to understand what it is that he is seeing: "What on earth, I thought, looking about me. What on earth? The old woman sobbed, pointing to the stuff piled along the curb. 'Just look what they doing to us. Just look,' looking straight at me. And I realized that what I'd taken for junk was actually worn household furnishings" (268). The old woman's words have forced him to refocus his vision, and, as he continues to observe the scene, its surface of chaos resolves itself into distinct legible signs. Ellison gives us a catalog of objects that, like Pynchon's, fills the observer with images of the lives of their owners:

> My eyes fell upon a pair of crudely carved and polished bones, "knocking bones," used to accompany music at country dances, used in black-face minstrels; the flat ribs of a cow, a steer or sheep, flat bones that gave off a sound, when struck, like heavy castenets [sic] (had he been a minstrel?) or the wooden block of a set of drums. Pots and pots of green plants were lined in the dirty snow, certain to die of the cold; ivy, canna, a tomato plant. And in a basket I saw a straightening comb, switches of false hair, a curling iron, a card with silvery letters against a background of dark red velvet, reading "God Bless Our Home"; and scattered across the top of a chiffonier were nuggets of High John the Conqueror, the lucky stone; and as I watched the white men put down a basket in which I saw a whiskey bottle filled with rock candy and camphor, a small Ethiopian flag, a faded tintype of Abraham Lincoln, and the smiling image of a Hollywood star torn from a magazine. And on a pillow several badly cracked pieces of delicate china, a commemorative plate celebrating the St. Louis World Fair . . . I stood in a kind of daze, looking at an old folded lace fan studded with jet and mother-of pearl. (271; ellipsis in original)

When he discovers the old man's tattered "free papers," which have fallen out of a drawer, the narrator is overcome and, like Mucho, is sickened by what he has seen: "A bitter spurt of gall filled my mouth and splattered the old folk's possessions" (273).

As the scene progresses, the narrator finds himself torn by mixed emotions: he is disgusted by the realization that eighty-seven years of "labor" can amount to nothing more than so much junk, "strewn in the snow like chicken guts," but he also comes to realize that these shabby possessions are familiar to him, that they represent the shared cultural experience of black people in the United States. And, as a result, they cause him "discomfort so far beyond their intrinsic meaning as objects" (273) because they force him to face up to the heritage that he has spent his life trying to escape in order to mold himself to fit white culture's definition of the successful black man. Having resolved itself into legibility, the pile of junk once more recedes into abstraction: "I turned and stared again at the jumble, no longer looking at what was before my eyes, but inwardly-outwardly, around a corner into the dark, far-away-and-long-ago, not so much of my own memory as of remembered words, of linked verbal echoes, images, heard even when not listening at home" (273). The feeling that he is struggling to articulate is the feeling of involuntary dispossession: "It was as though I myself was being dispossessed of some painful yet precious thing which I could not bear to lose; something confounding, like a rotted tooth that one would rather suffer indefinitely than endure the short, violent eruption of pain that would mark its removal" (273). Here, the image of the rotten tooth becomes a symbol for the shared experience of African American culture: almost too painful to endure, yet much more painful to lose.

The narrator's revelation moves him to address the crowd in a haphazard attempt to get it to do something about this intolerable situation, yet he is not immediately able to articulate his feelings. Only when a member of the crowd uses the word *dispossessed* does the narrator find a guiding trope with enough rhetorical force to sway the crowd:

"What's happened to them. They're our people, your people and mine, your parents and mine. What's happened to 'em."

"I'll tell you!" a heavyweight yelled, pushing out the crowd, his face angry. "Hell, they been dispossessed, you crazy sonofabitch, get out the way!" (278)

Attempting to get the crowd to think abstractly about the eviction in progress, the narrator sparks an exasperated, literal-minded response, which he is nonetheless able to use abstractly in order to articulate his new understanding: "That's a good word, 'Dispossessed'! 'Dispossessed,' eighty-seven years and dispossessed of what? They ain't got nothing, they caint *get* nothing, they never *had* nothing. So who was dispossessed?" (279). The narrator concludes that all of them—the black people being evicted and the black people watching—are among the dispossessed. The narrator's experiences up to this point in the novel have shown him that American culture only appears to encourage black people to take part in its individualistic success ethic; in reality, it has little intention of letting them participate. To be black in America is to be always already dispossessed. For further comparisons between Morrison and Ellison, see Awkward 1988; Butler-Evans 1995; Harris 1988, 75; Smith 1987.

5   For a lucid discussion of the Stencil portions of V., see Patteson. Tanner notes, "It is suitable that the last clue [Stencil] picks up, which will keep him moving on (approaching and avoiding), this time to Stockholm, is about a certain Mme. Viola, who is an 'onei-

213

romancer and hypnotist.' She will not only be able to divine his dreams, but also induce and prolong them" (33).

6   For a discussion of postmodern detective fictions and a comparison of Pynchon's *The Crying of Lot 49* to William Hjorstberg's *Falling Angel*, see Tani.

7   As James Cox puts it, "If 'Self-Reliance' was a ringing exhortation to trust the self, 'Experience' turns out to disclose that, after the last disillusion, there is nothing to rely on *but* the self" (81).

8   Chandler sets the hard-boiled detective story onto the pedestal of American myth by creating a hero who is simultaneously a man of the streets and a figure of legend, a modern version of both the knight in shining armor and the gunslinger. In contrast to Dashiell Hammett, who depicts a cynical and corrupt version of the quest for the Holy Grail in *The Maltese Falcon*, Chandler uses romance to temper the hard-boiled naturalism of *Black Mask* fiction. When openly displayed in names like Helen Grayle, Orfamay Quest, or *The Lady in the Lake*, the allusions to romance can sometimes seem like parody, but Chandler steadfastly depicts Marlowe's sense of honor as a modern form of chivalry, fortified by a healthy dose of cynicism, but never corrupt.

In the second paragraph of *The Big Sleep* (1939), for example, Marlowe notices a stained-glass window "showing a knight in dark armor rescuing a lady who was tied to a tree and didn't have any clothes on but some very long and convenient hair. The knight had pushed the vizor of his helmet back to be sociable, and he was fiddling with the knots on the ropes that tied the lady to the tree and not getting anywhere. I stood there and thought that if I lived in the house, I would sooner or later have to climb up there and help him" (589). A few chapters later, he does in fact find himself rescuing the drugged and naked Carmen Sternwood from a pornographer's studio, although when he subsequently discovers her naked in his bedroom, he realizes that she is a temptress rather than a damsel. "Knights had no meaning in this game," he thinks to himself, looking at a chessboard, while she looks at him. "It wasn't a game for knights" (95). Chandler's novels simultaneously validate and undermine the analogy to chivalric romance: Marlowe is the closest thing to a knight that the modern world can produce, a "shop-soiled Galahad" (*The High Window*; 1942, 120).

9   For a study of Pynchon's aesthetics in comparison to those of Jorge Luis Borges, see Castillo.

10 The slippery syntactic style of the novel serves to reinforce this idea of revelation. At the beginning of the third chapter, for example, Pynchon sets the word *revelation* into a grammatically conditional and ambiguous syntactic context. The chapter opens with this assessment of Oedipa's unexpected fling with Metzger, the actor turned lawyer who is the coexecutor of Pierce's estate: "Things then did not delay in turning curious. If one object behind her discovery of what she was to label the Tristero System or often only The Tristero (as if it might be something's secret title) were to bring to an end her encapsulation in her tower, then that night's infidelity with Metzger would logically be the starting point for it; logically. That's what would come to haunt her most, perhaps: the way it fitted logically, together. As if (as she'd guessed that first minute in San Narciso) there were revelation in progress all around her" (44).

The only unqualified declarative sentence in this paragraph is the first one, and it is tainted by the vagueness of the noun (*things*) and adjective (*curious*) that frame it. The second sentence is conditional, beginning with the word *if*; the mood of its verb is subjunctive; its internal phrasings are vague ("what she was to label," "something's secret title"); it contains a potential verb phrase introduced by *as if*; and it ends with a repetition that serves to undermine the validity of logical reasoning, which nevertheless seems to remain persuasive to Oedipa in the third sentence. This sentence breaks the subjunctive mood, but its use of the indicative is tempered by the qualifying word *perhaps* and by the peculiar sense of time generated by the tense of its verb. The first sentence of the passage seems to locate us at a particular moment in time—"Things then did not delay in turning curious"—but the retrospective vagueness of the word *then* is amplified by the injection of futurity into past action with the noun phrase *what she was to label*, an effect repeated and complicated by the third sentence, which begins with temporal ambiguity (is *That's* a contracted form of *That is* or *That was*?) and uses the word *would* not as a conditional but as a modal auxiliary that implies both past habitual action and futurity within the past (*would* being the past tense of *will*). Pynchon thus uses verb mood and tense to inject into the passage not only ambiguity but also a sense of ongoing revelation from which Oedipa and the reader are excluded.

11   For fuller discussions of Pynchon's use of Pentecostal and related sacred imagery, see Mendelson 1978 and Nohrnberg 1978.

12   The description of Sula's death also recalls the chapter devoted to the dead mother, Addie, in Faulkner's *As I Lay Dying*; Faulkner, of course, was a crucial influence for Latin American surrealists and magical realists. Skerrett notes that "Morrison's work has been singled out for a variety of creative characteristics—narrative experimentation in the great Faulknerian modernist tradition, the successful absorption of the lessons of Latin American 'magical realism,' the masterful presentation of black women of all ages and conditions as figures of capable imagination" (192). Bayles views Morrison's use of "magical realism" as a calculated attempt to appeal to a highbrow audience after "her tentative but promising first novel, *The Bluest Eye*, was blown to obscurity by the firestorm of García Márquez" (34). According to Bayles, Morrison's "embrace of magic realism has led her to neglect her strengths and indulge her weaknesses" (35). This is, needless to say, not a widely shared view among critics of Morrison's writing, and Bayles's argument is weakened by its tacit assumption that, while magical realism may well be appropriate for communities situated in "the Colombian interior," it has little relevance for communities in the United States: "Whatever the similarities between [the fictional village of] Macondo and Aracataca, García Márquez's actual birthplace, it is safe to say that neither resembles Lorain, Ohio, where Toni Morrison was born" (37).

FOUR. Contemplating Community

1   Richard Patteson points out a similar pattern at work in *V.*: "In *V.* children scarcely know their parents; some do not even know who their parents are. Stencil knows his father primarily through his journals, and although Pynchon hints that V. may have been Stencil's mother, one has no way to be sure; Stencil himself calls the question 'ridiculous' [54]. Victoria is estranged from her father, Sir Alastair Wren, and Paola is separated from Fausto. Evan Godolphin, although 'fond of his father' [156], rarely sees him. When Benny Profane goes to his old neighborhood to visit his parents—his sole journey home

in the entire novel—they are out. Personal history is the most logical beginning of any quest for a pattern in history at large. If more definitive connections than these or a greater degree of knowledge of the most immediate kind of cause and effect relationship cannot be found, what can be known?" (28–29).

2. Eva thus follows in the footsteps of such famous male antiheroes as Faulkner's Thomas Sutpen and Fitzgerald's Jay Gatsby.

3. In his analysis of the dynamics of hegemonic cultural formations, Williams argues that "a lived hegemony is always a process. . . . It has continually to be renewed, recreated, defended, and modified. It is also continually resisted, limited, altered, challenged by pressures not at all its own. . . . The reality of any hegemony . . . is that, while by definition it is always dominant, it is never total or exclusive. At any time, forms of alternative or directly oppositional politics exist as significant elements in the society." To remain in power, "any hegemonic process must be especially alert and responsive to the alternatives and opposition which question or threaten its dominance" (112–13).

4. Sula's indictment of Nel and the community whose values she has adopted is a version of Emerson's belief that power "resides in the moment of transition from a past to a new state" ("Self-Reliance"; 1841c, 271). Morrison writes:

> Nel was the first person who had been real to her, whose name she knew, who had seen as she had the slant of life that made it possible to stretch it to its limits. Now Nel was one of them. One of the spiders whose only thought was the next rung of the web, who dangled in dark dry places suspended by their own spittle, more terrified of the free fall than the snake's breath below. Their eyes so intent on the wayward stranger who trips into their net, they were blind to the cobalt on their own backs, the moonshine fighting to pierce their corners. If they were touched by the snake's breath, however fatal, they were merely victims and knew how to behave in that role (just as Nel knew how to behave as the wronged wife). But the free fall, oh no, that required—demanded—invention: a thing to do with the wings, a way of holding the legs and most of all a full surrender to the downward flight if they wished to taste their tongues or stay alive. But alive was what they, and now Nel, did not want to be. Too dangerous. Now Nel belonged to the town and all of its ways. She had given herself over to them, and the flick of their tongues would drive her back into her little dry corner where she would cling to her spittle high above the breath of the snake and fall. (119–20)

5. The fact that Shadrack doesn't "cuss" Sula but instead seems to respect her convinces the community that she, like he, is a devil. Unlike Shadrack, however, Sula is a devil who cannot be assimilated into the life of the Bottom.

6. In his review, Rushdie makes the following ironic comments about Pynchon's legendary obsession with privacy: "One thing that has not changed about Mr. P. is his love of mystification. The secrecy surrounding the publication of this book—his first novel since *Gravity's Rainbow* in 1973—has been, let's face it, ridiculous. I mean, rilly. So he wants a private life and no photographs and nobody to know his home address. I can dig it, I can relate to that (but, like, he should try it when it's compulsory instead of a free-choice option). But for his publisher to withhold reviewers' copies and give critics maybe a *week* to deal with what took him almost two decades, now that's truly weird, bad craziness, give it up" (1). Compared in this way, the authors' lives look like two morbidly comic forms of the unencumbered self.

7   In his "Thomas Pynchon and Postmodern Liberalism," Jerry A. Varsava argues that "Pynchon's work embrac[es] a determinate political stance [and] political philosophy." In particular, he contends that "Pynchon's two domestic novels [The Crying of Lot 49 and Vineland] provide a powerful, if often diffuse and indirect, defense of American political liberalism." The liberalism that Varsava has in mind here is, not "a retro-liberalism determined by the social and political exigencies of 1776 or the 1930s, but a 'postmodern' version shaped by both liberal traditions and those cultural circumstances and impetuses peculiar to the late twentieth century. Certainly, irony, self-doubt, and even self-deprecation figure more prominently in Pynchon's liberalism than in classical manifestations" (64).

Varsava and I disagree, however, about the extent of Pynchon's commitment to traditional liberalism and most particularly in our interpretations of the attitude toward communitarianism implicit in Vineland. Varsava reads Vineland as a defense of liberalism from the antagonistic communitarian philosophy pursued by Brock Vond. I think that Pynchon's exploration of communitarian alternatives to liberalism is more subtle and balanced than Varsava suggests; as I will argue below, Pynchon finds an appealing communitarianism in the extended Traverse-Becker family while registering the ever-present danger that an untempered communitarianism can devolve into the oppressive majoritarianism that both Reagan and Vond represent.

8   Reagan's mythic aura was very much a conscious creation on the part of his handlers. For example, in a memo written during the 1984 campaign, Richard Darman advised Reagan's campaign staff to "paint RR as the personification of all that is right with, or heroized by, America. Leave Mondale in a position where an attack on Reagan is tantamount to an attack on America's idealized image of itself—where a vote against Reagan is, in some subliminal sense, a vote against a mythic 'AMERICA'" (Goldman, 88).

9   For the discussion of jazz that follows, I am indebted to Breitwieser 1991.

10 I am indebted for this reference to Lhamon 1991, 237. In a footnote, Lhamon notes, "Brown composed 'Daahoud' as early as 1953 (Daahoud MFCD 826), but Pynchon probably heard him play it in the period 1954–56, when Brown was touring with a now-legendary quintet that included Max Roach, Richie Powell (Bud Powell's younger brother), and sometimes Sonny Rollins. Nearly every recording of this group includes 'Daahoud'" (264).

11 In retrospect, the link between the novels can be seen in an interview conducted while Morrison was still writing Beloved, in which Morrison described two "little fragments of stories" that had served as her starting point for that novel. The first, "a newspaper clipping about a woman named Margaret Garner in 1851" who had attempted to kill her children "because she had been caught as a fugitive," became the basis for the act of violence that lies at the center of Beloved. But, according to Morrison, the import of that story did not become clear until she remembered a story from a book called The Harlem Book of the Dead, which presented pictures by Van der Zee:

> In one picture, there was a young girl lying in a coffin and he says that she was eighteen years old and she had gone to a party and that she was dancing and suddenly she slumped and they noticed there was blood on her and they said, "What happened to you?" And she said, "I'll tell you tomorrow. I'll tell you tomorrow." That's all she would say. And apparently her ex-boyfriend or somebody who was jealous had come

into the party with a gun and a silencer and shot her. And she kept saying, "I'll tell you tomorrow" because she wanted him to get away. And he did, I guess; anyway, she died. (Naylor, 207)

What linked these two stories in her mind, according to Morrison, was that "in both instances . . . [a] woman loved something other than herself so much. She had placed all of the value of her life in something outside herself" (207). The second incident has no analogue in *Beloved*, but it does serve as the model for the central act of violence around which *Jazz* turns.

12 For feminist responses, see Ehrenreich and Albert.

CONCLUSION. Beyond Individualism

1 In its annual report on 151 countries for 1993, Amnesty International finds summary executions in 61 countries, with a total of 10,000 people killed, half of them in Africa; prisoners of conscience held in 63 states; prisoners tortured or mistreated in 112 countries, including several Western democracies; 600 dead of torture in 49 countries; 100,000 political prisoners detained without trial in 53 countries; and human rights activists and defenders increasingly subjected to the kinds of imprisonment, torture, and abuse that they are trying to investigate and prevent (Darnton, A13).

2 Fowler argues that we should view Pynchon as a "vastly capable writer of science fiction (which Leslie Fiedler accurately identified as 'the gothicism of the future')" rather than as "a humanistic novelist, or a satirist bent on mending the world. The impulses that created *Gravity's Rainbow* seem to me to have been largely gothic, and the novel makes extensive use of the only gothic locale that retains any mystery and terror for us in a thoroughly secular, disenchanted age: the laboratory" (51–52). I am suggesting, however, that Pynchon is, in fact, "a satirist bent on mending the world" who uses Gothicism to critique the Enlightenment's flawed construction of humanism. His goal, I believe, is a reformulated humanism that can account for and embrace the irrational and the miraculous.

3 For example, what happens when multiculturalist agendas come into conflict with feminist agendas over such issues as polygamy or clitoridectomy? Susan Okin takes issue with multiculturalists who argue for group rights for minority cultures within liberal states. If, Okin argues, "a culture endorses and facilitates the control of men over women in various ways," then, "under such conditions, group rights are potentially, and in some cases actually, antifeminist. They substantially limit the capacity of women and girls of that culture to live with human dignity equal to that of men and boys, and to live as freely chosen lives as they can" (Okin et al., 12). According to Okin, "What we need to strive toward is a form of multiculturalism that gives the issues of gender and other intragroup inequalities their due—that is to say, a multiculturalism that effectively treats all persons as each other's moral equals" (131). These comments—part of the debate that takes place in the volume *Is Multiculturalism Bad for Women?*—suggest that what I am calling *bad multiculturalism* may well end up sacrificing the individual dignity of some in order to promote the cultural dignity of others.

WORKS CITED

Adams, James Truslow. 1931. *The Epic of America*. Boston: Little, Brown.
Albert, M. Elizabeth. 1988. "In the Interest of the Public Good? New Questions for Feminism." In *Community in America: The Challenge of "Habits of the Heart,"* ed. Charles H. Reynolds and Ralph V. Norman, 84–96. Berkeley and Los Angeles: University of California Press.
Althusser, Louis. 1969. "Marxism and Humanism." In *For Marx*, trans. Ben Brewster, 219–47. New York: Random House.
Appleby, Joyce. 1992. *Liberalism and Republicanism in the Historical Imagination*. Cambridge, Mass.: Harvard University Press.
Arieli, Yehoshua. 1964. *Individualism and Nationalism in American Ideology*. Cambridge, Mass.: Harvard University Press.
Awkward, Michael. 1988. "Roadblocks and Relatives: Critical Revision in Toni Morrison's *The Bluest Eye*." In *Critical Essays on Toni Morrison*, ed. Nellie Y. McKay, 57–68. Boston: G. K. Hall.
Bailyn, Bernard. 1967. *The Ideological Origins of the American Revolution*. Cambridge, Mass.: Harvard University Press.
Bailyn, Bernard, Robert Dallek, David Brion Davis, David Herbert Donald, John L. Thomas, and Gordon S. Wood. 1985. *The Great Republic: A History of the American People*. 3d ed. Lexington, Mass.: Heath.
Baker, Houston A., Jr. 1984. *Blues, Ideology, and Afro-American Literature: A Vernacular Theory*. Chicago: University of Chicago Press.
Barthes, Roland. 1977. "The Death of the Author." In *Image, Music, Text*, ed. and trans. Stephen Heath, 142–48. New York: Hill and Wang.
Bayles, Martha. 1988. "Special Effects, Special Pleading." *New Criterion* 6, no. 5:34–40.
Bedau, Hugo Adam. 1972. "Founding Righteousness on Reason." *Nation*, 11 September, 180–81.

Beer, Samuel H. 1996. "Ragged Individualism." *Wilson Quarterly* 20, no. 3:89–91.

Beiner, Ronald. 1992. *What's the Matter with Liberalism?* Berkeley and Los Angeles: University of California Press.

Bellah, Robert N., Richard Madsen, William M. Sullivan, Ann Swindler, and Steven M. Tipton. 1985. *Habits of the Heart: Individualism and Commitment in American Life.* Updated ed. Berkeley and Los Angeles: University of California Press, 1996.

———. 1991. *The Good Society.* New York: Knopf.

Bercovitch, Sacvan. 1978. *The American Jeremiad.* Madison: University of Wisconsin Press.

———. 1986. "The Problem of Ideology in American Literary History." *Critical Inquiry* 12: 631–53. A revised version appears in *The Rites of Assent: Transformations in the Symbolic Construction of America,* 353–76 (New York: Routledge, 1993).

———. 1993. *The Rites of Assent: Transformations in the Symbolic Construction of America.* New York: Routledge, 1993.

Berlant, Lauren. 1991. *The Anatomy of National Fantasy: Hawthorne, Utopia, and Everyday Life.* Chicago: University of Chicago Press.

———. 1997. *The Queen of America Goes to Washington City: Essays on Sex and Citizenship.* Durham, N.C.: Duke University Press.

Berlin, Isaiah. 1958. "Two Concepts of Liberty." In *Four Essays on Liberty,* 118–72. Oxford: Oxford University Press, 1979.

Birnbaum, Pierre, and Jean Leca, eds. 1990. *Individualism: Theories and Methods.* Translated by John Gaffney. Oxford: Oxford University Press.

Breitwieser, Mitchell. 1991. "*The Great Gatsby*: Grief, Jazz, and the Eye-Witness." *Arizona Quarterly* 47:17–70.

Brosh, Aline. 1988. "Stomping on Individualism." *Harvard Crimson,* 11 October, 2.

Brown, Gillian. 1990. *Domestic Individualism: Imagining Self in Nineteenth-Century America.* Berkeley and Los Angeles: University of California Press.

Bryce, James. 1888. *The American Commonwealth.* Rev. ed. New York: Macmillan, 1910.

Butler-Evans, Elliott. 1995. "The Politics of Carnival and Heteroglossia in Toni Morrison's *Song of Solomon* and Ralph Ellison's *Invisible Man*: Dialogic Criticism and African American Literature." In *The Ethnic Canon: Histories, Institutions, and Interventions,* ed. David Palumbo-Liu, 117–39. Minneapolis: University of Minnesota Press.

Cabot, J. E. 1883. Introductory note to *Lectures and Biographical Sketches,* by Ralph Waldo Emerson. Cambridge, Mass.: Riverside.

Carruth, Hayden. 1986. "Eleven Memoranda on the Culture of Jazz." *Conjunctions* 9:67–91.

Castillo, Debra A. 1991. "Borges and Pynchon: The Tenuous Symmetries of Art." In *New Essays on "The Crying of Lot 49,"* ed. Patrick O'Donnell, 21–46. Cambridge: Cambridge University Press.

"Catholicism." 1841. *Boston Quarterly Review* 4:320–39.

Cavell, Stanley. 1981. *The Senses of Walden.* San Francisco: North Point.

———. 1990. *Conditions Handsome and Unhandsome: The Constitution of Emersonian Perfectionism.* Chicago: University of Chicago Press.

Cayton, Mary Cupiec. 1987. "The Making of an American Prophet: Emerson, His Audiences, and the Rise of the Culture Industry in Nineteenth-Century America." *American Historical Review* 92:598–620.

Chandler, Raymond. 1939. *The Big Sleep*. In *Stories and Early Novels*, ed. Frank MacShane, 587–764. New York: Library of America, 1995.
———. 1942. *The High Window*. In *Stories and Early Novels*, ed. Frank MacShane, 985–1177. New York: Library of America, 1995.
———. 1943. *The Lady in the Lake*. In *Later Novels and Other Writings*, ed. Frank MacShane, 1–200. New York: Library of America, 1995.
———. 1944. "The Simple Art of Murder." In *Later Novels and Other Writings*, ed. Frank MacShane, 1016–19. New York: Library of America, 1995.
Cohen, Marshall. 1972. "The Social Contract Explained and Defended." *New York Times Book Review*, 16 July, 1.
Collier, James Lincoln. 1978. *The Making of Jazz: A Comprehensive History*. New York: Delta.
Connolly, William E. 1987. *Politics and Ambiguity*. Madison: University of Wisconsin Press.
———. 1991. *Identity/Difference: Democratic Negotiations of Political Paradox*. Ithaca, N.Y.: Cornell University Press.
Constant, Benjamin. 1988. *Political Writings*. Edited and translated by Biancamaria Fontana. Cambridge: Cambridge University Press.
"The Course of Civilization." 1839. *U.S. Magazine and Democratic Review* 6:208–11.
Cox, James. 1975. "R. W. Emerson: The Circles of the Eye." In *Emerson: Prophecy, Metamorphosis, and Influence: Selected Papers from the English Institute*, ed. David Levin, 57–81. New York: Columbia University Press.
Cronin, Ciaran. 1995. Translator's introduction to *Justification and Application Remarks on Discourse Ethics*, by Jürgen Habermas. Cambridge, Mass.: MIT Press.
Curry, Richard O., and Lawrence B. Goodheart, eds. 1991. *American Chameleon: Individualism in Trans-National Context*. Kent, Ohio: Kent State University Press.
Cushman, Robert. 1621. *Self-Love: The First Sermon Preached in New England; and the Oldest Extant of Any Delivered in America*. Reprint. New York: J. E. D. Comstock, 1847.
Darnton, John. 1994. "Group Finds Widespread Violations Continuing in World." *New York Times*, 7 July (late ed.), A13.
Davis, David Brion. 1975. *The Problem of Slavery in the Age of Revolution, 1770–1823*. Ithaca, N.Y.: Cornell University Press.
Dickstein, Morris. 1986. "Popular Culture and Critical Values: The Novel as a Challenge to Literary History." In *Reconstructing American Literary History*, ed. Sacvan Bercovitch, 29–66. Cambridge, Mass.: Harvard University Press.
Dienstag, Joshua Foa. 1996. "Serving God and Mammon: The Lockean Sympathy in Early American Political Thought." *American Political Science Review* 90:497–511.
Dimock, Wai-chee. 1989. *Empire for Liberty: Melville and the Politics of Individualism*. Princeton, N.J.: Princeton University Press.
Douglass, Frederick. 1845. *Narrative of the Life of Frederick Douglass, Written by Himself*. Edited by Benjamin Quarles. Cambridge, Mass.: Harvard University Press, 1960.
Dworkin, Ronald. 1978. *Taking Rights Seriously*. Cambridge, Mass.: Harvard University Press.
———. 1989. "The Original Position." In *Reading Rawls: Critical Studies on Rawls' "A Theory of Justice,"* ed. Norman Daniels, 16–53. Stanford: Stanford University Press.
Eagleton, Terry. 1991. *Ideology: An Introduction*. London: Verso.
Ehrenreich, Barbara. 1983. "On Feminism, Family and Community." *Dissent* 30:103–6.

Elliott, Emory, ed. 1988. *The Columbia Literary History of the United States.* New York: Columbia University Press.

———, ed. 1991. *The Columbia History of the American Novel.* New York: Columbia University Press.

Ellison, Ralph. 1952. *Invisible Man.* Reprint. New York: Vintage, 1989.

Elster, Jon. 1990. "Marxism and Methodological Individualism." In *Individualism: Theories and Methods,* ed. Pierre Birnbaum and Jean Leca, trans. John Gaffney, 46–61. Oxford: Oxford University Press.

Emerson, Ralph Waldo. 1836. *Nature.* In *Essays and Lectures,* ed. Joel Porte, 5–49. New York: Library of America, 1983.

———. 1837a. "The American Scholar." In *Essays and Lectures,* ed. Joel Porte, 51–71. New York: Library of America, 1983.

———. 1837b. "The Individual." In *The Early Lectures of Ralph Waldo Emerson, 1836–1838,* ed. Stephen E. Whicher, Robert E. Spiller, and Wallace E. Williams, 173–88. Cambridge, Mass.: Harvard University Press, 1964.

———. 1838. "Letter to Martin Van Buren." In *Emerson's Antislavery Writings,* ed. Len Gougeon and Joel Myerson, 1–5. New Haven, Conn.: Yale University Press, 1995.

———. 1841a. "Circles." In *Essays and Lectures,* ed. Joel Porte, 401–14. New York: Library of America, 1983.

———. 1841b. "History." In *Essays and Lectures,* ed. Joel Porte, 235–56. New York: Library of America, 1983.

———. 1841c. "Self-Reliance." In *Essays and Lectures,* ed. Joel Porte, 257–82. New York: Library of America, 1983.

———. 1841d. "Self-Reliance." In *The Norton Anthology of American Literature,* ed. Nina Baym et al., 1:1126–41. 5th ed. New York: Norton.

———. 1842. "The Transcendentalist." In *Essays and Lectures,* ed. Joel Porte, 191–209. New York: Library of America, 1983.

———. 1844a. "An Address . . . on . . . the Emancipation of the Negroes in the British West Indies." In *Emerson's Antislavery Writings,* ed. Len Gougeon and Joel Myerson, 7–33. New Haven, Conn.: Yale University Press, 1995.

———. 1844b. "Experience." In *Essays and Lectures,* ed. Joel Porte, 469–92. New York: Library of America, 1983.

———. 1844c. "New England Reformers." In *Essays and Lectures,* ed. Joel Porte, 589–609. New York: Library of America, 1983.

———. 1844d. "Politics." In *Essays and Lectures,* ed. Joel Porte, 557–71. New York: Library of America, 1983.

———. 1854. "The Fugitive Slave Law." In *Emerson's Antislavery Writings,* ed. Len Gougeon and Joel Myerson, 73–89. New Haven, Conn.: Yale University Press, 1995.

———. 1855. "Lecture on Slavery." In *Emerson's Antislavery Writings,* ed. Len Gougeon and Joel Myerson, 91–106. New Haven, Conn.: Yale University Press, 1995.

———. 1856. *English Traits.* In *Essays and Lectures,* ed. Joel Porte, 763–936. New York: Library of America, 1983.

———. 1878. "The Sovereignty of Ethics." In *Lectures and Biographical Sketches,* vol. 10 of *The Complete Works of Ralph Waldo Emerson,* ed. Edward Waldo Emerson, 175–205. Centenary Edition. Cambridge, Mass.: Riverside.

———. 1903–4. *The Complete Works of Ralph Waldo Emerson*. Centenary Edition. Edited by Edward Waldo Emerson. Cambridge, Mass.: Riverside.
———. 1926. *The Heart of Emerson's Journals*. Edited by Bliss Perry. Boston: Houghton Mifflin.
———. 1957. *Selections from Ralph Waldo Emerson*. Edited by Stephen E. Whicher. Boston: Houghton Mifflin.
———. 1960–82. *The Journals and Miscellaneous Notebooks of Ralph Waldo Emerson*. Edited by William H. Gilman, Alfred R. Ferguson and J. E. Parsons. Cambridge, Mass.: Harvard University Press.
———. 1982. *Emerson in His Journals*. Edited by Joel Porte. Cambridge, Mass.: Harvard University Press.
———. 1995. *Emerson's Antislavery Writings*. Edited by Len Gougeon and Joel Myerson. New Haven, Conn.: Yale University Press.
Ferguson, Robert. 1994. "The American Enlightenment, 1750–1820." In *The Cambridge History of American Literature, Volume 1: 1590–1820*, ed. Sacvan Bercovitch and Cyrus R. K. Patell, 345–537. Cambridge: Cambridge University Press.
Fiedler, Leslie A. 1982. *Love and Death in the American Novel*. Rev. ed. New York: Stein and Day.
Fiscus, Ronald J. 1992. *The Constitutional Logic of Affirmative Action*. Edited by Stephen L. Wasby. Durham, N.C.: Duke University Press.
Fitzgerald, F. Scott. 1931. *The Crack-Up*. Edited by Edmund Wilson. Reprint. New York: New Directions, 1945.
Foner, Eric. 1996. Review of *Democracy's Discontent*, by Michael J. Sandel. *Nation* 262, no. 18:34–38.
Fowler, Douglas. 1980. *A Reader's Guide to Gravity's Rainbow*. Ann Arbor, Mich.: Ardis.
Franklin, Benjamin. 1987. *Writings*. Edited by J. A. Leo Lemay. New York: Library of America.
Gans, Herbert J. 1988. *Middle American Individualism: The Future of Liberal Democracy*. New York: Free Press.
Giamatti, A. Bartlett. 1988. "Power, Politics, and a Sense of History." In *A Free and Ordered Space: The Real World of the University*, 94–105. New York: Norton.
Glendon, Mary Ann. 1991. *Rights Talk: The Impoverishment of Political Discourse*. New York: Free Press.
Goldman, Peter. 1984. "Campaign '84: The Inside Story." *Newsweek*, special issue (November/December), 32–112.
Gonnaud, Maurice. 1987. *An Uneasy Solitude: Individual and Society in the Work of Ralph Waldo Emerson*. Translated by Lawrence Rosenwald. Princeton, N.J.: Princeton University Press.
Gougeon, Len. 1990. *Virtue's Hero: Emerson, Antislavery, and Reform*. Athens: University of Georgia Press.
Green, Geoffrey, Donald J. Greiner, and Larry McCaffery, eds. 1994. *The Vineland Papers: Critical Takes on Pynchon's Novel*. Normal, Ill.: Dalkey Archive.
Guinier, Lani. 1994. *The Tyranny of the Majority: Fundamental Fairness and Representative Democracy*. New York: Free Press.
Habermas, Jürgen. 1990. *Moral Consciousness and Communicative Action*. Translated by Christian Lenhardt and Shierry Weber Nicholsen. Cambridge, Mass.: MIT Press.
———. 1995. *Justification and Application: Remarks on Discourse Ethics*. Translated by Ciaran Cronin. Cambridge, Mass.: MIT Press.

Hall, Stuart. 1985. "Signification, Representation, Ideology: Althusser and the Post-Structuralist Debates." *Critical Studies in Mass Communication* 2:91–114.

Hammett, Dashiell. 1930. *The Maltese Falcon*. In *Complete Novels*, ed. Steven Marcus, 387–585. New York: Library of America, 1999.

Harper, Phillip Brian. 1994. *Framing the Margins: The Social Logic of Postmodern Culture*. New York: Oxford University Press.

Harris, Trudier. 1988. "Reconnecting Fragments: Afro-American Folk Tradition in *The Bluest Eye*." In *Critical Essays on Toni Morrison*, ed. by Nellie Y. McKay, 68–76. Boston: G. K. Hall.

Hart, H. L. A. 1989. "Rawls on Liberty and Its Priority." In *Reading Rawls: Critical Studies on Rawls' "A Theory of Justice,"* ed. Norman Daniels, 230–53. Stanford, Calif.: Stanford University Press.

Hartz, Louis. 1955. *The Liberal Tradition in America: An Interpretation of American Political Thought since the Revolution*. New York: Harcourt, Brace.

Heimert, Alan, and Andrew Delbanco, eds. 1985. *The Puritans in America: A Narrative Anthology*. Cambridge, Mass.: Harvard University Press.

Heller, Thomas C., and David E. Wellbery. 1986. Introduction to *Reconstructing Individualism: Autonomy, Individuality, and the Self in Western Thought*, ed. Thomas C. Heller, Morton Sosna, and David E. Wellbery. Stanford, Calif.: Stanford University Press.

Hofstadter, Richard. 1965. *The Paranoid Style in American Politics and Other Essays*. New York: Knopf.

Hollinger, David A. 1995. *Postethnic America: Beyond Multiculturalism*. New York: Basic.

Holmes, Stephen. 1993. *The Anatomy of Antiliberalism*. Cambridge, Mass.: Harvard University Press.

Holmes, Steven A. 1998. "Washington State Is Stage for Fight over Preferences." *New York Times*, 4 May (late ed.), A1, A15.

Hutcheon, Linda. 1988. *A Poetics of Postmodernism: History, Theory, Fiction*. New York: Routledge.

Jahanbegloo, Ramin. 1992. *Conversations with Isaiah Berlin*. London: Peter Halban.

James, William. 1987. *Writings, 1902–1910*. Edited by Bruce Kuklick. New York: Library of America.

Jameson, Fredric. 1988. "On *Habits of the Heart*." In *Community in America: The Challenge of "Habits of the Heart,"* ed. Charles H. Reynolds and Ralph V. Norman, 97–112. Berkeley and Los Angeles: University of California Press.

Jauss, Hans Robert. 1982. "Literary History as a Challenge to Literary Theory." In *Towards an Aesthetic of Reception*, trans. Timothy Bahti, 3–45. Minneapolis: University of Minnesota Press.

Jefferson, Thomas. 1982. *Writings*. Edited by Merill D. Peterson. New York: Library of America.

Jehlen, Myra. 1986. *American Incarnation: The Individual, the Nation, and the Continent*. Cambridge, Mass.: Harvard University Press.

Johnson, Samuel. 1977. *Selected Poetry and Prose*. Edited by Frank Brady and W. K. Wimsatt. Berkeley and Los Angeles: University of California Press.

Kant, Immanuel. 1784. "Idea for a Universal History with a Cosmopolitan Purpose." In *Political Writings*, ed. Hans Reiss, trans. H. B. Nisbet. 2d ed. Cambridge: Cambridge University Press, 1991.

———. 1793. "On the Common Saying: 'This May be True in Theory, but It Does not Apply in Practice.'" In *Political Writings*, ed. Hans Reiss, trans. H. B. Nisbet. 2d ed. Cambridge: Cambridge University Press, 1991.

———. 1795. "Perpetual Peace: A Philosophical Sketch." In *Political Writings*, ed. Hans Reiss, trans. H. B. Nisbet. 2d ed. Cambridge: Cambridge University Press, 1991.

Kaplan, Amy. 1993. " 'Left Alone with America': The Absence of Empire in the Study of American Culture." In *Cultures of United States Imperialism*, ed. Amy Kaplan and Donald E. Pease, 3–21. Durham, N.C.: Duke University Press.

Kateb, George. 1989. "Democratic Individuality and the Meaning of Rights." In *Liberalism and the Moral Life*, ed. Nancy L. Rosenblum, 183–206. Cambridge, Mass.: Harvard University Press.

———. 1992. *The Inner Ocean: Individualism and Democratic Culture*. Ithaca, N.Y.: Cornell University Press.

———. 1995. *Emerson and Self-Reliance*. Thousand Oaks, Calif.: Sage.

Lasch, Christopher. 1979. *The Culture of Narcissism: American Life in an Age of Diminishing Expectations*. Reprint. New York: Warner.

Leinberger, Paul, and Bruce Tucker. 1991. *The New Individualists: The Generation after the Organization Man*. New York: HarperCollins.

Leverenz, David. 1989. *Manhood and the American Renaissance*. Ithaca, N.Y.: Cornell University Press.

Lhamon, William T. 1991. *Deliberate Speed*. Washington, D.C.: Smithsonian Institution Press.

Locke, John. 1698. *Two Treatises of Government*. Edited by Peter Laslett. Cambridge: Cambridge University Press, 1988.

Lukes, Stephen. 1973. *Individualism*. Oxford: Basil Blackwell.

MacIntyre, Alasdair. 1984. *After Virtue*. 2d ed. Notre Dame, Ind.: University of Notre Dame Press.

Macpherson, C. B. 1962. *The Political Theory of Possessive Individualism: Hobbes to Locke*. Oxford: Oxford University Press.

Martin, John Frederick. 1991. *Profits in the Wilderness: Entrepreneurship and the Founding of the New England Towns in the Seventeenth Century*. Chapel Hill: University of North Carolina Press.

Marx, Leo. 1987. "A Visit to Mr. America." *New York Review of Books*, 12 March, 36–38.

———. 1990. "George Kateb's Ahistorical Emersonianism." *Political Theory* 18:595–99.

Mason, Charles, and Jeremiah Dixon. 1969. *The Journal of Charles Mason and Jeremiah Dixon*. Edited by A. Hughlett Mason. Philadelphia: American Philosophical Society.

Matthiessen, F. O. 1941. *American Renaissance: Art and Experience in the Age of Emerson and Whitman*. New York: Oxford University Press.

McCarthy, Thomas. 1990. Introduction to *Moral Consciousness and Communicative Action*, by Jürgen Habermas, trans. Christian Lenhardt and Shierry Weber Nicholsen. Cambridge, Mass.: MIT Press.

McDonald, Forrest. 1985. *Novus Ordo Seclorum: The Intellectual Origins of the Constitution*. Lawrence: University Press of Kansas.

Melley, Timothy J. 2000. *Empire of Conspiracy: The Culture of Paranoia in Postwar America*. Ithaca, N.Y.: Cornell University Press.

Mendelson, Edward. 1978. "The Sacred, the Profane, and *The Crying of Lot 49*." In *Pynchon: A Collection of Critical Essays*, ed. Edward Mendelson, 112–46. Englewood Cliffs, N.J.: Prentice-Hall.

———. 1990. "Levity's Rainbow." *New Republic*, 9, 16 July, 40–46.

Mill, John Stuart. 1859. *On Liberty*. Edited by David Spitz. New York: Norton, 1975.

Morgan, Edmund S. 1975. *American Slavery, American Freedom: The Colonial Ordeal of Virginia*. New York: Norton.

Morrison, Toni. 1970. *The Bluest Eye*. Reprint. New York: Plume, 1994.

———. 1973. *Sula*. New York: Knopf.

———. 1977. *Song of Solomon*. New York: Knopf.

———. 1984. "Rootedness: The Ancestor as Foundation." In *Black Women Writers (1950–1980)*, ed. Mari Evans, 339–45. New York: Anchor.

———. 1987a. *Beloved*. New York: Knopf.

———. 1987b. "The Site of Memory." *Inventing the Truth: The Art and Craft of Memoir*, ed. William Zinsser, 101–24. Boston: Houghton Mifflin.

———. 1989. "Unspoken Things Unspoken: The Afro-American Presence in American Literature." *Michigan Quarterly Review* 28 (winter): 1–34.

———. 1992a. "The History of *Beloved* and the Culture of Jazz." Lecture, Massachusetts Institute of Technology, 16 April.

———. 1992b. *Jazz*. New York: Knopf.

———. 1992c. *Playing in the Dark: Whiteness and the Literary Imagination*. Cambridge, Mass.: Harvard University Press.

———. 1994. *Lecture and Speech of Acceptance, upon the Award of the Nobel Prize for Literature, Delivered in Stockholm on the Seventh of December, Nineteen Hundred and Ninety-Three*. New York: Knopf.

———. 1997. "The Official Story: Dead Man Golfing." Introduction to *Birth of a Nation'hood: Gaze, Script, and Spectacle in the O. J. Simpson Case*, ed. Toni Morrison and Claudia Brodsky Lacour, vii–xxviii. New York: Pantheon.

———. 1998. *Paradise*. New York: Knopf.

Mouffe, Chantal, ed. 1992. *Dimensions of Radical Democracy: Pluralism, Citizenship, Community*. London: Verso.

———. 1993. *The Return of the Political*. London: Verso.

Nagel, Thomas. 1989. "Rawls on Justice." In *Reading Rawls: Critical Studies on Rawls' "A Theory of Justice,"* 1–16. Stanford, Calif.: Stanford University Press.

Naylor, Gloria. 1985. "A Conversation: Gloria Naylor and Toni Morrison." In *Conversations with Toni Morrison*, ed. Danille Taylor-Guthrie, 188–217. Jackson: University Press of Mississippi, 1995.

Newfield, Christopher. 1996. *The Emerson Effect: Individualism and Submission in America*. Chicago: University of Chicago Press.

Nicoloff, Philip. 1961. *Emerson on Race and History*. New York: Columbia University Press.

Nohrnberg, James. 1978. "Pynchon's Paraclete." In *Pynchon: A Collection of Critical Essays*, ed. Edward Mendelson, 147–61. Englewood Cliffs, N.J.: Prentice-Hall.

Nozick, Robert. 1974. *Anarchy, State, and Utopia*. New York: Basic.

Nussbaum, Martha J. 1995. *Poetic Justice: The Literary Imagination and Public Life*. Boston: Beacon.

Ogren, Kathy J. 1989. *The Jazz Revolution: Twenties America and the Meaning of Jazz*. New York: Oxford University Press.

Okin, Susan Moller. 1997. "Political Theory: Democracy's Discontent: America in Search of a Public Philosophy." *American Political Science Review* 91:440–42.

Okin, Susan Moller, et al. 1999. *Is Multiculturalism Bad for Women?* Edited by Joshua Cohen, Matthew Howard, and Martha Nussbaum. Princeton, N.J.: Princeton University Press.

Packer, Barbara. 1982. *Emerson's Fall: A New Interpretation of the Major Essays.* New York: Continuum.

Paine, Thomas. 1989. *Political Writings.* Edited by Bruce Kuklick. Cambridge: Cambridge University Press.

Patell, Cyrus R. K. 1993. "Baseball and the Cultural Logic of American Individualism." *Prospects* 18:401–63.

—. 1994. "Emersonian Strategies: Negative Liberty, Self-Reliance, and Democratic Individuality." *Nineteenth-Century Literature* 48 (March): 440–79.

—. 1999. "Emergent Literatures." In *The Cambridge History of American Literature, Volume 7: Prose Writing, 1940–1990,* ed. Sacvan Bercovitch, 541–716. Cambridge: Cambridge University Press.

Patterson, Orlando. 1982. *Slavery and Social Death.* Cambridge, Mass.: Harvard University Press.

Patteson, Richard. 1981. "What Stencil Knew: Structure and Certitude in Pynchon's V." In *Critical Essays on Thomas Pynchon,* ed. Richard Patteson, 20–31. Boston: G. K. Hall.

Pease, Donald E. 1994. "New Americanists: Revisionist Interventions into the Canon." In *Revisionary Interventions in the Americanist Canon,* ed. Donald E. Pease, 1–37. Durham, N.C.: Duke University Press.

Pellegrini, Angelo. 1986. *American Dream: An Immigrant's Quest.* San Francisco: North Point.

Pocock, J. G. A. 1975. *The Machiavellian Moment: Florentine Political Thought and the Atlantic Republican Tradition.* Princeton, N.J.: Princeton University Press.

—. 1980. "The Myth of John Locke and the Obsession with Liberalism." In *John Locke: Papers Read at the Clark Library Seminar,* 1–24. Berkeley and Los Angeles: University of California Press.

Poirier, Richard. 1987. *The Renewal of Literature: Emersonian Reflections.* New York: Random House.

[Posner, Richard. 1983.] *Jackson v. City of Joliet* (7th Cir. 1983), 715 F.2d 1200–1208.

Pynchon, Thomas. 1963. *V.* Philadelphia: J. B. Lippincott.

—. 1966. *The Crying of Lot 49.* Reprint. New York: Perennial, 1986.

—. 1973. *Gravity's Rainbow.* New York: Viking.

—. 1984a. "Is It O.K. to Be a Luddite?" *New York Times Book Review,* 28 October, 1, 40–41.

—. 1984b. *Slow Learner: Early Stories.* Boston: Little, Brown.

—. 1990. *Vineland.* Boston: Little, Brown.

—. 1997. *Mason & Dixon.* New York: Holt.

Rawls, John. 1958. "Justice as Fairness." In *Collected Papers,* ed. Samuel Freeman, 47–72. Cambridge, Mass.: Harvard University Press, 1999.

—. 1971. *A Theory of Justice.* Cambridge, Mass.: Harvard University Press.

—. 1977. "The Basic Structure as Subject." *American Philosophical Quarterly* 14:159–65.

—. 1985. "Justice as Fairness: Political not Metaphysical." In *Collected Papers,* ed. Samuel Freeman, 388–414. Cambridge, Mass.: Harvard University Press.

—. 1993. *Political Liberalism.* New York: Columbia University Press.

—. 1999a. *Collected Papers.* Edited by Samuel Freeman. Cambridge, Mass.: Harvard University Press, 1999.

—. 1999b. *The Law of Peoples; with "The Idea of Public Reason Revisited."* Cambridge, Mass.: Harvard University Press.

—. 1999c. *A Theory of Justice.* Rev. ed. Cambridge, Mass.: Harvard University Press.

Reagan, Ronald. 1984. *A Time for Choosing: The Speeches of Ronald Reagan, 1961–1982*. Edited by Alfred A. Baltizer and Gerald M. Bonetto. Chicago: Regnery Gateway.

———. 1989. *Speaking My Mind: Selected Speeches*. New York: Simon and Schuster.

Reynolds, Larry J. 1988. *European Revolutions and the American Literary Renaissance*. New Haven, Conn.: Yale University Press.

Robbins, Bruce. 1998. "Introduction Part I: Actual Existing Cosmopolitanism." In *Cosmopolitics: Thinking and Feeling beyond the Nation*, ed. Pheng Cheah and Bruce Robbins, 1–19. Minneapolis: University of Minnesota Press.

Rogin, Michael Paul. 1976. *Fathers and Children: Andrew Jackson and the Subjugation of the American Indian*. New York: Knopf.

———. 1987. *Ronald Reagan: The Movie and Other Episodes in Political Demonology*. Berkeley and Los Angeles: University of California Press.

Rorty, Richard. 1989. *Contingency, Irony, and Solidarity*. Cambridge: Cambridge University Press.

———. 1998a. "Human Rights, Rationality, and Sentimentality." In *Truth and Progress: Philosophical Papers*, 3, 167–85. Cambridge: Cambridge University Press.

———. 1998b. "Justice as a Larger Loyalty." In *Cosmopolitics: Thinking and Feeling beyond the Nation*, ed. Pheng Cheah and Bruce Robbins, 45–58. Minneapolis: University of Minnesota Press.

Rousseau, Jean Jacques. 1762. *On the Social Contract*. Edited by Roger D. Masters. Translated by Judith R. Masters. New York: St. Martin's, 1978.

Rowe, John Carlos. 1997. *At Emerson's Tomb: The Politics of Classic American Literature*. New York: Columbia University Press.

Rushdie, Salman. 1990. "Still Crazy after All These Years." *New York Times Book Review*, 14 January, 1, 36–37.

Ryan, Alan. 1997. "Republican Nostalgia." *Dissent* 44, no. 1:119–24.

Sanborn, F. B., ed. 1885. *The Genius and Character of Emerson*. Boston: Concord School of Philosophy.

Sandel, Michael J. 1982. *Liberalism and the Limits of Justice*. 2d ed. Cambridge: Cambridge University Press, 1998.

———. 1984a. "Morality and the Liberal Idea." *New Republic*, 7 May, 15–17.

———. 1984b. "The Procedural Republic and the Unencumbered Self." *Political Theory* 12:81–96.

———. 1988. "Democrats and Community." *New Republic*, 22 February, 20–23.

———. 1996. *Democracy's Discontent: America in Search of a Public Philosophy*. Cambridge, Mass.: Harvard University Press.

Sarat, Austin, and Dana R. Villa, eds. 1996. *Liberal Modernism and Democratic Individuality: George Kateb and the Practices of Politics*. Princeton, N.J.: Princeton University Press.

Schumpeter, Joseph. 1954. *History of Economic Analysis*. Edited by Elizabeth Boody Schumpeter. New York: Oxford University Press.

Shiffrin, Steven H. 1990. *The First Amendment, Democracy, and Romance*. Cambridge, Mass.: Harvard University Press.

Shklar, Judith N. 1984. *Ordinary Vices*. Cambridge, Mass.: Harvard University Press.

———. 1987. Review of *The Needs of Strangers*, by Michael Ignatieff. *Political Theory* 15:141–45.

Skerrett, Joseph, Jr. 1985. "Recitation to the Griot: Storytelling and Learning in Toni Morrison's *Song of Solomon.*" In *Conjuring: Black Women, Fiction, and Literary Tradition*, ed. Marjorie Pryse and Hortense J. Spillers, 192–202. Bloomington: Indiana University Press.

Skinner, Quentin. 1986. "The Paradoxes of Political Liberty." In *The Tanner Lectures on Human Values*, vol. 7, ed. Quentin McMurrin, 224–50. Salt Lake City: University of Utah Press.

Slater, Joseph, ed. 1964. *The Correspondence of Emerson and Carlyle.* New York: Columbia University Press.

Smith, Henry Nash. 1950. *Virgin Land: The American West as Symbol and Myth.* Rev. ed. Cambridge, Mass.: Harvard University Press, 1970.

Smith, Ralph Stuart. 1992. Letter to the editor. *Atlantic Monthly,* July, 8.

Smith, Valerie. 1987. *Self-Discovery and Authority in Afro-American Narrative.* Cambridge, Mass.: Harvard University Press.

Sollors, Werner. 1986. "A Critique of Pure Pluralism." In *Reconstructing American Literary History,* ed. Sacvan Bercovitch, 250–79. Cambridge, Mass.: Harvard University Press.

Steiner, Wendy. 1986. "Collage or Miracle: Historicism in a Deconstructed World." In *Reconstructing American Literary History,* ed. Sacvan Bercovitch, 323–51. Cambridge, Mass.: Harvard University Press.

——. 1999. "Postmodern Fictions, 1970–1990." In *The Cambridge History of American Literature: Volume Seven: Prose Writing, 1940–1990,* ed. Sacvan Bercovitch, 425–538. Cambridge: Cambridge University Press.

Stepto, Robert. 1979. "'Intimate Things in Place': A Conversation with Toni Morrison." In *Conversations with Toni Morrison,* ed. Danille Taylor-Guthrie, 10–29. Jackson: University Press of Mississippi, 1995.

Tani, Stefano. 1982. "The Dismemberment of the Detective." *Diogenes* 120:22–41.

Tanner, Tony. 1978. "V. and V-2." In *Pynchon: A Collection of Critical Essays,* ed. Edward Mendelson, 16–55. Englewood Cliffs, N.J.: Prentice-Hall.

Taylor, Charles. 1985a. "Atomism." In *Philosophy and the Human Sciences: Philosophical Papers 2.* Cambridge: Cambridge University Press.

——. 1985b. "What's Wrong with Negative Liberty?" In *Philosophy and the Human Sciences: Philosophical Papers 2,* 211–29. Cambridge: Cambridge University Press.

——. 1989. "Cross-Purposes: The Liberal-Communitarian Debate." *Liberalism and the Moral Life,* ed. Nancy L. Rosenblum, 159–82. Cambridge, Mass.: Harvard University Press.

Thomas, Evan. 1984. "Every Region, Every Age Group, Almost Every Voting Bloc." *Time,* 19 November, 45.

Tocqueville, Alexis de. 1961. *Democracy in America.* Translated by Henry Reeve. New York: Schocken.

——. 1969. *Democracy in America.* Edited by J. P. Mayer. Translated by George Lawrence. Garden City, N.Y.: Doubleday-Anchor.

Unger, Roberto Mangabeira. 1975. *Knowledge and Politics.* New York: Free Press.

——. 1987. *Politics, a Work in Constructive Social Theory.* Vol. 1: *Social Theory: Its Situation and Task.* Vol. 2: *False Necessity: Anti-Necessitarian Social Theory in the Service of Radical Democracy.* Vol. 3: *Plasticity into Power: Comparative-Historical Studies on the Institutional Conditions of Economic and Military Success.* Cambridge: Cambridge University Press.

Varsava, Jerry A. 1995. "Thomas Pynchon and Postmodern Liberalism." *Canadian Review of American Studies* 25, no. 11:63–100.

von Frank, Albert J. 1999. "Mrs. Brackett's Verdict: Magic and Means in Transcendental Antislavery Work." ESQ 45:385–407.

Wald, Priscilla. 1995. *Constituting Americans: Cultural Anxiety and Narrative Form*. Durham, N.C.: Duke University Press.

Wasby, Stephen L. Introduction to *The Constitutional Logic of Affirmative Action*, by Ronald J. Fiscus, ed. Stephen L. Wasby. Durham, N.C.: Duke University Press.

Weinstein, David. 1997. Review of *Liberal Modernism and Democratic Individuality*, ed. Austin Sarat and Dana R. Villa. *American Political Science Review* 91:953–54.

West, Cornel. 1989. *The American Evasion of Philosophy: A Genealogy of Pragmatism*. Madison: University of Wisconsin Press.

——. 1991. "Postmodern Culture." In *The Columbia History of the American Novel*, ed. Emory Elliott, 515–20. New York: Columbia University Press.

Whitman, Walt. 1982. *Complete Poetry and Collected Prose*. Edited by Justin Kaplan. New York: Library of America.

Williams, Patricia J. 1991. *The Alchemy of Race and Rights*. Cambridge, Mass.: Harvard University Press.

Williams, Raymond. 1977. *Marxism and Literature*. Rev. ed. Oxford: Oxford University Press.

Wills, Garry. 1978. *Inventing America: Jefferson's Declaration of Independence*. Garden City, N.Y.: Doubleday.

——. 1987. *Reagan's America: Innocents at Home*. Garden City, N.Y.: Doubleday.

Winthrop, John. 1630. "A Modell of Christian Charity." In *Winthrop Papers, 1623–1630*, ed. Stewart Mitchell, 282–95. Boston: Massachusetts Historical Society, 1931.

Wood, Gordon S. 1969. *The Creation of the American Republic*. New York: Norton.

Young, James P. 1996. *Reconsidering American Liberalism: The Troubled Odyssey of the Liberal Idea*. Boulder, Colo.: Westview.

INDEX

Abolitionism, 53, 57
Abortion, 13, 190
Abstraction: community and, 10, 46, 65; domination and, 31, 32; Emerson and, 13, 40–41, 50–52; methodological individualism and, xiv, 10; moral reason and, 51; narrative and, xviii; philosophy and, xv, xix, 6–7, 10, 36, 50, 58, 61, 63, 65; and universalism, 28. *See also* Individual: abstract
Adams, James Truslow, 201 n.15
Adventures of Huckleberry Finn, The (Twain), 84
Affirmative action, xiii–xiv, 13, 188
Althusser, Louis, 4
American dream, 201 n.15
American Revolution, 22, 59
American studies, 5, 193
Amnesty International, 218 n.1
Appleby, Joyce, 21
Arieli, Yehoshua, 37, 39, 40, 200 n.11
Aristotle, 6, 28
Armstrong, Louis, 174, 175, 177
Augustine, St., 1

Bailyn, Bernard, 19, 22, 59, 188
Baker, Houston, 211 n.2
Barber, Benjamin, 11
Barthes, Roland, 192

Bedau, Adam, 61
Beer, Samuel H., 73
Beiner, Ronald, xv, 6, 34
Bellah, Robert N., 8–10, 33, 142–44
Berlant, Lauren, 198n. 1, 202 nn.15, 16, 18
Berlin, Isaiah, 15, 17–19, 25, 73, 74, 89, 96, 200 n.7
Bible, 49, 158
Birnbaum, Pierre, 11, 12, 14
Border studies, 5, 193
Boston Quarterly Review, 38
Brown, Gillian, 202 n.16
Brownson, Orestes, 40
Bryce, James, 11
Buddhism, 49

Calhoun, John C., 203 n.18
Cardinal, Marie, 174–75, 177, 179
Carlyle, Thomas, 57
Carruth, Hayden, 175
Carter, Jimmy, 168
Cavell, Stanley, xv, 6, 206 n.10
Chandler, Raymond, 72, 113, 114, 214 n.8
Channing, William Ellery, 40
Cherokee removal, 54
Civil War, xi
Cohen, Marshall, 61
Coleridge, Samuel Taylor, 49, 205 n.6

Collier, James Lincoln, 174
Columbus, Christopher, 49
Communism, 18, 186
Communitarianism, 1, 28, 68–69, 210 n.27; critique of individualism and, 8, 11, 25, 25–26, 73–74, 76, 186; Jefferson and, 19–20; Kateb and critique of, 75–77; liberalism and, 1, 8; literary criticism and, 192–93; in Morrison, 139–40, 141, 153, 180, 182–84; positive liberty and, 18; in Pynchon, 2, 30–31, 141, 146, 152, 168, 171–73; critique of Rawls and, 67–68, 70; rights and, 27; Sandel and, 67–68, 73; situated self and, 37, 165, 193

Community: abstract version of, 10, 34, 46, 65; cosmopolitanism and, 194–95; *Crying of Lot 49, The*, and, 147–50, 152, 173; Emerson and, 41, 44, 46, 47, 60; family and, 23–24; identity and, xvi, 29, 34, 74, 140, 180, 196; ideology and, xii, 9; individualism and, xvii, xix, 13, 15, 19, 25–26, 60, 68, 152, 169; jazz and, 173–76, 180; Morrison and, xviii, xx, 31, 32, 141, 142, 153; narrative and, 6, 10; negative aspects of, xix, xx, 141, 142; *Paradise* and, 139–40, 180–82, 184; patriarchy and, 23–24, 181–82; positive liberty and, 14, 17–19, Pynchon and, xx, 31, 32, 141, 147–50; Rawls and, 62, 65–67; Reagan and, ix–x; *Sula* and, 153–59, 161, 165–67; *Vineland* and, 167–68, 171–73, 179; Winthrop and, x, 43–44

Connolly, William, 35, 204 n.1, 209 n.19
Contradiction: Declaration of Independence and, 24; Emerson and, 47–48; individualism and, ix, 32, 33; philosophy and, xv
Cosmopolitanism, xix, xx, 48–50, 180, 194–95, 196; Emerson and, xix, 48, 60; Kant and, 48
"Course of Civilization, The," 36, 187
Cowboy, figure of, 30, 71, 72
Critical legal studies, 26
Cronin, Ciaran, 28
Cultural mythology, xviii, 4, 13, 71
Cultural relativism, xvi, 49, 191–94
Cushman, Robert, 43

Davis, David Brion, 3–4
Declaration of Independence, 16, 22–24, 46, 59, 63, 91, 188, 195, 204 n.18; contradiction and, 24; Lockeanism of, 16; patriarchy and, 24; race and, 24; slavery and, 24
Declaration of Sentiments, 23
Democracy: individualism and, xviii, 38; liberalism and, xvi; national narratives and, 3; pluralism and, xvi
De Maistre, Joseph, 37
Derrida, Jacques, 192
Detective, hard-boiled, 71–72; *Crying of Lot 49, The*, and, 111–16, 126
Dickinson, John, 202 n.18
Dickstein, Morris, 72
Difference: cultural, 200 n.6; jazz and, 179–80; pluralism and, 67, 194. *See also* Cosmopolitanism; Multiculturalism; Pluralism
Dirty Harry, 72
Dispossession, 212 n.4; in Morrison, 85, 97–103, 107–10
Discrimination, xiii–xiv, 200 n.6; remedies for, 190–91
Douglass, Frederick, 27, 56, 60, 85, 86, 211 n.2
Du Bois, W. E. B., 139
Dworkin, Ronald, 62, 75, 190

Economic individualism. *See* Individualism: economic
Egoism, and individualism, 36, 37–38, 39, 60, 76, 78, 148
Eliot, Emory, 198 n.5
Ellison, Ralph, 99–100, 212 n.4
Elshtain, Jean Bethke, 182
Elster, Jon, 12
Emancipation Proclamation, 98
Emerson, Ralph Waldo, ix, xi, xii, xviii, xix, 10, 13, 36, 40–60, 78, 167, 197; abstraction and, xiv, xix, 13, 40–42, 46, 50–52, 55–60; in the American imagination, xi–xii, 60; contradiction and, 47–48; *Crying of Lot 49, The*, and, 110, 112, 146, 152; idealism in, 42–45, 47–57; Kant and, 43, 205 n.6; Kateb and, 81; Locke and, 41–42; materialism in, 42–47; methodological individualism and, xiv–xv, 50, 56, 59, 188; race and, 53–59, 206 n.13; John Rawls and, 61, 63, 65–67; revelation in, 116–17; rhetorical style, xix, 42, 44, 50; slavery and, 54–57, 206 n.13; universalism and,

xix, 47, 50; in *Vineland*, 132–34; Winthrop and, 43, 44; ix, xii. Works: "American Scholar, The," 34, 41, 42, 44, 45, 54, 66, 93, 146; "Emancipation of the Negroes in the British West Indies," 55; "Experience," 112, 113; "History," 50; Journals, 37, 38, 40, 41, 47, 50, 52, 53, 54, 55, 56, 57, 58; "Lecture on Slavery," 58, 59; "Letter to Martin Van Buren," 54, 57, 187; *Nature*, 39, 49, 51, 59, 110, 116, 117–18, 124–25; "New England Reformers," 37, 41, 46, 47; "Politics," xi, 45, 46; "Self-Reliance," xii, xx, 36, 38, 40, 41, 42, 44, 47, 52, 73, 124, 159, 161, 162, 178; "Sovereignty of Ethics, The," 58, 59, 134, 208 n.16. *See also* Emersonianism; Emersonian liberalism

Emersonian liberalism, xiii, xv, 33, 34, 35, 83, 169, 191; as idealized narrative, xviii–xx; jazz as revision of, 174, 180; Kateb and, 75–78, 80; methodological individualism and, 34, 35, 191; Morrison and critique of, xviii–xx, 10–11, 29, 33, 83, 140–41; official narrative and, xix, 77; Pynchon and critique of, xviii–xx, 10–11, 29, 33, 83, 92, 110, 123, 126, 140, 141; Rawls and, 65; slavery and, 29. *See also* Emerson, Ralph Waldo; Emersonianism

Emersonianism: abstraction and, 35–36, 51, 59; *Crying of Lot 49, The*, and, 110, 112, 114, 116, 117, 119, 123, 124, 126, 145, 146; Enlightenment roots of, 35; individualism and, xiii, xv, 13; Kateb and, 74–81; *Paradise* and, 185; influence on Reaganism, xi; *Sula* and, 105, 154, 159, 164, 174. *See also* Emerson, Ralph Waldo; Emersonian liberalism

Enlightenment: Emersonianism and, 35, 92, 140; individualism and, 92; liberalism and, xix, 21, 68, 92, 140, 196; Morrison and critique of, 82, 83–84, 136, 138–40, 141, 191, 195; Pynchon and critique of, 82–83, 111, 140, 141, 191, 195, 218 n.2; racism and, xix, 22, 84; Sandel on, 8, 68

Etzioni, Amitai, 11

Family, 13, 15, 19, 23–24, 31–32, 37; communitarians on, 77; in *Crying of Lot 49, The*, 49, 95, 146–49, 152; deformation of,

in Morrison, 88, 104, 106, 153–54, 160, 165–67, 178; in *Paradise*, 180–84; Reagan and, x, 168–69; in *Vineland*, 31, 130, 132, 136–37, 170–73, 179

Faulkner, William: Morrison and, 104, 156, 215 n.12, 216 n.2

Fiedler, Leslie, 86, 218 n.2

First Amendment, 190–91

Fiscus, Ronald J., xiii, xiv, 190, 197 n.3

Foucault, Michel, 192

Fowler, Douglas, 218 n.2

Foner, Eric, 73

Fourteenth Amendment, xiv

Fox-Genovese, Elizabeth, 182

Franklin, Benjamin, 15, 73

Freedom, 14–22, 25–27; communitarian view of, 4; dangerous, 108, 177–79; Emerson and, 40, 45; Emersonianism and, xix, xx, 7, 36; individual, ix–x, xvi, 6, 7, 8, 10, 29, 31, 172; individualism and, 8, 11, 14–15, 187–88; Morrison and, 177–79, 183, 196; national narrative and, 7, 71, 196; oppression linked to, 22, 25, 29, 31, 83–84, 99, 152; possessive individualism and, 20–21, 98; Pynchon and, xviii, 92; rights and, 26–27; self-mastery and, 17–18. *See also* Negative liberty; Positive liberty

Frontier, 4, 5, 193, 194

Frontiersman, figure of, 30, 71, 72

Fundamentalism, religious, 18, 186, 192

Gabel, Peter, 26–28, 30, 84, 152

Gans, Herbert, 72, 201 n.14, 202 n.17

García Márquez, Gabriel, 136

Giamatti, A. Bartlett, xi, 72

Gibbon, Edward, 49

Gonnaud, Maurice, 57, 206 n.9

Good: concept of, 9, 14–16, 18, 20, 32, 38, 42, 62; of the governed, 16

Good Society, The (Bellah et al.), 142

Gothic: American, 60; novel, 60, 82–83, 85–86, 136, 218 n.2

Great Republic, The (Bailyn et al.), 22

Guinier, Lani, 189

Habermas, Jürgen, 28, 29, 191

Habits of the Heart (Bellah et al.), 8–11, 72, 142

233

Hall, Stuart, 4
Harper, Phillip Brian, xvii, xxi
Hartz, Louis, 19, 20
Harvard Crimson, xii
Hawthorne, Nathaniel, 181
Hegel, G. W. F., 28
Hegelianism, 17
Hinduism, 49
Hobbes, Thomas, 12, 61, 75, 168, 186
Hollinger, David, 49, 50, 194
Holmes, Stephen, 141, 210 n.31
Homer, 6, 49
Homophobia, xiv, 188
Human rights, 22, 59, 188, 194–95, 210 n.27
Hume, David, 84
Hutcheon, Linda, xvii

Idealism: Emerson and, 10, 35, 42–45, 47, 51; Kateb and, 76, 78, 188; Rawls and, 61, 188; Winthrop and, 43–44
Identity, communal construction of. *See* Self: situated
Ideology, 3–4, 9–12; defined, 3–4; individualism as, xii, xiii, 9, 10, 11–12, 19, 22, 39, 61, 188; methodological individualism and, 12, 14, 188, 190; Morrison on, 3; national and official narratives and, 4, 33
Indian removal, 91, 187
Individual: abstract, 13, 63, 71, 79, 144; inviolability of, 61, 63, 159, 188, 190
Individualism, ix–xiii, xv, xviii–xx, 1, 8–16, 19–47, 59–61, 63, 65–67, 71–84, 186–93; communitarian critique of, 8–11, 73–74, 143, 182; conformity and, xii; contradiction and, ix, 32; *Crying of Lot 49, The*, and, 111, 116, 126, 144, 148–49; economic, 12, 20, 21, 80, 105, 178; Emerson and, 40–43, 45–47, 59–60; ideology of, xii–xiii, 9, 19, 81; jazz and, 174–77, 180; *Jazz* and, 178–79; Kateb and, 75–81; limits of, 25–29; Morrison and, 29–32, 33, 83, 84; ontological, 12, 14–15, 20, 47, 61, 67; oppression and, 22–25, 88, 91, 92, 188–89; political, 12, 16, 20, 23; popular culture and, ix, xi–xiii, 30, 71–73; postliberalism and, 28–29; Pynchon and, 29–32, 33, 83, 84; Rawls and, 61, 63, 65–67; Reagan and rhetoric of, ix–xi, 168–69; rights-based, 71–84; *Sula* and, 152–54, 163; de Tocqueville and, 36–40, 148–49; *Vineland* and, 167, 173; vs. conformity, xii, 41, 142, 166. *See also* Methodological individualism; Rugged individualism; U.S. individualism
Individualisme, 37
Individuality: conformity and, xii, 142, 167; *Crying of Lot 49, The*, and, 118, 125–26, 142–46, 148–49, 152, 173; democratic, xix, distinct from individualism, 39–40; Emerson and, 40–42, 47, 53; Emersonianism, 34, 36; family and, 24; Kateb on, 74–75, 76–78, 80–81; Morrison and, 32, 104, 138, 141, 180; official narrative and, 19, 23; possession and, 82, 93; Pynchon and, 82, 93, 97, 118, 141; overemphasis on, 23, 25; poststructural critique of, 11, 169; Rawls and, 28, 63; *Sula* and, 152, 162, 164, 166, 167; *Vineland* and, 31, 167, 171–73
Invisible Man (Ellison), 99–100, 212 n.4

Jackson v. City of Joliet, 1
James, William, 132, 134
Jameson, Fredric, 9–10
Jauss, Hans Robert, 193
Jazz: African American culture and, 174; Morrison and, 173, 174, 176–78; pluralism and, 174; Pynchon and, 91, 176
Jefferson, Thomas, 16, 18, 19, 20–21, 22, 23, 24, 73, 76, 84, 202 n.18; Locke and, 16, 18, 20, 201 n.14; property, 20, 21
Jones, Indiana, 71, 72
Justice: distributive, 70, 190, 197 n.3; principles of, 62–64, 188, 192

Kant, Immanuel, 8, 28, 43, 48–49, 50, 61, 76, 84, 110, 195; cosmopolitanism and, 48. Works: "Idea for a Universal History with a Cosmopolitan Purpose," 48, 49; "Perpetual Peace," 48, 49; "Theory and Practice," 48, 208 n.18
Kaplan, Amy, 193, 194
Kateb, George, xv, xviii, 1, 10, 26, 34, 47, 74–81, 96, 145, 146, 187, 188, 210 n.28; critique of communitarianism, 75–77; on democratic individuality, xix, 74–81; idealism and, 35; on "Song of Myself" (Whitman), 78–79

Keats, John, 192
Kingston, Maxine Hong, xvii

Laissez-faire, 41, 64, 168
Lasch, Christopher, ix, 73, 74, 142, 168, 182
Leca, Jean, 11, 12, 14
Leonidas, 49
Leroux, Pierre, 39, 40
Levellers, 75
Literary criticism, 3, 192–94
Liberalism, 8, 21, 60, 61, 69; Appleby on, 21; communitarianism and, 1, 8, 67–74, 141, 180; economic liberalism and, 21, 29; Emersonian influence on U.S., xiii; Enlightenment and, xix; individualism as basis of, 1, 8, 11–25; *individualisme* as critique of, 37; Jefferson and, 19–21; Kateb on, 74–81; Mouffe on, xv–xvi, 29, 74, 191; Rawlsian contribution to, 60–67; pluralism and, xvi, 21, 70, 194; traditional view revised, xv, 10, universalism and, 21. See *also* Emersonian liberalism
Libertarianism, 63–64, 168
Lincoln, Abraham, 76
Locke, John, 8, 43, 84, 110, 200 n.13; Emerson and, 41, 42; influence on U.S. culture, 16, 18–20; Jefferson and, 16, 18, 19–20, 201 n.14; negative liberty and, 16, 18, 19; possessive individualism and, 20, 93, 109; property, theory of, 16, 20, 101; Rawls and, 61, 75; slavery and, 202 n.18
Lukes, Steven, 12, 37, 63

MacIntyre, Alasdair, xv, 6, 11, 30, 73, 74, 182
Macpherson, C. B., 20
Madison, James, 76, 189
Madsen, Richard, 8
Magical realism, 83, 131, 136, 140, 184. See *also* Pynchon, Thomas: the miraculous
Malcolm X, 139, 176
Manifest Destiny, 91
Marginalization, xvii, xviii; negative effects of, xx
Marlowe, Philip, 71, 72, 114
Marx, Karl, 4
Marx, Leo, xx, xxi, 79, 210 n.28
Materialism, 20–21, 47, 79, 201 n.15; Emerson and, 42–45; slavery and, 29
Matthiessen, F. O., 206 n.9

McCarthy, Thomas, 28
Melley, Timothy, 204 n.20, 212 n.3
Mendelson, Edward, 167
Methodological individualism, xiii–xv, 12–14, 188–91; abstraction and, xiv, xv, xix, 10, 12–13, 35, 50; defined, xiii; discrimination and, xiv, 10, 25, 188–90; Emerson and, xiv, xix, 10, 13, 50, 56, 59; ideology and, 12, 14; ontological individualism and, 12–13; Rawls and, 10, 63, 67, 71, 190
Mill, John Stuart, 8, 14, 76
Milton, John, 75
Misogyny, xix, 32, 188
Montesquieu, 76
Morrison, Toni: communitarianism and, 31, 74, 180, 193; community and, xviii, xx, 31, 32, 141, 142, 153–59, 161, 165–67; critique of Enlightenment and, 82–83, 136, 138, 140, 141, 191, 195; critique of individualism and, 10, 29–30, 31, 35, 163, 187–88; as cultural critic, 5, 199 n.2; cycle of violence, 88, 104, 108; dangerous freedom, 108, 177–79; degraded masculinity in the work of, 103–6, 178–79; dispossession in, 85, 97–103, 107–10; Emersonianism and, xix, xx, 7, 36, 164; family in, 88, 104, 106, 153–54, 160, 165–67, 178, 180–84; jazz and, 173–77, 180; limits of community and, xx, 141–42, 153–54; magical realism and, 83, 136, 140, 184; matriarchy, 153–57, 159; negative liberty and, 22, 186; official stories and, 2–8, 29, 32–33, 196; political engagement and, xv, xvii–xviii; postmodernism and, xvi–xvii; pluralism and, 179, 180; self-reliance and, xviii, 105, 141, 161–63, 165, 178–79; slave narrative, revision of: 85–86; slavery and, 29, 31, 84–87, 89, 92. Works: *Beloved*, 2, 7, 84–90, 97, 136, 177, 195; *Birth of a Nation'hood*, 2; *Bluest Eye, The*, 2, 32, 99–100, 102–5, 108, 153, 177–78; *Jazz*, 32, 173, 174, 176, 177, 179; *Paradise*, 2, 139, 140, 179–85; "Site of Memory, The," 85, 86; *Song of Solomon*, 101, 136, 138, 140; *Sula*, 2, 98, 105, 106, 136, 139, 153–67, 178, 179, 195
Mouffe, Chantal, xv, xvi, 29, 67, 70, 74, 191, 192, 194

Multiculturalism, xvi, 193, 194, 195, 197 n.4, 218 n.3

Nabokov, Vladimir, 95
Nagel, Thomas, 68, 209 n.20
Narcissism, 210 n.29
Narrative: cultural function of, 5–8; slave, 85–86. *See also* Official narrative; Storytelling
National narrative. *See* Official narrative
Natty Bumppo, 71
Negative capability, 192
Negative liberty, 1, 15–17, 20, 22, 26, 27, 28; defined, 14; Enlightenment origins of, 82; Kateb on, 78; Locke on, 16, 18, 19; Morrison and, 32, 141, 179, 181, 186; oppression and, 25; relation to positive liberty, 14, 17–20, 32, 71, 73, 77, 80, 81, 180; Pynchon and, 32, 141, 186; race and, 26–27; Rawls and, 61, 67; Sandel and, 73; slavery and, 25, 83–84, 92, 203 n.18; taxation and, 201 n.14; U.S. individualism and, 15–17, 35, 71, 186. *See also* Freedom
New Criticism, 192, 193
Newfield, Christopher, 197 n.2
Nicoloff, Philip, 53
Night of the Living Dead, 131
Nozick, Robert, 63–64, 75
Nussbaum, Martha, xv, 34, 35, 140; interpretation of *Hard Times* (Dickens), 6–7

Official narrative, xx, 2–5, 8, 10, 20, 25, 30, 196, 202 n.15; contradiction and conflict in, 23, 32–33, 59, 74; Emerson and, 59–60; Emersonianism and, xi, xiii, xviii–xix, 7, 29, 36, 77; ideology and, 3–4, 14, 199 n.1; jazz and, 174, 180; methodological individualism and, xii, xiii, 14; Morrison and, 2–4, 5, 7, 29, 32–33, 74, 82, 83, 154, 174, 180, 181; negative liberty and, 15, 19, 22, 35, 73, 82, 181; oppression and, 22, 29, 83; Pynchon and, 4–5, 29, 32–33, 74, 82–83, 126, 152, 173; rugged individualism and, 71–72, 169. *See also* Narrative; Storytelling
Ogren, Kathy J., 174
Ontological individualism. *See* Individualism: ontological

Oppression: negative liberty and, 22, 25; race and, 6, 8, 10, 156. *See also* Slavery
Original position. *See* Rawls, John: original position

Packer, Barbara, xx, 50, 56, 206 n.13, 207 n.14
Paine, Thomas, 76, 204 n.18
Parker, Charlie, 176
Patriarchy, 22–24, 156, 178, 181
Patterson, Orlando, 25, 83, 202 n.18
Peabody, Elizabeth Palmer, 40
Pepper, Vangie, xiv
Philosophy: abstraction and, xv, 6, 34–35; literature and, xiv–xv, 6; methodological individualism and, xiv; official narratives and, xviii, 7, 8, 33; storytelling and, xiv, 6, 7, 33, 34. *See also* Enlightenment; Idealism; Materialism; *individual philosophers*
Phocion, 49
Pindar, 49
Plato, 49, 61
Platonism, 17
Plotinus, 49
Pluralism, 28–29, 48–50, 74; conflict and, 29; cosmopolitanism and, 48–49, 60, 194; jazz and, 171; liberalism and, xvi, 21, 70; Morrison and, 179; Mouffe and, 29, 67, 74, 191–92; Pynchon and, 171; Rawls and, 62, 67; Sandel and, 67, 74; universalism and, 28
Pocock, J. G. A., 19, 200 n.12
Poirier, Richard, 206 n.10
Political individualism. *See* Individualism: political
Popular culture, ix, 8; rugged individualism and, 30, 71–73
Positive liberty, 1, 14–15, 17–20; community and, 15, 18, 78; defined, 14; relation to negative liberty, 14, 17–20, 32, 71, 73, 77, 80, 81, 180; individualism and, 14, 19, 20, 32, 71, 73, 180; Kateb and, 77, 78, 80, 81; Morrison and, 32, 74; official narrative and, 32, 71, 73, 77, 180; oppression and, 74, 80, 141; Pynchon and, 32, 74. *See also* Freedom
Posner, Richard, 1
Possessive individualism, 12, 29; defined, 20, Emerson and, 42, 78; Locke and, 12,

42, 78, 93, 109; materialism and, 29, 42, 78, 94, 95; Morrison and, 30, 109, 136, 138–39; Pynchon and, 30, 93, 94, 95; slavery and, 29, 109. *See also* Individualism; Methodological individualism; Rugged individualism

Postmodernism, xvi–xvii, 198 n.5, 204 n.1

Poststructuralism: as critique of individuality, 11

Privacy, right to, xvi, 14, 16, 181, 190

Property, 20–21; body as, 20, 82; Emerson on, 42–43, 45, 46, 53; Locke on, 16, 20, 42, 93, 101, 109; slavery and 28, 84–85; self-possession and, 100–101. *See also* Possessive individualism

Puritans, xi, 43, 46. *See also* Winthrop, John

Pynchon, Thomas: ambiguity in, 111, 115–16; border studies and, 5; communitarianism and, 2, 30, 31, 74, 141, 142–44, 152, 171–73; critique of Enlightenment, 82–83, 111, 140, 141, 191, 195, 218 n.2; critique of individualism, 10, 29, 30, 35, 81, 91, 116, 152, 163, 167–68, 187; detective fiction and, 111, 112, 114, 123, 126; Emersonianism and, xix, xx, 10, 36, 110, 112, 114, 116, 117, 119, 123, 124, 126, 145, 146; Emerson quoted in, 132; erosion of community in, 146–50; family in, 31, 49, 95, 130, 132, 136–37, 146–49, 152, 170–73, 179; frontier mythology and, 4; jazz and, 176, 177; the miraculous and, 83, 118, 126–27, 129, 136, 140; narcissism and paranoid narcissism in, 116, 122–23, 125–26, 152, 146, 150, 152, 173; narrative technique, 150–51; negative liberty and, 22, 186; objectification and dehumanization in, 93–97; official stories and, 4, 29, 32–33, 126, 152, 173; paranoia and, 111, 115–16, 126, 150–52, 204 n.20; political engagement, xv, xvii–xviii; positive liberty and, 32, 74; postmodernism, xvi–xvii, 111; revelation in, 111, 113, 116–22, 124, 128, 134, 151; slavery and violence, 5, 29, 31, 32, 84, 88, 92, 195; "Song of Myself" (Whitman) and, 145–46; technology and, xviii, 118, 135. Works: *Crying of Lot 49, The*, 30, 95, 111–26, 127, 128, 129, 130, 131, 133, 134, 135, 142–52, 171, 173; *Gravity's Rainbow*, 7, 30, 84, 96–97, 118, 126, 132, 167, 168, 176; "Is It O.K. To Be a Luddite?" 82, 83, 118; *Mason & Dixon*, 1, 4, 5, 32, 84, 196; *Slow Learner*, 167; *V.*, 2, 30, 84, 88–95, 110–11, 126, 144, 176, 196; *Vineland*, 2, 31, 127–36, 167–68, 170–73, 179, 180

Racism: Emerson and, 53, 55, 206 n.13, 207 n.14; Declaration of Independence and, 22; individualism and, xiv, 22, 26, 29, 31–32, 141, 188, 189; liberalism and, xix; Morrison and, 2, 22, 31–32, 83, 84, 102, 136, 141, 153, 166, 177; Pynchon and, 22, 31, 83, 91, 92, 141

Rambo, 72

Rationalism, xix, 7, 21, 35, 83, 126, 139, 140, 191, 195; domination and, xix

Rawls, John, 28, 34, 35, 60–71, 81, 110, 192; abstraction and, xv, 34, 61, 145, 146; critiqued by Sandel, 8, 67–69; difference principle, 63, 65, 69, 70, 79, 190; Emerson and, xv, xviii, xix, 10, 61, 63, 65, 66, 67; individualism and, xv, xix, 23, 26, 35, 60–71, 75–77; justice as fairness, 61, 63, 65, 67, 69, 209 n.22; Kant and, 61; Kateb on, 75–77, 79; maximum rule, 64; methodological individualism and, 188, 190; original position, 35, 62–70, 79; veil of ignorance, 62, 63. Works: "Justice as Fairness: Political not Metaphysical," 69; *Law of Peoples, The*, 61; *Political Liberalism*, 61; *Theory of Justice, A*, 61, 65, 67

Reagan, Ronald, xiii, 128, 129, 132, 167, 168, 169, 172, 197 n.1, 217 n.8; communal role, ix; rhetoric of individualism and, ix–xi; as rugged individualist, 72

Reeboks, advertising campaign, xi–xii

Reeve, Henry, 36

Republican Party, ix, x, 13, 169, 197

Reynolds, Larry J., 205 n.8

Rights, xiv, xviii, 1, 8, 12, 13, 14, 16–18, 20, 25, 26–28, 186–91; basis in negative liberty, 14; Declaration of Independence and, 22–23; Emerson on, 45, 46, 52–54, 58–59, 134; human, 59, 188, 194–95; Kateb on, 74–81; Locke on, 8, 16, 93, 144, 152, 180, 182; Morrison on, 81, 84; Pynchon and, 81, 93, 134; Rawls on, 62, 64, 67; Sandel on, 69, 73; slavery and, 84, 195

Romero, George, 131
Rorty, Richard, xv, 6, 194, 195
Rousseau, Jean-Jacques, 18, 61, 76
Rugged individualism, 71–73; Morrison and, 30, 178–79; mythology of, 29–30, 71–73; popular culture and, 30, 71–73; Pynchon and, 30, 144; Reagan and, x, 169; Sandel and, 35, 71, 73
Rulfo, Juan, 136
Rushdie, Salman, 167, 216 n.6
Russell, William, 49

Saint-Cheron, Alexandre, 39, 40
Saint-Simon, Comte de, 37
Saint-Simonism, 37
Sallust, 49
Sandel, Michael J., xv, 6, 8, 11, 35, 67–71, 73, 74, 168, 180, 209 n.19; on John Rawls, 8, 67–69
Scarlet Letter, The (Hawthorne), 181
Schumpeter, Joseph, 12
Self: Saint-Simonian, 37; situated, 37, 69, 193; unencumbered, xviii, 67–69, 71, 158, 165, 178
Self-autonomy, 14, 173, 196
Self-expression, 14, 18, 19, 23, 24, 78, 94, 173, 180, 196
Self-fulfillment, 14, 15, 19, 23, 73, 82, 165
Self-mastery, 14, 17, 18
Self-realization, 14, 18, 81
Self-reliance, xii; *Crying of Lot 49, The*, and, 112–14, 116, 122, 141, 146, 152; Emerson on, 40, 42, 54, 56, 59, 60, 78; Morrison and, xviii, 141, 178–79; negative liberty and, 75, 82; official narrative and, xiii, xviii; Pynchon and, xviii, 141; rugged individualism and, 71; *Sula* and, 105, 161–63, 165. *See also* Emerson, Ralph Waldo, Works: "Self-Reliance"
Seneca Falls (first Woman's Rights Convention), 23
Sexism, xiv, 22, 23; in Emerson, 52
Shakespeare, 6, 49
Shane, 71
Shiffrin, Steven, xv, 6
Shklar, Judith, xv, 1, 6, 7, 199 n.4
Signification, 123, 150, 163
Simpson, O. J., 2, 3
Situated self. *See* Self: situated

Slavery, xix, 5, 24–26, 28, 29, 31–32, 98, 109, 110, 138, 195, 196, 202 n.18; Emerson on, 53–58; in Morrison's work, 83–85, 87–88; in Pynchon's work, 88, 92–93; negative liberty and, 25, 83; as trope, 31, 92, 203 n.8
Smith, Henry Nash, 193
Skinner, Quentin, 200 n.10
Socialism, 18, 19, 25, 26, 37, 39–40, 46; Emerson and, 205 n.3
Socrates, 49
Sollors, Werner, 49, 194
"Song of Myself" (Whitman): and *Crying of Lot 49, The*, 145–46; Kateb on, 76, 78, 79
Steele, Claude M., 199 n.6
Steiner, Wendy, 122, 198 n.5
Storytelling, xiv, 3, 6, 7, 184; cultural dominance and, 2–3; philosophy and, xiv, 6–7, 33. *See also* Narrative; Official narrative
Stowe, Harriet Beecher, 56
Subject position, xvi, 27, 153, 193
Sullivan, William M., 8
Swedenborg, Emmanuel, 49
Swidler, Ann, 8

Taylor, Charles, 11, 17, 70, 74
Thoreau, Henry David, 71, 76, 78
Tipton, Steven M., 8
Transcendentalism, 205 n.8
Tocqueville, Alexis de, 11, 23, 25, 36–39, 41; *Crying of Lot 49, The*, and, 148, 149; Kateb on, 75, 76, 78, 80, 81
Trenchard, 76
Twain, Mark, 84

Uncle Tom's Cabin (Stowe), 56
Unger, Roberto, 209 n.19, 210 n.31
Unencumbered self. *See* Self: unencumbered
Universalism, xix, 21–22, 28, 47–50, 52, 59, 60, 191, 195; abstraction and, 28
U.S. individualism, xii–xiii, 12–13, 23–24; critiques of, 11, 25, 26, 186; defined, 12; Emerson and, 36, 59; ideology and, ix, 12; Morrison and, 29–30; 83, 154, 180; official narrative and, xiii, xx, 15, 32, 73, 83; oppression and exclusion in, 22, 83, 188; Rawls and, 59, 67; rugged individualism and, 71. *See also* Individualism; Method-

ological individualism; Possessive individualism; Rugged individualism
Utilitarianism, 6–7, 62, 63, 69

Van Buren, Martin, 54, 55, 57, 187
Van der Zee, James, 217 n.11
Vane, Henry, 49
Varsava, Jerry A., 217 n.7
Veil of ignorance. *See* Rawls, John: veil of ignorance
Vinet, Alexandre, 39
Von Frank, Albert J., 206 n.13, 208 n.18

Wald, Priscilla, 198 n.1
Walzer, Michael, 11, 74
Wasby, Stephen L., xiii
Washington, Booker T., 139

Weinstein, David, 74–75
West, Cornel, 53, 198 n.5
Whiteman, Paul, 173, 174
Whitman, Walt, ix, 145–146; Kateb on "Song of Myself," 76, 78–79. *See also* "Song of Myself" (Whitman)
Williams, Patricia, 26, 27, 28, 30, 152
Williams, Raymond, 158
Williams, Roger, 75
Wills, Gary, ix, 19, 169
Winkelried, Arnold, 49
Winthrop, John, x, xi, 43, 44, 46
Wood, Gordon S., 19, 21
Worcester Women's Convention, 53

Zoroastrianism, 49

Cyrus R. K. Patell is Associate Professor of English at New
York University. He is the author of *Joyce's Use of History in
Finnegans Wake* and a contributor to the *Cambridge History of
American Literature, Volume 7: Prose Writing, 1940–1990*.

Library of Congress Cataloging-in-Publication Data
Patell, Cyrus R. K.
Negative liberties : Morrison, Pynchon, and the problem of
liberal ideology / Cyrus R. K. Patell.
p. cm. — (New Americanists)
Includes bibliographical references and index.
ISBN 0-8223-2664-7 (cloth : alk. paper)—ISBN 0-8223-2669-8
(pbk. : alk. paper)
1. American fiction—20th century—History and criticism.
2. Politics and literature—United States—History—20th
century. 3. Political fiction, American—History and criticism.
4. Morrison, Toni—Political and social views. 5. Pynchon,
Thomas—Political and social views. 6. Individualism in
literature. 7. Liberalism in literature. 8. Liberty in literature.
I. Title. II. Series.
PS374.P6P37 2001   813'.5409358—dc21   00-046269

www.ingramcontent.com/pod-product-compliance
Lightning Source LLC
Chambersburg PA
CBHW070758230426
43665CB00017B/2407